James Hannay

The Life and Times of Sir Leonard Tilley

Being a political history of New Brunswick for the past seventy years

James Hannay

The Life and Times of Sir Leonard Tilley
Being a political history of New Brunswick for the past seventy years

ISBN/EAN: 9783744743242

Printed in Europe, USA, Canada, Australia, Japan

Cover: Foto ©Suzi / pixelio.de

More available books at **www.hansebooks.com**

THE

LIFE AND TIMES

OF

SIR LEONARD TILLEY

BEING

A POLITICAL HISTORY

OF

NEW BRUNSWICK

FOR THE PAST SEVENTY YEARS.

BY

JAMES HANNAY,

AUTHOR OF A HISTORY OF ACADIA.

ST. JOHN, N. B:
1897.

CONTENTS.

CHAPTER I.

CHAPTER II.

CHAPTER III.

CHAPTER IV.

CHAPTER V.

of the governor to make appointments. Sir Charles Metcalfe's conduct applauded in New Brunswick. The Reade appointment in 1845. Indignation of the family compact. The Assembly passes an address to the Queen on the subject. The appointment cancelled. The Wilmot appointment to the bench. The battle of responsible government won.

CHAPTER VI.

Sir Leonard Tilley's ancestry. His great grandfather a loyalist. His grandfather and father. Place of birth. Education. Ancedote of Sir Howard Douglas. Goes to St. John in 1831. His business life. Became a total abstainer. The election of 1850. Mr. Tilley elected to the legislature. Some of his colleagues : L. A. Wilmot, Charles Fisher, W. H. Needham, W. J. Ritchie, John H. Gray, R. D. Wilmot, John R. Partelow. The government still Tory. Gray and Wilmot enter it. A new education bill. The college. Mr. Ritchie's resolution. The St. John bye-election. Mr. Tilley resigns his seat. Railway resolutions. The reciprocity treaty. General election of 1854. Mr. Tilley again elected to the legislature. Defeat of the Street-Partelow government. New government formed by Mr. Fisher. Mr. Tilley becomes Provincial Secretary. Responsible government becomes a reality.

CHAPTER VII.

The prohibitory liquor law. A bold experiment. Strength of the liquor interest. The governor dissolves the legislature. Defeat of Mr. Tilley in St. John. A new government formed by Messrs. Gray and Wilmot. The election of 1857. Mr. Tilley returned for St. John city. Joins Mr. Fisher in the formation of a government. A strong administration. Railway legislation. The Intercolonial negotiations. Immigration. State of the finances. Completion of the railway from St. John to Shediac. Voting by ballot. Re-organization of the college. The Connell episode. The crown lands investigation. The general election of 1861.

CHAPTER VIII.

CHAPTER IX.

CHAPTER X.

CHAPTER XI.

CHAPTER XII.

CHAPTER XIII.

CHAPTER XIV.

PREFACE.

This work was commenced some six years ago, for
the purpose of relating, in a brief space, the political
history of New Brunswick, during the period of Sir
Leonard Tilley's life, and telling the story of a New
Brunswick public man, who was a member of the first
government under the responsible system, and who
attained to a greater distinction, both in his own province
and in Canada, than any other statesman whom New
Brunswick has yet produced. The story of the battle
for responsible government has not before been told in
any book that has been published in this province, yet
New Brunswick's share in that struggle was a most
interesting phase of a contest which was waged in every
one of the provinces that formed the original Dominion
of Canada.   It is the story of the progress of a people
from political infancy to a political manhood, and no
person who is not informed in regard to it, can have any
idea of the real worth of the institutions under which he
lives, or of the blessings which he enjoys under a system
of government·which tolerates no privileged class, and
places all men upon an equal footing.

Sir Leonard Tilley was not born early enough to take
any conspicuous part in the contest for responsible government, but he was a member of the administration
which first worked it out in practice, and he was, during

the whole of his public career, one of its most strenuous supporters and advocates. The opposition which he met with, as a public man, in the early part of his career, was the opposition of those who were opposed to responsible government, and who used all sorts of contemptuous phrases in describing the new system which had come into force, and which has done so much to strengthen the loyalty of the people of Canada to the mother country. His life is, therefore, united to the story of the growth of responsible government, and is now given to the people of this province, in the hope that it will lead to a closer study of their own political history, and of the lives of the distinguished men who have taken a conspicuous part in it.

In preparing this life of Sir Leonard Tilley, the author had the advantage of his active assistance in the collection of the necessary documents, both public and private, which were used for that purpose. Sir Leonard also granted the author numerous private interviews, and was at all times accessible for the purpose of answering any question which might be propounded to him on the subjects connected with this book. At the same time it ought to be stated that no portion of this volume was ever submitted to him for approval or otherwise, and that, therefore, he is not in any sense responsible for any of the opinions which are expressed in it, either in regard to political questions or the characters of public men. The writer felt that, in preparing a work of this kind, he should not be hampered by the supervision of any other person, and that it would have been embarrassing to himself, and to the distinguished person whose life he commemorates, if it had been revised by the latter, and he had been made in any sense responsible for it.

It was intended that this book should have appeared in the year 1891, and a considerable portion of it was actually printed at that date, but circumstances which need not be mentioned here, prevented its publication at that time, and this will account for one or two references in it to dates which seem to imply an earlier publication than the present one.   It was also expected that this volume should have made its appearance during the life of Sir Leonard Tilley, and it would, under any circumstances, have been published during the present year, but his sudden death, which was wholly unexpected, changed all this, and made it necessary to add to the story of his life an account of his lamented death.   It may be added that this Life of Sir Leonard Tilley is not written from the point of view of one who believed that he was always right in everything he did.   The author was with him in the great struggle for Confederation, and he was decidedly opposed to him with respect to the National Policy.   So far as possible, however, there has been no controversial matter introduced into this volume in regard to any question which can now be considered as a live one, of which is likely to be again fought out at the polls.

LIFE AND TIMES

OF

SIR LEONARD TILLEY.

CHAPTER I.

THE SOCIAL AND INDUSTRIAL CONDITION OF NEW BRUNSWICK IN 1818.

Sir Samuel Leonard Tilley, who was destined to be twice Finance Minister of Canada, and twice Lieutenant Governor of New Brunswick, was born at Gagetown, in the County of Queens and Province of New Brunswick on the 8th May, 1818. At that time New Brunswick had existed as a separate province for thirty-four years, and thirty-five years had elapsed since the arrival of the first great immigration of loyalists at St. John. Only fifty-six years before, the first English settlers of New Brunswick had reached the mouth of the St. John river, and the township of Maugerville, the oldest agricultural settlement in New Brunswick, only dated back fifty-five years. The Province was young not only in years but in character; it was undeveloped and unprosperous, politically and economically. It becomes necessary, therefore, to a right understanding of the career of the subject of our biography, to describe the condition of New Brunswick at the date of his birth, and the social and political state of its people. Any one who imagines that life in New Brunswick in 1818 was at all like what it is in 1891 will be guilty of a grievous error, for changes of the most revolutionary character have taken place in respect to almost everything which enters into the lives of the people.

In 1818 the population of the province did not exceed 50,000 souls. The first census was taken in 1824, when it was found that New Brunswick had 74,176 inhabitants. But the immigration had been large between 1818 and the year of the census, so that the population in 1818 was probably less than the figure named. The city of St. John at that period had fewer than 6,000 inhabitants, and the entire county, including Portland, and exclusive of the city, not more than 3,000 persons. Fredericton had then a population of about 1,500 or less than one fourth its present number. The entire County of York, including the capital of the Province, had not more than 8000 people. Northumberland with about 12,000 inhabitants was the most populous county, but its area then included what is now Kent, Gloucester and Restigouche.

Westmoreland, which included the territory which is now Albert county, had 6,000 inhabitants, and Charlotte about the same number. The County of Queens in which Sir Leonard Tilley was born had not more than 4,000 people. It was the day of small things in New Brunswick, seventy-three years ago.

The population of New Brunswick was much more homogeneous in 1818 than it is at present. The original settlers were from Massachusetts and largely came from a stock which had been settled in New England for a century or more at the time of their emigration to the River St. John in 1762 and 1763. The Simondses, Hazens, Burpees, Perleys, Coys, Barkers, Whites, Quintons and other families which then settled in New Brunswick were all of New England growth, and brought with them the peculiarities and customs which prevailed among the people who were settled around Massachusetts Bay. The Loyalist immigration largely added to the number of persons from New England, but it also introduced a still greater number from New York, the Middle States and the South. Still the stock was mainly English and substantially the same in origin as that which came from New England, although differing from it in some minor points of custom and speech. The only elements that came in the Loyalist immigration which differed radically from the old stock were the disbanded soldiers of the regiments raised in the British Islands, and a few Hessians who preferred to remain on this side of the Atlantic rather than trust themselves again to the tender mercies of their hereditary prince.   It was not until 1817 that the immigration to New Brunswick from the United Kingdom commenced which was destined so materially to modify the character of our population.   This immigration has now practically ceased or rather has become insignificant in proportion to the number of natives, so that the population of New Brunswick has again largely grown to be a native one, and its characteristics are becoming fixed.   The old struggle between the Loyalist element and the new comers has ceased ; numerous inter-marriages with Loyalist families have immensely added to the number of those who claim descent from the immigrants of 1783, and, except where religion is involved, race animosities have died away.   But throughout the greater part of Sir Leonard Tilley's career these race animosities were active and potent and exercised no small influence on the politics of the Province.

In 1818 the homes of the people of New Brunswick presented a marked contrast to their present aspect.   In the cities, wood was the universal building material, the number of buildings of brick and stone being so few as to be hardly worthy of mention.   St. John did not possess a single brick residence until the year 1817, when the Disbrow house on the corner of Germain and Church streets was built.   The great majority of the residences were quite plain in appearance and not too well provided with conveniences.   Bath rooms were hardly known; there were no sewers worthy of the name, and the supply of water for domestic use had to be obtained from wells. In 1818, and for many years afterwards, water was hawked about the streets of St. John at a half penny a pail. The houses of the better class in the cities were generally two stories in height with a high pitch roof. Some of these buildings exist at the present day and enable a striking contrast to be drawn between the best houses of that age and of this. A few very rich men, however, who were ambitious to have fine mansions, erected houses of a more pretentious character shortly after the era of which I have been speaking. The Wright house, built by the collector of the port of St. John in 1819, was the finest of these, but it was destroyed in the great fire of 1877. The Peters house on Coburg street, which was built by Attorney General Peters, and is now owned by the Hatheway family, is almost the only survivor of the better class of houses of that day. Both of these mansions were built of stone. The Hazen house, on the corner of Charlotte street and King Square, which is now the Hotel Dufferin, is another survivor of that time.

The average country house of the year 1818 in the older settled parts of the Province was a story and half wooden building with a narrow hall in the middle, giving four rooms on each floor. A high chimney with two or more fire-places connected with it afforded the means of heating the kitchen and sitting rooms. These great fire-places were very pleasant to look at when the fire was blazing brightly, and in moderate weather in winter were not uncomfortable. But when the mercury fell to zero and the cold winds whistled about the unsheltered house, the fire-place as a means of heating failed. The hapless individual who sought it for warmth was roasted on one side and frozen on the other. The only thing the fire-place insured was good ventilation, and the great majority of country houses were quite too well provided in this respect, and admitted the cold air with a degree of freedom which was very unfavorable to the comfort of their inhabitants. In the newer settlements log houses predominated and they were still more uncomfortable than those just described. Only a vast consumption of fuel, which was everywhere abundant, rendered them habitable.

All the cooking of those days was done at the big fire-place. A swinging crane hung over the fire and it was provided with hooks of various lengths upon which the pots could be hung. Bread was baked and meat cooked in a large flat pot with a cover which was known as the bake-kettle, and with a good fire and plenty of live coals on the hearth, where the bake-kettle was placed, and on the cover of this important utensil, the cooking was usually well done. But with this system cooking of all kinds was extremely laborious. The fire-place itself was frequently five feet in width and the back-log which formed the basis of the fire, and without which a good fire could not be built, was generally so huge and heavy that it could not be lifted but had to be rolled into its place. Swinging a heavy pot filled with potatoes on to the crane was laborious work, and required lifting powers beyond the strength of ordinary women. When the farm was extensive and large quantities of food had to be cooked, not only for the persons who lived and worked upon it but for the cattle and pigs, the work of the women became so heavy that it was injurious to their health and made them prematurely old. There is a belief in many quarters that the people of that time lived better and reached a more vigorous age than those of the present day are likely to attain, but this is a delusion. The few rugged survivors of the period of which I have been speaking are no more to be taken as types of the average individual of that time than some Hercules of the present day is to be taken as a sample of the average man. It is one of the beneficent consequences of our improved way of living that the weakly and frail now have a chance of existence, and, although their lives may not be prolonged to great age, they can do much good work for themselves and for the world while they are with us.

Seventy years ago the people of New Brunswick were neither so well fed nor so well clad as they are at present. The farmers of those days grew a great deal of Indian corn and this grain entered very largely into the food of the people. Among working men corn meal porridge was much used, and at many of their meals it was the principal dish. The Legislature gave a bounty for the growing of corn on new land, and thus its production was stimulated especially in the river counties. There was no oatmeal in the province in those days because there were no mills in which it could be ground, but oats were

grown in considerable quantities for the lumbermen.
Wheat was grown to a limited extent, but wheat flour
was much less generally used as food than is the case at
present. In the year 1819 there were 32,857 barrels of
flour imported into New Brunswick and 8,109 were exported, leaving a net consumption of 24,748 barrels, so that
no great quantity of wheat could have been grown in the
province at that time. Barley was grown to some extent and also rye. Very little buckwheat was then produced by our farmers, but potatoes, beets, carrots and
other vegetables were grown in considerable quantities.
There are no figures of the live stock owned by the farmers of New Brunswick until the year 1840, but in a general way it may be said that swine and sheep were more
plentiful in proportion to the population in 1818 than
they are at present.

With respect to clothing, the people of the rural districts supplied the largest part of it for themselves.
Large flocks of sheep were kept by the farmers and
their wool was made into homespun by the labor of the
women of the family. The wool was in 1818 carded by
hand, but, in the course of time, carding mills were introduced and the women relieved of this laborious work.
The spinning and weaving, however, remained a part
of their tasks, no house being without a spinning wheel
and few without a loom. The homespun thus produced
was worn by both men and women and was thought good
enough for any person. Homespun was made of the
wool of white and black sheep mixed, five or six of the

latter being kept on every farm to color the cloth, which was called sheep's grey. There was a sort of Kersey cloth, blue and white, which was made into blouses for the men. The blue dye-tub was a feature of every kitchen, and, as it was necessarily closed with a tight cover, frequently served as a seat. Women had their dresses made in plaid patterns and frequently wore what were called camlet cloaks, a sort of Scotch plaid with very bright colors. Their dresses had mutton leg sleeves and their bonnets were of the coal scuttle order. Men wore surtouts that came to their feet, enormous capes covered with pleats and bell crowned hats. The waists of both men and women were just under their arms. When a man wished to have a fashionable Sunday suit he had his homespun fulled and pressed, there being a few mills in the province at which this work could be done. This thickened the cloth and made it more presentable, but suits made of fulled cloth were seldom well fitting or attractive. A tailor was employed to come to the farm-house and make up the suit, and one suit of this kind was generally required to last several years. In respect to dress neither the men nor the women of that day could bear any comparison with those of the present time. All kinds of imported cloths were costly, especially cotton which is now so cheap. In lieu of cotton many of the thrifty farmers' wives manufactured linen out of home grown flax, a laborious and slow process, which seldom yielded good results. In nothing is the advance of civiliza-tion more marked, and with it the increase of comfort, than in the cheapness of cotton goods which now enter so largely into the domestic economy of every inhabitant of this province. Ready-made shoes were not to be had in New Brunswick in the year 1818, and the foot-wear for both men and women was a product of the farm. The hide of the slain beeve or calf was tanned into leather, and the shoemaker, who like the tailor, was a nomadic individual, did the rest. There was not much style about the shoes made under this system and ladies with small feet had but little opportunity of displaying their neatness in calfskin shoes of home manufacture.

Great as is the contrast in the clothing of the people between 1818 and 1891, the contrast in the furniture of the houses is greater still. Few houses in the country had carpets and when there was a carpet in the parlor it was invariably home-made, woven out of the wool grown on the farm. Chairs of painted wood were considered good enough for the best room, and very frequently they were of home manufacture with bottoms of split ash woven in by the Indians. In the kitchen, which was the living room of the house, benches were the ordinary seats. A box about six feet long, two feet wide and two feet high and with a high back, answered for storing fuel and for a bed at night. Frequently the children slept in trundle beds, which to economize space were pushed under the beds of the older people during the day and drawn out at night. Such a thing as a piano, organ or other similar musical instrument could hardly be found in a country house in the province of New Brunswick in the year 1818; now there are few country houses without them. In the matter of books there was also a great contrast between that time and the present. The average farm house was well equipped with reading matter, if, besides a Bible, it had a book of sermons, the Pilgrim's Progress and Doddridge's Saints Rest. Newspapers were seldom to be seen in the country and where they were taken no one was allowed to read them on a Sunday.

The agricultural implements used by the farmers in 1818 were of the most primitive description. Labor-saving farm machinery was unknown. The ploughs were not much in advance, so far as efficiency went, of those in use in Europe a thousand years before. Their mould-boards were of wood sheathed with iron and they had but one handle. The harrows were home made and most of the other implements were clumsy and inefficient. Mowing machines and reapers had not been invented and all the grain had to be cleaned by the wind, after the manner of the Egyptians three thousand years ago. Oxen were much more used than horses in all agricultural operations and much time was wasted by the farmers in following their tardy footsteps. The science of agriculture was but little understood and the proper rotation of crops received hardly any attention. The cattle on the farms were of inferior breeds and yielded but a poor return for the food they consumed. No attention whatever was paid to housing them properly. Any kind of a shed was considered good enough for a barn, and, while they frequently suffered from insufficiency of food, they invariably were exposed to the cold.   The same inferiority of breed which marked the cattle of the country extended to the horses, sheep and swine, especially the latter which were mostly of the racer variety and yielded a minimum of flesh and fat from a maximum of food.

Farm wagons were almost the only wheeled vehicles in use in the rural districts.   A few persons possessed what was termed a chaise, a high two wheeled affair on leather springs, but these chaises were not common and were rather thought to savor too much of luxury.   The ordinary mode of travelling was on horseback and when a lady went to market or to church she usually rode behind her husband on a pillion.   Most of the inhabitants however, were settled on the banks of large rivers, so that boats and skiffs were available for much of their travelling.   There were about five hundred miles of so-called roads in the Province at this period, but most of them were mere bridle paths, only suitable for persons on horseback.   The mail from Fredericton to Gagetown and St. John was carried by a courier on horseback who gave due notice of his approach by vigorously blowing a horn.

The principal road from St. John to Fredericton in 1818 followed the west side of the river past Oak Point, Hampstead, Gagetown and Oromocto.   It was $82\frac{1}{2}$ miles in length and a ferry had to be used at the mouth of the Nerepis and at Oromocto.   The Nerepis road, which reduced the distance to Fredericton by about 17 miles, was not opened until some years later in the time of Sir Howard Douglas. There were two other roads between St. John and Fredericton in those days, one on the east side of the river by Gondola Point, Kingston, the Head of Bellisle, Washademoak, Jemseg and Sheffield, which was 86 miles in length; the other by Hampton Ferry and Head of Bellisle to Vanwart's, where the St. John river was crossed and the road on the west side of the river followed to Oromocto and Fredericton. The other roads of the Province at this time were one to Fort Cumberland by Hampton Ferry, Sussex and the Bend 144½ miles in length; a road from St. John to St. Andrews 67 miles in length, and a road from Fredericton to Miramichi 108½ miles in length. There was no road north of Fredericton on either side of the St. John river; no road between the Bend and Miramichi, and no road north of the Miramichi River. The roads of the province were always an object of interest to its people and in 1816, 1817, 1818 and subsequent years the Legislature made liberal grants for their improvement, but the great size of the rivers, necessitating long and costly bridges, and the other difficulties incident to the construction of roads in a forest country, made progress slow and for many years kept the roads in a backward state. The only mitigating circumstance was that the people used the roads as little as possible and relied almost entirely on water communication where there were any considerable loads to be carried. At that date the distinction between great roads of communication and bye roads

was recognized, but there is no information available as
to the number of the latter, or their aggregate length.
When the great roads were in so bad a condition the
state of the bye roads may be imagined. Many of
them had merely a nominal existence and some were
little better than blazed paths through the forest.

The year in which Sir Leonard Tilley was born was
the third year that a steamboat ran on the river
between St. John and Fredericton. Prior to that time
the only means of travelling of a public character had
been by small sloops and schooners. In 1784 Ne-
hemiah Beckwith established the first scow or tow-
boat on the river between St. John and Fredericton and
in 1786 the schooner Four Sisters began to make regular
trips between the two places, leaving St. John every
Tuesday, wind and weather permitting. Sloops and
schooners continued to run long after steamboats were
introduced and did not cease their trips until the year
1843. The passenger sloop of the year 1818 was not a
very comfortable kind of vessel. Bishop Plessis of
Quebec who travelled from St. John to Fredericton in
the sloop Minerva, commanded by Captain Segee, in 1815,
gives a very amusing account of his voyage. They em-
barked at Indiantown on Thursday morning the 17th.
August at 8 o'clock and did not reach Fredericton until
Saturday afternoon at 4 o'clock. It thus took the Bishop fifty-six hours to accomplish a voyage which is performed by the steamboats of the present day in less than
seven hours. This sloop had twenty-one persons on

board, of whom four were women and four children, and
she was so small that this number crowded her uncom-
fortably.   The captain, a mate and two negroes formed
the crew.   A small-after cabin was reserved for ladies
and the forward one was for the men and was also used
as a dining room.   It was too small to allow all the
twenty-one passengers to eat at once so that they had to
be accommodated at two tables.   The sleeping conveniences were wretched.   The good bishop says patheti-
cally in his journal:—"Dirty beds without clothes and
without blankets were the lot of whoever did not wish
to sleep in the common room and in view of the other
passengers, men and women, who were enjoying themselves at cards far into the night.   The first was so disa-
greeable to the prelate that he retired in his little cabin
with Messrs. Broncherville and Gadreau which scarcely
sufficed to hold them, much less their baggage which had
been piled into a heap.   The following night, the weather
being fine and the moon bright, he determined to remain on deck where towards morning he enjoyed a few
hours of uncomfortable rest on overcoats and other
articles of apparel gathered up from one place and another,
for since leaving Halifax he found himself deprived of all
his articles of night use.   It was under all these inconveniences that two nights and nearly three days were
to be passed in this miserable sloop."

The experience of the Bishop of Quebec was by no
means singular, for the Rev. George J. Mountain, who was
afterwards Episcopal Bishop of Montreal, was three days

on the river between St. John and Oromocto in the year 1814, and being becalmed at the latter place had to make the remaining part of the journey to Fredericton on horseback. It will convey to the modern reader some idea of the difficulties of travel in those days to learn that the journey of this clergyman from Quebec to Fredericton occupied almost six weeks, and cost as much money as a trip to Europe and back would at the present day. He first set sail in a transport from Quebec to Charlottetown, P. E. I. From thence he crossed to Pictou and proceeded by land to Halifax. From the latter place he went to Annapolis and crossed in a schooner to St. John. No one travelled for pleasure in the year 1818.

The first steamer on the St. John river was the General Smyth, and she reached Fredericton on her initial trip on the 21st. May 1816. This vessel was named after the Administrator of the province, General George Stacey Smyth, and like most enterprises of that time had her origin in a provincial bounty. In 1812 the Legislature passed an act "To encourage the erection of a passage boat to be worked by steam for facilitating the communication between the city of St. John and Fredericton." This act was amended and its provisions extended by a statute of 1813 and it was still further amended and extended in 1819. By this last act the owners of the General Smyth were granted the exclusive right of navigating the St. John river by steam for a period of ten years. This monopoly expired in 1829 and was not renewed. The General Smyth only made one trip a week to Fredericton and therefore did not seriously interfere with the sloops which did not abandon the river until many years after a steam tug was thoroughly established. This pioneer steamer took fifteen hours to make the trip from St. John to Fredericton. The trip cost four dollars each way or just four times the present fare. The General Smyth was very unlike the steamboats of the present day, all her cabins being below the main deck. The St. George, owned by the same company, followed the General Smyth but the latter was the only steamboat on the river when Sir Leonard . Tilley was born.

The people who resided on the St. John River, however, did not rely on either the steamer or sloops to take their produce to St. John. They had what were called market boats, these boats being like those used in the whale fishery, sharp at both ends, but considerably larger than a whale boat. They had a cuddy forward, in which a couple of people could find shelter, and carried a mainsail and jib rigged on one mast. Dozens of these boats were to be seen in the market slip at St. John during the summer and nearly all the produce that was consumed in that city was carried in these market boats. For people to whom time seems to have been of little value they answered well enough, but they would not be regarded with favor by the farmers of to-day, who look upon time as money and send their produce to market in the most expeditious manner possible.

Communication was maintained in 1818, and for

B

many years afterwards, between St. John and Digby, by
means of a packet schooner which received a subsidy of
£150 a year from the Government of this Province and a
similar amount from the Government of Nova Scotia. It
was not until the year 1827 that the first steamer was
placed on this route. The steamboat service across the
Bay was steadily maintained from that time for the growing
trade of St. John was vitally interested in it being kept
up. In 1818 a packet sloop named the Wellington owned by Noah Disbrow ran to New York, and several small
sloops with accommodations for passengers sailed between
St. John and Eastport. In 1824 this service was supplemented by a small steamer, the Tom Thumb, which made
trips from St. John to the ports on Passamaquoddy Bay.
In 1825 a packet schooner of considerable size commenced to run to New York, and for many years the
packet service to New York was continued. At a later
period steamers were put on the route between St. John
and Boston, but even so late as the year 1838 persons going
from St. John to Boston had to disembark at Eastport
and drive by stage to Bangor, where they took passage
in a steamboat for Portland or Boston. It is hardly
necessary to remind the reader that in 1818 slow and uncertain sailing vessels were the only means of reaching
Europe from St. John, it being then thought quite impossible for a vessel wholly depending on steam to cross
the Atlantic.

The hotels of New Brunswick in the year 1818 were
few in number and of inferior character. Bishop Plessis,

whom we have already quoted, gives a very unflattering account of those he encountered at Fredericton in the year 1815. Judging from his description the city hotels of that day must have been much worse than the most inferior country inns of the present time. The bar was the most prominent feature in all of them and the name "tavern" which was usually given to them very properly described their character. It was not until the year 1837 that the people of St. John had in the old St. John hotel a place where a traveller could live in comfort and decency. In the country the fewness of the travellers and the universal hospitality of the people made hotels almost unnecessary, but when a new road was opened up it was essential that houses should be provided at which a traveller could find food and shelter. Thus when the Nerepis road from St. John to Fredericton was completed in 1824 two persons were induced to settle on it and keep houses of entertainment, receiving pay from the Government for doing so. This custom was continued for many years with all the new roads that were opened up, and no better proof could be adduced of the primitive state of affairs which existed at that day. The keepers of these subsidized wayside inns usually received from £25 to £50 a year, and considering that they had to live remote from their fellow men they were not overpaid.

Education was in a very unsatisfactory condition in the Province of New Brunswick in the year 1818, and it continued in that condition for many years afterwards.

If we may judge from the statute book the founders of the province had very little appreciation for the advantages of education, for no law was passed with a view to the establishment of public schools until the year 1805. In that year "An act for encouraging and extending literature in this Province" was passed under the provisions of which a public grammar school was established in the city of St. John which received a grant of £100 for the purpose of assisting the trustees to procure a suitable building for school uses, and also an annual grant of £100 for the support of the master. The same act provided for the establishment of County schools, and the sections relating to them being limited in respect to time were continued by 50th Geo. 3rd, cap. 33 to the year 1816 when they expired and were replaced by "An act for the establishment of schools in the province." This act expired in 1823 and in its place "An act for the encouragement of Parish schools" was passed the same year. This last act was repealed by "An act relating to Parish schools" passed in 1833 which continued in force for many years. All these acts were essentially the same in principle as they provided for government aid to teachers who had been employed to teach schools in the parishes under the authority of the school trustees. The act of 1833, which was considered to be a great improvement on former acts, provided for the appointment of three school trustees in each parish by the sessions and these trustees were charged with the duty of dividing the parishes into districts and directing the discipline of the schools. They

were required to certify once a year to the Lieutenant
Governor as to the number of schools in their parish,
the number of scholars and other particulars, and on
their certificate the teacher drew the government money.
This money was granted at the rate of £20 for a male
teacher who had taught school a year, or £10 for six
months, and £10 for a female teacher who had taught
school a year, or £5 for six months, provided the inhabitants of the school district had subscribed an equal
amount for the support of the teacher, or supplied board,
washing and lodging to the teacher in lieu of the money.
Thus, a male teacher, in a district where a school was
always kept, would receive for his year's work his board,
lodging and washing, and £20 in money, and a female
teacher £10. Such a rate of remuneration was not well
calculated to attract competent persons and the result
was very unsatisfactory. Most of the teachers employed
were old men who had a mere smattering of learning and
who were very incompetent instructors. They usually
boarded around among the parents of the pupils, living at
each house in proportion to the number of scholars sent.
This system, which raised them but one degree above
the condition of paupers, was not conducive to their
comfort or self-respect. As there was no uniformity in
the books prescribed and no sufficient educational test,
the results of such teaching were not likely to be
satisfactory. Sometimes the teacher was a woman who
eked out a scanty subsistence by communicating her
small learning to a few scholars whom she gathered in

her kitchen.   Generally, however, the school building was a log hut without any of those appliances which are now regarded as essential to the proper instruction of youth.

In the year 1818 the sum of £3,000 was granted by the Province for the support of public schools; and in 1819 the same amount was granted, but a return made to the House of Assembly shows that only about one half of these amounts was expended, so that there were probably less than one hundred schools in operation throughout the Province, and perhaps 4,000 would be a high estimate of the number of pupils.   Thus it will be seen that, not only were the educational qualifications of the teachers low, but the schools, such as they were, never became numerous enough to meet the educational wants of the children.   This condition of affairs was somewhat improved by subsequent legislation, but it was not until a Normal School was established for the training of teachers that New Brunswick can be said to have had good schools.   The free school act of 1872 finally gave this Province, what it needed most, a first-class school system by which every child born in it could obtain an education.

In 1816 an act was passed providing for the establishment of grammar schools in the several counties of the Province.   At that period St. John and St. Andrews had already grammar schools which had been established under separate acts, and Fredericton had an Academy or College which was founded by a Provincial Charter

granted by Lieutenant Governor Carleton in 1800. The
counties of St. John, Charlotte and York were therefore
excepted from the operation of the general act for the
establishment of grammar schools. This act, after being
amended in 1823, was finally repealed by the act of 1829
which endowed Kings College at Fredericton and made
new provisions for the establishment and support of
grammar schools throughout the Province. Kings College, at a later period, developed into the University of
New Brunswick, which is the only Provincial institution
for higher education that we possess. It had its beginning in the original charter of 1800, already referred to,
which established the College of New Brunswick. In the
same year the Governor and Trustees of the College of
New Brunswick received a grant, under the great seal of
the Province, of a considerable tract of land in and near
Fredericton for the support of that institution of learning.
In the year 1818 the New Brunswick College was merely
a classical school receiving from the Legislature annually
£250, which was the same amount then allowed to the
St. John grammar school. Its principal preceptor was
Rev. James Somerville, a Church of England clergyman,
who was also chaplain to the garrison at Fredericton and
chaplain of the House of Assembly. This gentleman
afterwards became Professor of Divinity and Metaphysics
in Kings College, under its new charter. In 1818, part
of the work of the so-called New Brunswick College was
done by a tutor named Shelton. The St. John grammar
school was then conducted by James Paterson, who took

charge of it that year and who continued to be its head master for upwards of forty years. The Fredericton school and the St. John grammar school were the only institutions in the Province where anything like a good classical education could be acquired in the year 1818, but in the course of a few years grammar schools were established in all the counties, and that at Gagetown was the one at which Sir Leonard Tilley completed his education.

About this time the attention of the people of this Province was directed to what was called the Madras system of national schools as conducted by Dr. Bell, the real founder of the system being Joseph Lancaster. This system depends for its success on the use of monitors, who were selected from among the senior pupils, to instruct the younger ones. It was supposed at the time to be a notable discovery, but like other short cuts to learning, it has fallen out of favor. In July, 1818, the first Madras school was established in St. John by a Mr. West from Halifax. This was a boy's school, and a school for girls, on the same system, was opened a year or two later. In 1819 a Madras School Charter was procured, under the great seal of the Province, and the Madras school system established on a substantial foundation. The province gave a grant of £250 for the erection of a suitable school building in St. John and the National Society in England contributed to its support. This charter was confirmed by an act passed in 1820. The St. John school was to be regarded as the central school, but it was the design of the charter that the benefits of the system should be extended to other parts of the Province, and this was accordingly done. The Madras schools received liberal appropriations of money, and large grants of land, and they continued to exist until the introduction of the free school system. One or two of them indeed continue in operation up to the present time, but they have lost their original character and have become simply Church of England schools, that denomination having appropriated the Madras school endowments to the support of schools in which its principles and creed are taught. It is clearly the duty of the Legislature to take over the Madras school property for the benefit of the common schools.

The Church of England was the leading religious body in the Province in 1818. A majority of the influential settlers among the Loyalists belonged to the Church of England, and for a time it was virtually regarded as an established church. One of the first acts of the Legislature of New Brunswick, 26th Geo. 3rd, Cap. 4, was "An act for preserving the Church of England as by law established in this Province, and for securing liberty of conscience in matters of religion." This act was not quite so sweeping in its provisions as its title would seem to indicate, its principal feature being a provision requiring beneficed clergymen to read the service in their parishes at least once a month. Liberty of conscience was granted to all dissenters, and they were also given the right to erect meeting houses and conduct public worship. The principal disability from which ministers of other denominations suffered was that they were denied the right to solemnize marriages. By 31st Geo. 3rd, Cap. 5, the right to solemnize marriages was restricted to clergymen of the Church of England, ministers of the Kirk of Scotland, Roman Catholic clergymen and Justices of the Peace. Quakers were permitted to marry according to the usages of their sect, but all other ministers were forbidden to solemnize marriages under a penalty of one hundred pounds and twelve months imprisonment. This obnoxious law was not repealed until 1834, when the right of marrying was extended to ministers and teachers of all other religious denominations, provided they obtained a license from the Lieutenant Governor for that purpose. Thus New Brunswick had been a separate Province for about fifty years before ministers of Protestant denominations, other than the Church of England and the Church of Scotland, were granted this important right. The bill was specially reserved for the approval of the King, but fortunately the King's advisers at that time were the reform government of Earl Gray, so the bill became law.

The Church of England had been highly favored in the matter of glebes and grants, but it cannot be said to have made the best use of its opportunities. In 1818 it had but nine settled clergymen, who were stationed at St. John, Fredericton, St. Andrews, St. Stephen, Sussex, Maugerville, Gagetown, Woodstock and Kingston. The Church of Scotland had but one minister, who was stationed at St. John. It is evident that at this time the

Church of England was either very far from doing its duty to its people or that its adherents were much less numerous, in proportion to the rest of the population, than they had been when the Province was first settled. There was no bishop of the Church of England residing in New Brunswick in 1818, nor for many years afterwards, the appointment of the first bishop of Fredericton, who exercises ecclesiastical jurisdiction over the entire province, taking place in 1845. The New Brunswick clergy were in 1818, and up to the year 1845, under the jurisdiction of the Bishop of Nova Scotia, and that ecclesiastic was, until the year 1833, a member of the Council of New Brunswick which, besides being a legislative body, had also executive functions. The Bishop of Nova Scotia appears to have been present at only one meeting of the New Brunswick Council, the date being the 3rd July, 1826. His visit to this province at that time was in connexion with his proper duties as a bishop, and on that occasion he consecrated St. John's Church in this city. The appointment of the Bishop of Nova Scotia as a member of the Council of New Brunswick sufficiently shows, if any proof was needed, that the Church of England was regarded as established in this Province. This idea is also embodied in the charter of Kings College, which was granted in 1828. This charter makes the bishop of the diocese the Visitor of the College and declares that the president shall always be a clergyman, in holy orders, of the United Church of England and Ireland. No religious test was required of students

matriculating or taking degrees in arts, but the Council of
the College, which was the governing body, was to be
composed of members of the Church of England, who,
previous to their appointment, had subscribed to the
thirty-nine articles. The professors to the number of
seven, who were members of the Church of England, were
to be members of the Council, so that although no
religious test was required of them it was reasonably
certain that none but persons of that denomination would
be appointed to professorships. This much can be said
in favor of Kings College, that its charter was much less
illiberal than that of its namesake at Windsor, Nova
Scotia, yet surely it was a rank absurdity to place a
provincial college under the control of a single denomination which could not claim more than one-third of the
population of the Province as belonging to its communion.
This injustice to the other denominations was finally
redressed, but not until after the lapse of many years
and when the usefulness of the College had become
seriously impaired and its very existence threatened.
Even at this day it is doubtful if the University has
ever recovered from the malign effects of the narrow and
sectarian spirit which sought to make it the College of
one denomination instead of a University for all classes
and creeds.

In 1818 the majority of the men who had come with
the Loyalists, and who had occupied influential positions
in the early years of the Province, were dead. Many of
these men were well educated, and some of them had

filled offices of high responsibility in the old colonies. Their sons, who had fewer educational advantages and who had perhaps less natural energy, were the leading men in New Brunswick at the time of which I have been speaking. It is no discredit to the latter to say that they were hardly equal to their fathers either in ability or force of character, and they were beginning to be exposed to the competition of new-comers who had perhaps but little sympathy with the Loyalists or their traditions. In the rural districts the tone of society was very free and easy, and the distinctions of class were but little observed. Among the people who lived on their farms and worked every day for their living, as they had to do at that period, there was very little opportunity for one class to set itself above another. But it was otherwise in the cities. In Fredericton, and also in St. John and St. Andrews, the line which separated the society people from others was very marked. The best society in Fredericton consisted of the official element, with a sprinkling of the military element and the descendants of the old families who kept up the traditions of the past. These people had entree to the Government House, and formed quite an exclusive circle, into which it was difficult for a new-comer to enter. The professional men, lawyers, doctors and clergymen of the Church of England were recognized, for the most part, as belonging to this set, but tradesmen, or men who lived by commerce, were rigorously excluded. In St. John very much the same state of affairs prevailed, except that a

few merchants who were descended from influential
Loyalist families, and who had acquired considerable
wealth, were able to maintain their position in society
beside the official and professional classes. Those who
composed the official classes were not, as a rule, persons
who could claim any very ancient descent, if their pedi-
grees had been submitted to the inspection of a herald in
the United Kingdom. The officials who occupied
positions in Massachusetts and the other colonies before
the Revolution, and who afterwards filled public
positions in Nova Scotia and New Brunswick, were not
generally men of ancient lineage, but they succeeded in
establishing in both these colonies an aristocracy of their
own, and looked down with something like contempt upon
men who were engaged in mercantile pursuits, although
these men might far surpass them in the antiquity of
their families. It is easy to see that where society was
thus controlled on narrow and exclusive lines there was
but little opportunity for its development or for the
growth either of intellect or learning. When a set of
people have made up their minds that they are superior
by virtue of birth to all others, they are not usually in a
condition to advance very far forward in any direction, or
to add to the intellectual or industrial development of the
country in which they live. The regime of this class,
therefore, was rather injurious to New Brunswick, because
it taught the sons of persons who regarded themselves as
the aristocracy to look with contempt upon those pursuits
by the exercise of which the province alone could hope to

become wealthy and prosperous. One thing militated very much against a change in this respect, and that was the largeness of the official salaries in comparison with those of the present day, or with the gains of commercial men. It would be utterly impossible for any official class to occupy the same position now that was occupied by their predecessors in 1818, because as compared to the rest of the population the official classes are now in but indifferent circumstances, whereas they were then the wealthiest people in the Province. We have reached a time, fortunately, when broader views prevail, and when people are not excluded from society by reason of their occupations, where these occupations are honorable and respectable.

Among the customs of the year 1818, which have now utterly disappeared, was the practice of duelling. In those days when two men had a quarrel they thought the proper way in which to vindicate their honor was for them to stand up and avenge the real or supposed insult by pistol practice at each other. Of all the senseless and unchristian methods of settling a dispute the duel was the worst, and it is a singular proof of the original and persistent savagery of human nature that the duel should have existed in this Province within a period which many living men can remember. Duels were quite numerous in New Brunswick seventy years ago, and some of them were fatal. One which is recalled at the present day was that which took place between George Ludlow Wetmore and George Frederick Street, in the month of October, 1821, resulting in the death of the former. In this case the other principal, Mr. Street, and the seconds, Messrs. Davis and Winslow, had to fly from the Province to escape the penalties of murder. But a year afterwards they gave themselves up and were tried and acquitted, thus showing that public opinion was not sufficiently advanced to punish duelling as it ought to have been punished. The fact that George Frederick Street afterwards became a judge of the Supreme Court shows that he did not suffer in social or political influence merely because he had the blood of another man on his hands. One of the latest duels fought in New Brunswick, and fortunately a harmless one, was that which took place between Dr. Wilson, who was then a member for Westmorland, and Thomas Gilbert, a member for Queens, somewhere about the year 1840. After that, duelling gradually fell into disrepute, but the spirit which produced it still survived among some of the ancient inhabitants. This was shown by a singular occurrence which took place during the government of Manners Sutton in 1861, when the Rev. Dr. Jacobs, principal of the University of New Brunswick, becoming offended at some remarks made by the Lieutenant Governor as Visitor of the College, challenged the latter to fight a duel. The duel was not fought, and the challenger had to withdraw his challenge to avoid the penalty of being dismissed from the College. The people of the present day who are unfamiliar with the duel, and who fail to see the philosophy of it, can hardly understand the tone of a society in which such an institution could be tolerated.

In 1818, and for thirty-two years afterwards, the post office was an imperial institution in the British North American colonies. The postal facilities of that day were so very inferior in comparison with what we enjoy at present, as to make any contrast almost an absurdity. The postage on letters was so high that no one sent letters by mail, unless in cases of absolute necessity. It cost seven pence to send a letter from St. John to Fredericton, and a shilling to send one to Richibucto. The postage from St. John to Dorchester was nine pence, and the same rate took a letter to Halifax. But it cost one shilling and three pence to send a letter to Dalhousie, one shilling and six pence to send it from St. John to Quebec, and one shilling and eight pence to forward it to Montreal. These excessive rates of postage existed until the year 1850, when the post office department was transferred to the provincial government. A curious light is thrown on these high rates of postage by some correspondence which passed between the post office authorities and the government of New Brunswick in the year 1843 in regard to the postage charged on certain public documents which had been forwarded to the government of this Province from Nova Scotia and Prince Edward Island. A copy of the laws of Prince Edward Island, which had been sent from Charlottetown for the use of the provincial government, was charged £34 16s. 8d. postage, upon which the provincial

C

authorities here refused to take it out of the post office, and a long correspondence ensued in regard to it. The packet in which the law book was contained being closed, it was subject to letter postage, and the Postmaster General or his deputy was unable to relax or reduce the rate, so that the book in question probably never reached its destination. It is impossible to exaggerate the inconvenience which must have resulted from such excessive rates of postage; nor was this the only evil from which the Province suffered in connection with the post office department. Mails, which now go daily or twice or three times a week, at that day seldom went oftener than once a week, and these mails were usually so small that a courier on horseback was able to carry them with him. Those who had friends at a distance seldom resorted to the post office for the purpose of communicating with them, and depended on sending letters by private hand when some casual traveller journeyed between the places. The same difficulty, with regard to postage, retarded the circulation of newspapers, and prevented the transmission of intelligence throughout the country.

The newspapers of the year 1818 in the Province of New Brunswick were few in number and of very indifferent quality. Besides the "Royal Gazette," which was an official publication issued at Fredericton, there were not more than three or four weekly papers in existence throughout the Province. The principal of these was the "New Brunswick Courier," which was commenced by Henry Chubb & Company in the year 1811, and which existed for upwards of fifty years. The "City Gazette," published by William Durant & Co., was also in existence at that time, and the "Star and Commercial Intelligencer" began its short life about the same period. The newspapers of that day, however, were quite different from these of the present time. Their advertisements were few in number and not very attractive in appearance. Local news was remarkably scarce, and what there was of it was not always properly looked after. The average newspaper of seventy years ago contained a great deal more foreign intelligence, in proportion to its size, than the newspapers of the present day, and far less that had any bearing on New Brunswick. Its columns were usually filled with accounts of the doings of great people in Europe, and, except when the Legislature was in session, there was very little of provincial interest to be found in it. Even when the Legislature was sitting there were no debates published that were worthy of the name, the newspaper editors of that day having a very wholesome dread of being brought up before the bar of the House for breach of privilege. The gentlemen who composed the Legislature in those days thought very highly of their privileges, and were not disposed to deal leniently with any person who ventured to attack them. In 1818, William Durant, the publisher of the "City Gazette," was brought before the bar of the House, charged with the publication of an article which reflected on some of the members. This article was voted a high breach of privilege, but Durant escaped by declaring that the article in question was written by Stephen Humbert, one of the members for the city of St. John. The Legislature then proceeded against Humbert, who was called upon for an explanation of his conduct, and this proving unsatisfactory, he was expelled from the House and his seat declared vacant. The liberty of the press of New Brunswick was of very little value in the year 1818, and therefore there was not likely to be much freedom in the comments of the editors upon the conduct of those who were doing the public business. It was dangerous for a newspaper to offend "the powers that be," and thus any chance of improvement by bringing the force of public opinion to bear on wrong doers was lost. In nothing has the Province of New Brunswick advanced more materially, during the past seventy years, than in respect to its newspapers.

In the year 1818 the timber trade formed the great exporting business of New Brunswick. At that time spruce deals, which now form the staple of our exports, were almost wholly unknown, and it did not enter into the wildest dreams of the people of that period to imagine that the day was approaching when the pine timber trade would come to an end and the despised spruce take its place. Owing to the imperfect character of the returns presented to the Legislature, we have no means of ascertaining what the exports of timber were in the year 1818, but at the session of 1821, a return was made to the House

of Assembly, giving the exports and imports of New
Brunswick for the years 1819 and 1820. From this
return we learn that 1,283 vessels, of 251,538 tons,
entered the ports of New Brunswick in the year 1819,
and that during the same year 1,333 vessels, of 257,293
tons, were cleared from our ports. At that time all the
exports and imports of New Brunswick were included in
the returns of the port of St. John, West Isles, Miramichi
and St. Andrews, all being regarded as out-bays of St.
John. The returns for 1819 and 1820 make no distinction between the exports and imports from St. John and
those from the out-bays, all being lumped together; but
from the returns of 1821, in which they are distinguished,
it would appear that about half the exports of New
Brunswick went from the port of St. John. The exports
of the whole Province for the year 1819 comprised
247,398 tons of timber, 26,545,000 feet of pine boards
and plank, 10,910 oar rafters, 15,821 handspikes, 19,890
hogshead shooks, 6,616,000 shingles, 5,850,000 staves,
6,099 cords of lath wood, and 6,232 masts and spars. In
addition to these the Province exported that year 40,073
quintals of dry fish, 362 barrels of salmon, 11,436 barrels
of herring, and 523 barrels of fish oil. Among the
imports of the Province were 11,974,000 feet of pine
boards and plank, 3,587,000 staves, and 3,746,000
shingles; so that, as is the case at present, a certain
proportion of the lumber exports of New Brunswick
appears to have come from the Province of Nova Scotia.
The exports of timber for the year 1820 were 207,899

tons. The other exports of the Province at this period consisted of coal, gypsum, grindstones and potatoes. The quantities of coal exported were, however, quite small, not much more than 1,000 tons a year. But in 1819, 99,887 tons of gypsum were exported, and in 1820, 30,627 tons. Of grindstones 13,878 were exported in 1819, and 7,053 in 1820. Of potatoes 10,595 bushels were exported in 1819, and 1,657 bushels in 1820. In 1821 the exports of timber amounted to 262,597 tons, of which 145,963 tons went from the port of Miramichi. The most of the pine boards and plank, of which 25,000,000 superficial feet were exported that year, went from St. John, although St. Andrews and West Isles contributed largely. The export of grindstones that year fell to 2,088, but the export of gypsum went up again to 44,554 tons. These figures show what the extent of the timber trade was at the time this narrative opens, and also the fluctuating character of the business done in other articles. The timber trade was conducted in a very lavish and wasteful manner by the people of New Brunswick seventy years ago. The prices obtained for the timber were good, and if there had been but a little economy and care shown in the management of the business the results would have been vastly different and those engaged in it would have become opulent. But at that time timber was so abundant and so easily obtained that the people seem to have been impressed with the idea that the supply would never be exhausted. The men, instead of working closely and industriously at their business in the woods, frequently indulged in prolonged debauches, and there was always far too much rum used in getting out timber for the work to be done with the greatest amount of economy and efficiency. The timber trade largely depended upon the condition of the tariff in the mother country, and the discrimination which existed in our favor and against the countries in the north of Europe which sent timber to the British market.

In 1791, when the export of timber from New Brunswick may be said to have commenced, the duty on Baltic timber in England was only six shillings and eight pence a load of fifty cubic feet. This duty, however, was gradually raised, and in 1812 it amounted to two pounds, fourteen shillings and eight pence a load. In 1820 the duty was two pounds and fifteen shillings a load for Baltic timber, and for the first time a duty of ten shillings a load was placed on timber from British North America. These fluctuations in the rate of duty always produced a degree of uncertainty in the timber trade, but the existence of the duty was of immense advantage to the British North American colonies and to a large extent gave them the command of the market. It was not till a much later period that the system of duties was introduced which gradually placed the British colonies and the nations of the north of Europe on the same footing with respect to this matter. There can be no doubt that had there been the same economy and the same attention to details in the timber trade in the year 1818 which exist at present, the men of that day who

were engaged in it would have made splendid fortunes.*
As it was it is doubtful whether the trade was more
profitable than it is at present, notwithstanding the
enormous productiveness of the forests and the advantage
which New Brunswick and the other British colonies
then had in the markets of Great Britain.

In no one respect, perhaps, have the customs of our
people changed more in the past seventy years than in
regard to drinking. In 1818 such a thing as a total
abstinence society was unknown in New Brunswick and
the consumption of liquor was universal. In that year
there were imported into St. John 329,327 gallons of
rum and shrub, and 32,211 of wine, brandy and gin.
At Miramichi, in the same year, 75,410 gallons of rum

*The following prices of timber and lumber from 1824 to 1839
are taken from the books of the great firm of Robert Rankin
& Co. :—

Year.	Red Pine per ton.	White Pine per ton. 16 to 17 in.	Birch per ton 14 to 16 in.	Deals per M. sup. feet.
1824...28s. to 30s.		20s.	18s. to 20s.	60s. ......
1825...27s. to 31s. 3d.		18s. to 20s.	17s. 6d. to 20s.	56s. to 60s.
1826...27s. to 29s.		15s. to 20s.	18s. to 20s.	55s. to 60s.
1828...27s. 6d.		16s.	17s. 6d.	50s. ......
1829...27s. 6d. to 30s.		21s. 3d.	20s.	60s. ......
1830...25s.		21s. 3d to 22s. 6d.	21s. 3d.	50s. ......
1831...		22s. 6d.	20s. to 21s.	50s. ......
1833...		14s. to 30s.	20s.	50s. ......
1834...		15s. 6d to 26s. 6d.	20s.	45s. to 50s.
1838...		15s. to 22s.	20s.	50s. ......
1839...		19s. 6d to 26s. 6d.	20s.	55s. ......

The above were the prices paid to the producers here, and the
same was shipped at the same price, substituting sterling for
currency.

The sterling then carried no premium, nothing but the par
of 11 1-9.

were imported and 18,084 gallons of wine, brandy and gin. At St. Andrews, in the same year, 102,185 gallons of rum were imported and 2,471 gallons of wine, brandy and gin. That this large importation of liquor was not exceptional or peculiar to the year 1818 admits of easy proof. In 1821 a return was laid before the House of Assembly by the Lieutenant Governor, giving a list of the goods imported and exported at the port of St. John for the years 1819 and 1820. From this return it appears that in 1819 the importation of liquor at St. John alone reached the enormous aggregate of 844,996 gallons of rum, 31,183 gallons of brandy and gin, and 16,345 gallons of wine. But 327,930 gallons of this rum were exported, so that the net consumption of rum that year in the Province appears to have been 517,066 gallons. In 1820 the importations of rum were still greater, the number of gallons brought into the Province that year being 949,260. The export was also greater and amounted to 475,837 gallons, so that the net consumption was smaller than in 1819. That year, however, 19,368 gallons of wine were imported at St. John and 27,336 gallons of brandy and gin.

These figures go to show that the people of New Brunswick seventy years ago were much more addicted to drink than they are to-day. It was indeed an age of drinking. No work of any kind could be done in the field or in the forest, in the shipyard or in the workshop without the assistance of rum. Liquor was as much a staple article for use in the woods as was pork or flour.

The sloops that went up the river from St. John to Fredericton, in Sir Leonard Tilley's boyhood, had their decks piled up high with rum and pork, and the one was regarded as quite as much a necessary of life as the other. Total abstinence was an unheard of virtue in those days.

This sketch of the social condition of New Brunswick seventy years ago might be greatly extended, and fuller details might be supplied to illustrate the various phases of the subject, but it is not necessary to do so. Enough has been shown to prove that life in New Brunswick in 1818 was wholly different from what it is to-day, and that we have advanced since then quite as much in material prosperity as we have in political freedom. The people of to-day would no more endure the hardships and drawbacks which their fathers had to bear than they would the yoke of the family compact, or of a Governor who paid no heed to the wishes of the people.

CHAPTER II.

THE POLITICAL CONDITION OF NEW BRUNSWICK IN 1818.

In 1818 the political condition of New Brunswick and the system of government were very different from what they are at the present time. It would, indeed, have been impossible, with such a system as prevailed in the mother country, for New Brunswick to have enjoyed the same free institutions which exist now. In the United Kingdom, although the constitution was the same nominally which is now in force, its operation was entirely different. The throne was occupied by George III., who for many years had been insane, and whose functions were performed by his son the Prince Regent, afterwards George IV. The old king, who has earned a title to the contempt and hatred of the British people in both hemispheres by conduct which separated the British North American colonies from the mother country and produced a breach between the two great sections of the Anglo-Saxon race which has not yet been healed, was then within but a few months of the end of his life. During his reign, and while his faculties were active, he had introduced into British institutions a degree of personal

government which was wholly incompatible with the free
operation of the British constitution. Those who take
the trouble to read the correspondence between his favorite
minister, Lord North, and George III. will understand in
what fashion the British government was conducted
during the reign of that monarch, and how little the
wishes of the people were consulted or the representative
system of the mother country was retained, many petty
boroughs with small population being able to send members to parliament, while large and populous cities had
no representation or voice in the councils of the empire.
A few great families imagined that they had the hereditary right to rule and control affairs, not only in the House
of Lords, but also in that branch of the Legislature which
was supposed to represent the people. Great land-owners,
like the Duke of Newcastle, were extensive proprietors of
borough influence and were enabled to give support to
the crown in its measures in return for favors in the
shape of sinecure offices. It is a remarkable proof of the
state of affairs which existed at that period with respect
to the colonies that men were appointed to office in
places they had never seen, and who knew nothing whatever of their wants or requirements. Charles Greville, a
clerk of the Privy Council, whose memoirs, recently
published, have excited much interest, not only held that
important and lucrative position, but was also Secretary
for Jamaica, a sinecure office which was performed by
deputy but of which he received the emoluments. It
was not until fourteen years later that the reform bill

was carried in England, that charter of the people's liberties which gradually has brought Great Britain to be the most free and democratic country in the world, with the exception of her colonies. When the old king died the scandal which attended the quarrels between George IV. and his wife filled the land with excitement and horror. This debauched and worthless monarch, who was utterly without one redeeming quality, while he was attempting to obtain a divorce from Queen Caroline for her alleged infidelities, was living in shameless licentiousness with his mistress, Lady Conyngham. With such a spectacle on the throne it was not to be expected that the tone of good society in England could be either pure or satisfactory. Indeed it was not until the reign of Queen Victoria that the better classes of that country were obliged to conform to those rules of decency and good order which alone can make any society tolerable. The constitution of New Brunswick in 1818 was a bad copy of that of the United Kingdom. There was a House of Assembly, which was elected by the owners of a freehold worth £25, if residents of the county in which they voted, or £50 if non-residents. In the city of St. John the members were chosen by freemen as well as by freeholders. The qualification of members was the ownership of a freehold worth £200 in the county which they wished to represent. The term of the general assembly was seven years, and not four as at present. Elections were not by ballot but by open voting, and lasted fifteen days, the poll being removed from one section of the county to

another for the purpose of taking votes.   This system of
election naturally produced great disorders and much
rioting, and tended to convey the impression that the
people were not worthy to be entrusted with power. The
Council, however, which was nominated by the Crown,
and the Lieutenant Governor, who was appointed by the
British government, were the great ruling forces in New
Brunswick at that period.   The Council then exercised
legislative as well as executive functions, and absorbed
most of the authority which was not assumed by the
Governor.   The latter received his instructions from
England as to the manner in which he should conduct
the affairs of the Province, and these instructions, which
were very voluminous, embraced nearly every topic on
which he was likely to find his judgment exercised.   In
a general way they gave him authority over a great many
matters with which a Governor at the present day has
nothing to do.   The Governor virtually controlled the
appointments to office, although these appointments were
sometimes nominally made with the advice of his Council.
When, however, there came to be a question between the
Council and the Governor, the former always had to yield.
The royal prerogative, as it was termed, was supposed to
be pre-eminent and to override the wishes of both the
Council and the Assembly.   This condition of affairs, so
unfavorable to the development of popular government,
was greatly promoted by the fact that the Governor had
control of a large amount of public revenue quite independent of either branch of the Legislature.   The casual

and territorial revenues, which were the names given to the revenues derived from the crown lands of the Province, and also the imperial duties, which were collected by officers appointed by the British government, were at the disposal of the Governor without reference to the wishes of his advisers. The Imperial government also controlled the post office, and, though it was not a revenue-producing branch of the government, this fact still further emphasized the manner in which our affairs were governed from Downing Street.

In 1818 only one member of the original Council of the Province, which was appointed in November, 1784, was alive. This was the Rev. and Hon. Jonathan Odell, who occupied the position of Secretary of the Province from 1784 to June, 1812, when he was succeeded by his son, William Franklin Odell, who held the position until the year 1844. These two Odells, the father and son, filled the office of Provincial Secretary of this Province for more than sixty years, and no better illustration can be found of the manner in which the offices were held and patronage dispensed in those days than this single fact. The Hon. and Rev. Jonathan Odell had been originally an Episcopal clergyman in New Jersey. During the war he became chaplain in one of the Loyalist corps. Being possessed of considerable influence, he succeeded in obtaining the appointments of Provincial Secretary, Registrar, and Clerk of the Council of New Brunswick when the Province was first established, and he was not only able to hold on to that office so long as he wished to perform its duties, but to transfer it to his son, who held it for a period of thirty-two years. This fact shows how little the people had to say in regard to the dispensing of the patronage of the Crown at that period. The Secretary of the Province naturally obtained the ear of the Colonial minister, or what was perhaps more to the purpose, of the permanent clerks in the Colonial office. He was thus able to check any attempt on the part of the people, or of the popular branch of the Legislature, to interfere with him, and in this way all possibility of reform in the methods of government or improvement in the management of the public offices became impossible. The salaries of the officials of the Province were then large in comparison to what they are at present, and the occupants of these offices were able to live on a scale much beyond that of any ordinary merchant or lawyer. They were strong in social influence as well as in political power, and the masses of the people viewed their position as unassailable, and for the most part acquiesced in the claims which these magnates made on behalf of their right to govern the country. The Attorney General of the Province in 1818 was Thomas Wetmore, grandfather of the present judge of that name. He had held the office from the year 1809, and continued to hold it until the year 1828, when he died. The office at that time was not as it is at present—a political one, but generally its term was for the life of the occupant, or till his removal to a judicial position. Jonathan Bliss had been Attorney General of the Province from the year

1785 until the time of Attorney General Wetmore, and his resignation of the position was only due to the fact of his being appointed Chief Justice of the Province of New Brunswick. The Solicitor General in 1818 was William Botsford, who a few years later became a judge. The Advocate General was Ward Chipman Jr., afterwards Chief Justice of New Brunswick. His father, Ward Chipman, had held a position in connection with the pay office of the Loyalist regiments and became Advocate General in 1787, holding that office until he was appointed judge in 1809, when he was succeeded by his son. He was also appointed Solicitor General in 1785, and held that office until he became a judge. Thus it will be seen that the tendency was altogether in favor of making the high offices in the Province hereditary, and that these offices were distributed, not with a view to the greatest efficiency in the public service, but in such a manner as would best satisfy the demands of those who were clamorous for a public position and who had the ear of the Governor and his friends. The Treasurer of the Province in 1818 was John Robinson, who was also Mayor of St. John. The office of Treasurer at that time was one of great importance, he being head of the Provincial customs department, and most of the revenues of the Province coming into his hands. When Mr. Robinson died, in 1828, he was succeeded by Richard Simonds, but on the death of the latter, Beverly Robinson, son of John Robinson, was appointed to the treasurership, thus again illustrating the hereditary principle which prevailed with

D

respect to such offices. The composition of the Council at the period of which I have been speaking is of much interest as illustrating the peculiar system of government which prevailed. Jonathan Odell has already been mentioned as one of the Council from the beginning, and the only survivor of the original Council who was living in 1818. The other members of the Council were: Christopher Billop, John Saunders, Ward Chipman, Jonathan Bliss, John Coffin, John Murray Bliss, William Pagan, Thomas Wetmore and John Robinson. Jonathan Bliss was then the Chief Justice of the Province, and John Saunders, Ward Chipman and John Murray Bliss were judges of the Supreme Court. Thomas Wetmore was Attorney General and John Robinson was Treasurer, so that nearly all the members of the Council were officials of the Province in the receipt of salaries, and not depending upon the public for the positions they held. The relations of the Council to the Lieutenant Governor were generally of an amicable character, as it was natural they should be, considering how much his voice had to do with their appointment or removal. These men, although nominally his advisers, were in no position to thwart his wishes, nor did their desires ever go so far as cause them to set themselves in opposition to his will. On many occasions the Governor made appointments without consulting his Council in any way, it being his idea that he was the sole dispenser of the royal prerogative, and that, as all appointments were supposed to emanate from the Crown, he had the right to appoint without

reference to the views either of the Council or of the
people of the Province over which he presided. The
Lieutenant Governor of New Brunswick, for many years
after the creation of the Province, was Thomas Carleton,
a brother of Sir Guy Carleton, who was afterwards made
Lord Dorchester. Thomas Carleton held the office of
Lieutenant Governor from 1784 until 1817, when he died
in England. He had resided out of the Province for a
great number of years previous to his death, and was so
little known in it that when he died the event excited
hardly any notice. His successor in the office of Governor
was General George Stacy Smyth, who had filled the
office of President on several occasions in the absence of
Governor Carleton. General Smyth being a military
man, as Governor Carleton had been, naturally knew but
little of the civil needs of the Province, and it was not
until the year 1824 that New Brunswick found, in the
person of Sir Howard Douglas, a governor, who although
an officer in the army, was disposed to take an active
interest in the improvement of the Province with respect
to those matters which were outside the mere military
routine. One of the most flagrant evils in connection
with the system of government which prevailed at that
time was the union of legislative and executive functions
in the Council. It was bad enough to have a Council
acting as advisers of the Lieutenant Governor, composed
almost exclusively of office holders and other persons
who were interested in having no changes made, but
the evil became intolerable when the Council was invested

with legislative functions and could reject any bill which
came to it from the House of Assembly, the body chosen
by the people.   The members of the Council, being permanent in their positions and not removable except at
the pleasure of the Crown, naturally looked upon themselves as entirely independent of the people, and as
superior to the persons who composed the popular branch
of the Legislature.   Chief Justice Bliss or Judge Chipman would hardly think the representative of some rural
constituency his equal in point of learning or political
knowledge, and where the Council differed from the
members of the Assembly in regard to any act of legislation the chances were greatly against the opinion of
the House of Assembly prevailing.   This is why it
was so long before any reform could be effected in a
system of government which was essentially vicious, and
which did not in any respect reflect the views of the
inhabitants of the Province.   The House of Assembly
might pass as many resolutions as it pleased and send up
as many bills for the improvement of public affairs as it
found time to discuss, but the Council was not bound to
give them any attention or to do otherwise than suppress
whatever it regarded as a tendency towards popular
government.   At the present day in New Brunswick
government by the people is so firmly grounded in the
constitution that men who advocate any other system
than this are looked upon as relics of a past age ; but in
those days every man who advocated popular government
was regarded with suspicion, as a rebel, a Jacobin, a lev-

eller, a republican, and a malicious person.   A free press, which is now regarded as essential to popular liberty, was then the subject of animadversion and condemnation. Many instances might be cited of the manner in which the attempts of the House of Assembly to improve matters with respect to the system of government were frustrated, but some of these will be referred to more appropriately in future pages at the time of their occurrence. · One of the causes of quarrel between the two Houses had been the desire of the members of the Assembly to pay themselves for their attendance at the meetings of the Legislature, a most wise and sound provision, unless we are to surrender the right of legislation to those who have sufficient means to give up their time exclusively to the public without remuneration. But at that time the Council regarded the measures taken by the House of Assembly to reimburse themselves for their attendance as most reprehensible and blameworthy, and in this view they were upheld by the Governor.   In 1817 the members of the House of Assembly voted themselves fifteen shillings a day during the period of their attendance at the Legislature, or going to or coming from the House, reckoning twenty miles to a day's travel.   This vote seems to have passed without remark, but in 1818 they set the value of their services at twenty shillings a day, and there was a conflict between the two Houses in consequence.   Finally the matter was settled by the same allowance being made to the members of the Council.   In 1819 the amount voted was likewise twenty

shillings a day, and it seems to have been accepted by the
Council.   In 1820, however, when the members of the
new House voted themselves twenty shillings a day for
their services, the Council resolved, on motion of the
Attorney General, that the granting of a remuneration to
the members of the House of Assembly at so high a rate
as twenty shillings a day, is a lavish and improvident
grant, and that the further consideration of the bill
making this grant be postponed for six months.   This
resolve was passed on motion of Mr. Justice Chipman,
who had been careful in his time to obtain as many
offices as possible, and to exact as high a rate of remuneration for them as he could manage to squeeze out of
his employers, whether those employers were the British
government or the people of the Province of New Brunswick.   The members of the House, however, were not to
be so defeated, and they placed the obnoxious item in the
supply bill, so that the Legislative Council had not the
option of rejecting it.   The Lieutenant Governor, in
proroguing the Legislature, did not forget to remind the
members of the House of the words of the Council,
saying that he had not withheld his assent to the appropriation bill, although it contained an item of expense
which had been deemed by the Council a lavish and
improvident grant.   It was thus that the members of
the House of Assembly were accustomed to be lectured
by the Governor and by the members of the Council, who
regarded themselves as a superior order of beings.   This
matter serves to illustrate the manner in which the

business of legislation was conducted by the Governor and
his alleged advisers, the Council. The year 1819 furnished another instance of the bad temper of the Governor,
and of the manner in which he sought to go beyond his
proper authority. The House of Assembly discovered
that the Surveyor General had commenced to exact bonds
from the lessees of timber lands, requiring them to pay a
shilling a ton for all timber they might cut on the lands
leased to them. They naturally enquired of the Governor
what authority he had to make such an arrangement as
this, and he replied that it was done to prevent the waste
of timber on the Crown lands. This, however, was not
a proper answer to the demand, because it was virtually
levying an export duty on the timber of the Province
without the authority of the Legislature of New Brunswick, or of the British Parliament. The Assembly
persisted in their protests against the acts of the Governor,
and that functionary came down in a very bad frame of
mind, at the close of the session, and dissolved the House,
which had then five years to run, stating : " It is with
great concern that I notice your persistence in the
measure to which your attention has been very recently
called, which conduct I cannot suffer to pass unnoticed,
consistent with the duty I owe to my Sovereign. The only
mode which you have now left me to do this is by dissolving this General Assembly." Thus was the business
of New Brunswick conducted seventy years ago, when
Governors imagined themselves to be vested, not only
with the prerogatives of the Crown, but with the whole

power of the Imperial Parliament. The power of the Governor to regulate matters in the Province without the authority of the Legislature was greatly increased by the fact that a certain proportion of the revenue was collected under Imperial authority and could be expended by him without any reference whatever to the Legislature. The British government, under a number of acts of parliament, had been in the habit of levying import duties on certain products that were imported into the Province of New Brunswick. To do this they maintained their own customs establishments, so that the Imperial customs and the revenue officers of the Province both exacted duties upon the same article. The head of the Provincial customs establishment was termed the Province Treasurer, and his officers, who acted as collectors of duties at the several outports, were designated Deputy Treasurers. The Imperial officers, on the other hand, went by their proper names as Collectors and Deputy Collectors at the several ports. This arrangement lasted for many years after the time of which I have been speaking, and was productive of great inconvenience. One of its results was to seriously impair the export trade of the Province, for, while goods imported into New Brunswick from foreign parts were allowed to be bonded by the Provincial authorities, if intended for export, they were required to pay duty to the Imperial authorities, whether intended for export or not, and no drawback was allowed. It was also a subject of complaint, both in New Brunswick and Nova

Scotia, that the customs authorities charged enormous fees on shipping, so as to seriously embarrass the coasting trade between the two Provinces. The customs authorities treated New Brunswick, Nova Scotia, Prince Edward Island and Cape Breton as separate countries, charging fees on their intercourse with each other in the same manner as on foreign voyages; so that a vessel clearing at St. John for a port in Nova Scotia had to pay as high customs charges as if she was bound to the East Indies or to Liverpool. The fee charged on a coaster going from a New Brunswick port to a Nova Scotia port was £2 2s., which of itself was enough to put a stop to the trade which naturally existed between the two Provinces. It was not until the year 1825 that this enormous evil was rectified by the Imperial act, 6 George IV., Ch. 14, which abolished or reduced to reasonable proportions the fees chargeable on the coasting trade, and which placed the customs establishments in the several Provinces on a more liberal footing. By that act the net produce of the revenue collected under the several acts of parliament was to be applied to the use of the Colony, so that the Legislature of New Brunswick obtained control at once of a large amount of money which before had gone into the Imperial exchequer. Even this, however, did not prove altogether satisfactory, because the salaries of customs officials still continued to be paid out of the gross amount of revenue collected, and over these salaries the Legislature of the Province had no control. It was also a cause of complaint that, while the shipping interests of the Province derived great advantages from the reduction or abolition of the fees formerly payable to the officers of the customs, these advantages were neutralized to some extent by the fact that Colonial vessels still remained liable to heavy charges in foreign ports, while British ships and the ships of foreigners, which formerly paid fees towards the support of the custom house establishment in the Province, were admitted free from any fees or imposts whatever. In addition to this large source of revenue from customs the Imperial government retained all the lands of the Province, and the revenue collected from them, which was called the casual and territorial revenue, went into the Imperial exchequer. This revenue was chargeable with the salaries of certain officials in the Province, designated His Majesty's civil list, but it was altogether outside the control of the Legislature of New Brunswick, and the manner of collecting it and the amount collected were regulated by the authorities of Downing Street. Under this system corruption flourished, extravagance reigned supreme, and the Surveyor General, who was head of the Crown Land Department, became a great personage with a large revenue, sometimes greater than that of the Lieutenant Governor, and with more political influence than any official ought to possess.

In those days the fees exacted by the Surveyor General and other officials on land grants were also the subject of complaint. It appeared from a return which was made by the Governor in reply to an address of the Legislature in 1819, that the fees exacted on a grant of land not exceeding 300 acres in extent, amounted to £11 13s. 4d., equal to almost $47 of the money of the present day. Of this sum the Governor received £4 1s. 8d., the Secretary £3 7s. 6d., the Attorney General £1 10s. 10d., the Surveyor General £2, and the Auditor General £2 13s. 4d. It will be seen by this that these officials, who virtually controlled the affairs of the Province, had a direct pecuniary interest in the issuing of land grants, and that while on the one hand the fees exacted were enormous and excessive, on the other hand it was to their advantage to encourage the issuing of grants to as large an extent as possible. This was an almost certain means of defeating the object of the Legislature to effect the settlement of the Province by industrious workers, for the fees, while high on all grants, were excessive on the smaller ones, and the burthen diminished in proportion as the grants became large. In an address which was presented to the King in the year 1831 by the Legislature, the grievances under which the Province suffered from the operation of the system of dealing with the Crown lands, were duly set forth. It was stated that under this system very large sums were taken from the people of the Province for licenses to cut timber, and that enormous fees were exacted without the authority of Parliament or of the Legislature. It was complained that the Commissioner of Crown lands imposed on timber licenses a duty of 1s. 3d. per ton and exacted a fee of 45s., thereby injuring the subject without benefiting the revenue. It is no wonder that under the circumstances the members expressed their opinion that such a system of taxation, without authority, was incompatible with free government, and required redress.

Another great evil in connection with the system of government which existed in the year 1818 was the absence of executive responsibility. The money which was received by the Province went into the office of the Provincial Treasurer freely enough, but the manner in which it was to be disposed of was largely left to chance. There was no executive authority in the Province at that time, which exercised the same functions as the Executive Council of the present day. The Governor was not responsible to any person but the Crown or the British government. The members of the Council were not responsible to the people, and were selected without reference to the wishes of the people; and while the House of Assembly could withhold grants of money which were necessary for the public service, the manner in which these grants were made was highly unsatisfactory, and demoralizing in its tendency. At the present time the business of the Executive has to be considered as a whole, and the government is responsible for the due disbursement of the public money for the public services. The government is supposed to know how much money it will have at its disposal, and how much it can afford to pay, and any attempt on the part of the House of Assembly to force it to grant a larger sum than it considers the finances of the Province can afford, would be regarded as a vote of want of confidence, and would lead to its resignation. For that reason all money grants which are moved in the Assembly must be initiated by the Executive, and no private member can present a petition asking for money, or can introduce a bill requiring the payment of money, without the assent of the government. But in 1818 the disposal of the money was entrusted to a committee which doled out grants for the public services in such a manner that no one was responsible for them. This led to what was called a system of "log rolling," by which a member who desired grants for his own locality agreed to support the grants of members from other localities on condition that his demands were supported by them. Thus the member for Queens, who wished to have a new road opened in a country district, and wanted a grant for that purpose, agreed to support a similar demand from the member for York or the member for St. John, on condition that his grant was supported by them. It is easy to see that under this system there was no check whatever on extravagance, and that sums of money might be voted for grants far beyond the ability of the Province to pay, no one having any very clear idea of what the income of the Province was or might be during a certain year, and everybody being anxious to obtain as much money as possible for his own district. It will be seen by and by how strongly the effort to bring about a change of system and the introduction of responsible government was resisted even by those who were most opposed to the arbitrary and absurd restrictious imposed on the Province by the Colonial office. There were many men who were ready to resist the exactions of the customs authorities and denounce the extravagance of the Crown Land Depart-ment, who, when it came to the placing of the control of the finances of the Province in the hands of the Executive, exclaimed against the proposed innovation and denounced it as an infringement on their liberties. Fortunately for New Brunswick, these half-hearted friends of improve-ment who halted by the way, were not able to prevent altogether the introduction of responsible government in its integrity, although they contrived to retard it for a good many years.

Another great cause of complaint at the system of government which prevailed in this Province in the year 1818 was the predominance that was given to members of the Church of England. Of the nine members of the Council who were in office in that year, all but one belonged to the Church of England. Every judge of the Supreme Court belonged to the same communion, and indeed the first judge appointed in New Brunswick who was not a member of the Church of England was the Honorable L. A. Wilmot, who took his seat for the first time on the Bench in 1851, after the Province had been in existence for almost seventy years. The same state of things was found to exist with regard to the other offices, the fact that a man was a member of the Church of England placing him in a much more favorable position for obtaining an office than if he belonged to one of those

bodies which were called Dissenters. In the Province
of Nova Scotia, in the year 1809, the bishop was made a
member of the Council, and soon afterwards the Bishop
of Nova Scotia was appointed a member of the Council
of New Brunswick. In July, 1826, the Right Reverend
John Inglis, Lord Bishop of Nova Scotia, took his seat
as a member of the Council of New Brunswick, while on
a visit to this portion of his diocese. This was the first
and only instance of the Bishop of Nova Scotia exercising
his rights as a member of the New Brunswick Council,
but the fact that such an instance should have occurred
shows that the right might have been exercised at any
time, and also emphasizes, in a very marked manner, the
evil and injustice of the system of government which
permitted the head of one denomination of Christians to
exercise the functions of an executive councillor and a
member of the upper branch of the Legislature, while
ministers of other denominations were not only excluded,
but were expressly disqualified, by act of the Legislature,
from being elected members of the House of Assembly.
In Nova Scotia the bishop was given precedence in the
Council after the Chief Justice, but his appointment was
with the understanding that he was not to administer the
government in case of the death or absence of the
Lieutenant Governor, and this appears also to have been
his status in New Brunswick.

But while clergymen were disqualified from occupying
seats in the Legislature, office holders who were in the
receipt of a salary from the Province were eligible to be

members of the Council or members of the House. This still further tended to create an official class, and it also enabled certain greedy individuals to acquire numerous offices for themselves, so that sometimes one man in each county would absorb nearly all the official positions in it which were of any pecuniary value. At a period later than that when this history commences, there was one practising lawyer in New Brunswick, who afterwards became a judge of the Supreme Court, who at one time was a member of the House of Assembly for the County of Kent, Speaker of the House of Assembly, Postmaster of Richibucto, Deputy Treasurer of Richibucto, Issuer of Marriage Licenses for the County of Kent, Keeper of the Seals and Clerk of the Peace and of the Inferior Court of Common Pleas for the County of Kent, and Registrar of the Probate Court for the County of Kent. Nor was this a solitary instance of a plurality of offices in one individual. Many other examples could be given if it were necessary, in which one person absorbed half a dozen or more offices, and thereby acquired a powerful influence, altogether out of proportion to his merits and wholly incompatible with the efficiency of the public service. The manner in which appointments to office were made, and the utter powerlessness of the people to control the appointing power led to great abuses, and to a tyrannical exercise of authority on the part of those who held offices. Few men are so good or so conscientious that they will not abuse their authority if they are subject to no control, and the "insolence of office," of which Shakespeare

speaks, was very prevalent in the Province of New
Brunswick in the year 1818, and for many years afterwards. In these days by the aid of a free press and
under the system of appointment, by which the responsibility is placed on the government, no official dares to
presume to abuse his power or to treat the public with
incivility. But such was not the case seventy years ago,
when men were pitch-forked into power and authority
who treated the common people as if they were the dirt
beneath their feet, and regarded those who ventured to
criticize their conduct as seditious persons, who were
almost guilty of rebellion.

There were two circumstances connected with the time
of which I have been speaking, which it is necessary to
mention in this connection. The treaty of peace between
Great Britain and the United States, by which the independence of the latter was acknowledged, had left the
boundary question in a very unsatisfactory condition.
The person who represented Great Britain in that treaty
was evidently altogether ignorant of the topography of
the country between the United States and the remaining
British possessions on this continent, and as a consequene
of this, the description of the boundary was of such a
character as to be utterly inexplicable. The boundary line
of the United States was declared to be "from the northwest angle of Nova Scotia, to wit, that angle which is
formed by a line drawn due north from the source of the
St. Croix River to the highlands which divide those
rivers that empty themselves into the River St. Lawrence

E

from those which flow into the Atlantic Ocean, to the northwestermost head of Connecticut River, thence down along the middle of that river to the 45th degree of north latitude, etc." The first difficulty which presented itself in regard to this boundary line was the determination of which of the rivers that entered Passamaquoddy Bay was the St. Croix. This was finally determined by a commission, which concluded its labors in 1798, and which decided that the true St. Croix was the river which now bears that name. When this matter had been settled there still remained the further difficulty of discovering the highlands which divided the rivers which empty themselves into the River St. Lawrence from those which flow into the Atlantic Ocean. It has now long been known that no such highlands exist, and that the search for them was as vain as the quest for the philosopher's stone. But the matter for many years continued in controversy, and the boundary question was not settled until the Ashburton treaty in the year 1842. After the war between the United States and Great Britain, which commenced in 1812, the treaty of peace, which was arranged at Ghent, made provision for deciding as to the ownership of the lands in dispute, particularly with reference to the islands in Passamaquoddy Bay, Grand Manan, Campobello and other islands which were claimed by the United States. The treaty provided for the appointment of two commissioners, one to be selected by his Britannic Majesty, and one by the President of the United States, to decide the question. These commissioners were also charged with the duty of ascertaining the northwest angle of Nova Scotia, in order that that part of the boundary might be defined. The commissioners appointed were Colonel Barclay, who had for his agent the Hon. Ward Chipman of New Brunswick, and the Hon. John Holmes, of Massachusetts, for the United States. Their first meeting was held in September, 1816, and at the opening of the Legislature in January, 1818, Lieutenant Governor Smyth was able to congratulate that body on the fact that the final decision of the commissioners in respect to the islands in Passamaquoddy Bay had been made, and that Grand Manan, Campobello and other important islands had been found to belong to Great Britain; Moose Island and two other small islands of no importance being given to the United States. The fishery question at the same time became one of great consequence to the people of the Maritime Provinces. By the treaty of 1783 the people of the United States were allowed to continue to enjoy unmolested the right to take fish " off Quebec in the Gulf of St. Lawrence, and all other places in the sea where the inhabitants of both countries used at any time heretofore to fish." And they were also allowed to have liberty to take fish on such parts of the coast of Newfoundland as British fishermen should use, and also on the coasts, bays and rivers of all other of His Majesty's bays and dominions. In addition to this they had also liberty to dry their fish in any of the bays of Nova Scotia, the Magdalen Islands and Labrador. Thus it will be seen that the treaty of 1783 virtually gave to the people

of the United States concurrent rights of fishing with
the fishermen who were subjects of Great Britain, and
had that state of affairs continued to exist, the fishery
disputes which have since taken place would either never
have arisen, or would have assumed an entirely different
form.   But it was held by the British authorities, after
the war of 1812, that the provisions of the treaty of 1783
which related to fishing had been abrogated by the war,
and that new arrangements must be made in regard to
the fisheries.   Thus in 1817 a circular from the British
government to the collectors of customs and light dues at
the different ports of the Maritime Provinces stated that
American fishermen were not to be permitted to frequent
the harbors, bays or creeks of the Maritime Provinces,
unless driven into them by actual distress.   The difficulties between the two governments in regard to these
rights of fishing finally resulted in the arrangement of a
treaty, which was made at London, between Great Britain
and the United States, on the 20th of October, 1818, and
which was ratified at Washington in the following January.   This treaty, which is the one now in force, defined
the rights of the Americans with regard to fishing on our
coasts, and excluded them from our waters within three
marine miles of the coasts, bays and creeks of His
Majesty's dominions.   The Americans by this treaty
explicitly renounced forever any liberty before enjoyed or
claimed by them to take, dry and cure fish within three
marine miles of our coasts, bays or harbors.   The treaty
defined their rights to enter our bays or harbors to be "for

the purpose of shelter, of repairing damages therein, of purchasing wood and obtaining water, and for no other purpose whatever." The arrangement of this treaty, which has had such an important bearing on the relations of Canada and the United States since that time, was an important event connected with the history of the year 1818.

The revenue of the Province in 1818, and during the years which followed that period, was subject to great fluctuations. In 1818 the entire receipts of the Province, which went into the hands of the Provincial Treasurer, amounted to a total of £15,348 7s. 6d., while the expenditure was £22,859 7s. 9d. Fortunately there was a large balance from the previous year, so that notwithstanding the deficit in the revenue, there still remained a surplus at the close of the year. In 1819 the revenue received, exclusive of seizures, amounted to £23,338 10s. 8d., while the expenditure was £20,886 16s. 10d. That year £8,925 in treasury notes were issued, a device which was frequently resorted to when money was required. In 1820 the receipts, exclusive of a loan, amounted to £27,904 18s. 10d., and the expenditure to £20,408 15s. 3d. The revenue sometimes showed a handsome surplus over the expenditure, and at other times was deficient, the import trade apparently not being established on the same sound and stable lines which prevail at the present day, but much of it being of a speculative character. It is amusing to contrast the small sums which were deemed sufficient to defray the expenses of the Province at that period in comparison with what is now required even for our mere Provincial concerns, to say nothing of the amount expended on Dominion account, and the large sums disbursed by the municipalities. Small as the grants were for the different services at that period, it not infrequently happened that a large part of them were not expended, either in consequence of the lack of money in the treasury, or because the work for which the grants was made was postponed to a later day. In 1821 a committee was appointed to enquire and report what sums of money heretofore granted remained unpaid, and what would be the disposable funds of the Province, which had arisen or would be likely to arise from the revenue in the course of the current year. This committee found that during the previous two years no less than £23,732 14s. 4d. of money which had been appropriated to the public services had not been expended. Of this sum £1,845 was on account of bounties on fish, £425 was on account of bounties on grain, £2,700 was money granted for the encouragement of schools and £5,000 was money granted for bye-roads. As the balance in the Provincial chest was £121 16s. less than the total of these unexpended grants, the committee could only report that there were no disposable funds in the treasury. Thus the public services at that time were maintained in a very inefficient manner, mainly because of the smallness of the revenue available for public needs. When we take into account how much had to be done in the way of opening up the Province by the construction of roads, the

building of bridges, and in other ways, we must admire
the courage of those who undertook to reduce the wilderness into subjection with such inadequate resources.
Nothing but the adaptability of the people of that period
to their circumstances, and their willingness to endure
privations for the sake of living under the British flag,
would have sufficed to do the work which has since been
accomplished. It was fortunate that New Brunswick
had so hardy and self-reliant a population, even if they
were somewhat deficient in political discernment, and
thought too much of the prerogatives of the Crown, for,
after thirty-five years of settlement, the Province was, in
1818, little better than a wilderness, and the conveniences
for travel were of such a character as we should at the
present day regard as utterly inadequate. He would
have been a bold man who would have ventured to
predict that during the seventy years that were to follow,
not only would the constitution of the Province be
entirely changed, but that its material advancement would
be so great that the most distant point in it could be
reached from St. John in the course of a few hours, and
that no county within its boundaries would be without
rapid and regular communication.

The foregoing sketch of the political condition of New
Brunswick in 1818 is necessarily brief and somewhat
incomplete, because the subject will be more fully developed as our narrative advances, and as the story of
the means adopted to bring about responsible government is related. It is sufficient here to indicate

slightly, and in a general way, the leading features of the system of government at that period, and to leave the details to be told as they arise in the course of the narrative.

CHAPTER III.

AGITATION FOR A BETTER SYSTEM OF GOVERNMENT.

The Province of New Brunswick was always the most conservative of the British colonies of North America, and that feature of its condition has been retained until the present time. In Upper Canada the Loyalist element was smaller in number than in New Brunswick, and was mixed largely with immigrants from the United States who came after the Revoluntionary war for the sake of the fine lands of that Province ; and at a later period a very large immigration took place from the British Islabds of people who had no particular sympathy with the views of the Loyalists, and who were imbued with that spirit of political unrest which had begun to prevail in the mother country at that period. In the Province of Quebec, the French element, though conservative during the French regime, became radical under British rule, and was always arrayed in opposition to the governing classes, who were mainly British. Thus the French, in spite of themselves, became a valuable aid in the regeneration of the Provinces from the old system of government. In the Province of Nova Scotia the original settlers were

English, and they were largely reinforced by immigrants from the New England colonies who came prior to the Revolutionary war, and who were in sympathy, to a large extent, with the principles of the American revolution. The Loyalists were never as numerous in Nova Scotia as in New Brunswick, and never possessed one tithe of the influence there that they possessed here. In New Brunswick the original settlers from New England, who resided at Maugerville, Sheffield, and some parts of the County of Queens, were insignificant in numbers in comparison with the Loyalists, and they had become so cowed after their unsuccessful attempt to cast their lot with the Revolutionists in the year 1777 that they never possessed any political importance afterwards. For this reason, and because of the small dimensions of the immigration from Europe, the Loyalists possessed absolute control of the government of this Province for a period of more than half a century after its formation, and if the matter were now examined into closely, it would be found that they still possess a preponderating influence in Provincial affairs.

In those days the term "loyalty" was frequently mis-used in its application. Instead of being taken as another word for patriotism and devotion to the flag which floated over the Province, it was used merely as being applicable to a condition of mind which impelled a man to support the existing order of things, whether it was right or wrong. Nothing seems more absurd to us of the present day, who look back upon the long dreary period of family compact rule, than to find every person who desired to change this system and to make it more in accordance with the wishes of the people, denounced as an innovator, as a seditious person and a disloyal man. Our ancestors in New Brunswick seem to have had a great horror of the word "innovation," and any one who could raise that cry and shout it loudly and frequently enough was sure to obtain an attentive hearing and a large following. Yet for all that from the very beginning of the Province there were signs that many were not satisfied with things as they were. There were disputes at the very foundation of the Colony over land grants, which were thought to have been unfairly distributed, and not in accordance with the wishes of the home government. There were, likewise, difficulties in regard to the cost of surveying the lands, and also in reference to the fees that were exacted upon grants. When the Legislature was formed the dissatisfaction of many was practically expressed in riots at the polls, and in the return to the House of Assembly of members who were not in sympathy with the ruling classes. As early as 1795 we find great commotion caused in the Province by a Mr. Glennie, who was a candidate for the representation of the County of Sunbury, and who addressed a long speech to the freeholders on their grievances, which was printed in pamphlet form. In 1802 there were difficulties in regard to matters of appropriation between the House of Assembly and the Council, which led to a number of the members of the House withdrawing themselves from their attendance there and going home ; and these proceedings resulted in the issuing of more pamphlets for and against the course adopted. In those days, and for a long time afterwards, the Governors were in the habit of lecturing the Assembly, as if they were a set of school boys. This course was commenced by Governor Carleton, who, in 1795, expressed his indignation at the Assembly because they refused to pass some appropriations which had been recommended by him for the general defence of the Province. At that time, and for long afterwards, the House of Assembly and the Council were in disagreement, and this state of affairs continued more or less down to the time when responsible government became an acknowledged feature of the constitution. The home authorities always sided with the Governor, and reflected severely on the Assembly whenever that body was so unfortunate as to differ from the views of His Excellency. The House always claimed the right to make the appropriations for the public service, and rejected the claim of the Council to amend or modify such money bills as were passed by the Assembly. In 1796 the Duke of Portland, who then was at the head of the department which had the charge of Colonial affairs, laid down the rule that while the appropriation of monies voted was peculiarly within the province of the Assembly, the directing of the actual payment of the public accounts and contingencies by the House of Assembly was an improper encroachment on the functions of the Executive government. He condemned the practice which had been adopted of inserting different and distinct, as well as disputed points, in money bills, and said that persistence in this practice would result in absolute annihilation of the other deliberative branch of the Legislature. He quoted a standing order of the House of Lords, which had been made in 1702, in which it is declared "that the annexing any clause or clauses to a bill of aid or supply, the matter of which is foreign and different from the matter of the said bill, is unparliamentary, and tends to the destruction of the constitution of this government." He added that such matter should be brought forward as separate bills, thereby admitting a free and candid discussion. He thought that a steady adherence to this rule would heal the differences between the House and the Council. They do not seem to have healed their differences, however, because a year later, in June, 1797, the Duke of Portland is again addressing Governor Carleton on the subject, and expressing His Majesty's regret and displeasure that difficulties still exist between the Council and the Assembly of New Brunswick. The differences then seem to have arisen in consequence of the desire of the members of the Assembly to grant themselves a remuneration for their attendance, and the Duke of Portland expressed the opinion that such a measure could only tend to lessen the weight and dignity of the Assembly and to diminish the reverence and respect which he hoped the Province would always show to its Legislature. Another communication, dated a year later, June 5th, 1798, from the same nobleman, expressed still further concern at the differences which continued to prevail to the injury of the joint interests of the Crown and the Province. These references show the nature of the differences which existed between the Council and the Assembly, but they do not involve those principles of good government for which New Brunswick had to strive so earnestly in future years and which were finally triumphantly successful. We may therefore date the first awakening of the Assembly to the anomalous condition of their constitution, and the unsatisfactory. manner in which they were governed, to the year 1818. For some years before that time Governor Carleton had been absent from the Province, and public affairs had been administered by successive " Presidents," as they were called, who stood in the place of the Governor, but who probably had not the ear of the authorities at home to the same extent. But when a new Governor was appointed, in the person of General George Stacey Smyth, a man with very high views of the royal prerogative and of his own importance, then there began to be that friction between the Assembly and the Executive which finally resulted in an entire change of the system. The term " royal prerogative " was one which had a sweet sound to many of the old inhabitants of the Province at that period, they apparently being impressed with the idea that there was some connection between the maintenance of the royal prerogative and the maintenance of their liberties. But when the prerogative came to be used as a cover for scandals of the worst description, for robbery of the people by means of avaricious office holders, and for disregard of the wishes of the Legislature, then it ceased to be so popular.

General Smyth adroitly took advantage of his position as Lieutenant Governor of the Province and endeavored to manufacture a public opinion hostile to all reform. In the year 1820, at the opening of the Legislature, we find him addressing the gentlemen of the Council and the gentlemen of the House of Assembly as follows :—

"It cannot but be a subject of anxiety and regret that a spirit utterly hostile to our excellent constitution, and subversive of all order in society is so fully manifest in various parts of Great Britain, but I trust that the sentiments of veneration for His Majesty, and decided determination to resist all innovation, expressed in the addresses of the industrious and most respectable classes of society to His Royal Highness the Prince Regent, will dissipate this, I hope temporary, gloom, an event which would afford to none a more lively satisfaction than to the loyal inhabitants of this Province. And it would give me, gentlemen, much pleasure to have the honor of conveying to the throne, from you, their sentiments upon those proceedings, so highly interesting both to His Majesty and his people."

The trouble to which the Governor thus referred was the first wave of the reform movement which afterwards swept over England and buried feudalism beneath its waters. In 1819 and 1820 the people of England began to think that some change was needed in their representative system, and the constitutional agitation which they then commenced for that purpose, is what Governor Smyth found to be such "a subject of anxiety and regret," that he asked the Legislature to address His Majesty on the matter. In reply to this speech of Governor Smyth's, the Assembly expressed their unfeigned sorrow that a spirit of disaffection prevailed in many parts of Great Britain, and said that "they are astonished that men can be so blind to the blessings of our glorious constitution as to attempt the subversion of it." They trusted, however, "that the loyalty of the better informed part of the nation will speedily check this evil and avert from the country the destructive consequences which at one time were but too much to be apprehended." They thanked His Excellency for the high opinion he had expressed of the loyalty of the people of the Province, and for his offer to convey their sentiments to the throne, and closed in the following words:—

"Far removed from the suggestions of the seditious, His Majesty's dutiful subjects in this Province are fully sensible that their happiness here and hereafter must depend upon the cultivation of the principles of religion and a just subordination to lawful authority, always bearing in mind the moral precept 'To Fear God and Honor the King.'"

The very day this address was passed the House of Assembly resolved that a committee be appointed to request the Council to join the House in an humble address to His Royal Highness the Prince Regent, expressive of the sentiments they entertained of "the loyalty of His Majesty's subjects in New Brunswick, and of their firm and inviolate attachment to His Majesty's person and government." A joint address, couched in this strain, appears to have been agreed to by both Houses, without any protest being entered against it by any member of either House, and it was duly forwarded to the Prince Regent, as an expression of the sentiments of the people of New Brunswick in regard to the constitutional agitation for reform which was then going on in the British Islands. Such a proof of the slavishness and ignorance which characterized the proceedings of the Legislature of the Province of New Brunswick at that time will serve to emphasize the difficulty which reformers must have experienced in obtaining any substantial improvement in the constitution of the Province. Our Tories at that period, not content with insisting on the maintenance of the "family compact" and the irresponsible system of government which prevailed in New Brunswick, must needs extend the sphere of their influence to the British Isles, and attempt to give their moral support to the obstructionist party which sought to perpetuate all the monstrous evils of the unreformed British constitution, by which the whole power of the state was centred in a few privileged individuals; while the masses were wholly unrepresented.

In describing the various steps by which the constitution of the Province was improved until it reached the form in which it existed prior to the confederation of the

F

Provinces, it will be convenient to take up each particular reform separately, and trace its progress from the first agitation on the subject until the change asked for was effected.

Among the first of the grievances to which the attention of the House of Assembly was called in 1818, was the excessive fees charged on land grants. These fees, as already stated, amounted to the enormous sum of £11 13s. 4d. on a lot of land not exceeding three hundred acres, and where a lot of a thousand acres was granted to ten grantees in severalty, under the scale of fees that then existed, the amount chargeable was £49 12s. 7d., which was not very much less than the value of the land itself. By this system of enormous fees the officials of the Government became enriched, while the settlement of the Province was discouraged. The House of Assembly, in 1818, passed an address to His Excellency, the Lieutenant Governor, asking for copies of such parts of the royal instructions as related to the granting of Crown lands and fees on grants. It appears that the officials had been in the habit of compelling each applicant for Crown lands to take out a separate grant, thereby greatly increasing their profits, whereas the House maintained that the royal instructions contemplated the granting of lands to several grantees in a single grant. A committee of the House, which was appointed to examine the royal instructions, reported that they could find nothing in the instructions to justify the system adopted in the Crown land office, compelling each applicant to take out a sep-

arate grant, and that the table of fees showed that the
instructions contemplated more than one applicant being
included in a grant. They also reported that if this
system was pursued it would be injurious to the Province,
and a prohibition against future settlement. Acting
on this report, the House again requested His Excellency
to furnish them with such parts of the royal instructions
as directed that not more than one grantee should be
included in any one grant. In reply to this, His Excellency said that he had already communicated such parts
of the royal instructions as he deemed necessary, and he
sent them a copy of a letter from Lord Bathurst, relating
to the mode of passing the King's grants. This letter does
not appear in the journals of 1818, but committee of
the House reported that Lord Bathurst did not sufficiently
know the facts in regard to the mode of granting lands in
this Province, and that his letter did not sanction the
system then so universally complained of, compelling
each applicant to take out a separate grant. This was
followed up by a resolution of the House of Assembly for
a joint address, (with the Council) to the Prince Regent,
asking him to direct that the practice of including several
grantees in one grant, be again adopted. The Council,
however, with its usual obsequiousness to the authority
of the Governor, declined to concur in this address,
whereupon the House requested that official to
transmit their address to the Prince Regent,
without reference to the Council. This was done and,
the following year, a reply to the address was

received from Lord Bathurst, in which he stated that he saw no objection to continuing the system of including a number of grantees in one grant, provided that in every grant the lands were distinctly apportioned to the several grantees, and that each grantee was separately and as fully bound to fulfil the conditions of the grant as to his own lot, as if he had taken it out as his own particular grant. Thus one important reform was achieved, which materially reduced the gains of officials, and made it possible for a number of poor men to unite in a land grant, thereby saving large sums in fees, and so assisting in the settlement of the Province.

It has been already stated that under the original system, with respect to the solemnization of marriages, the only religious persons authorized to solemnize marriages were clergymen of the Church of England, ministers of the Kirk of Scotland, Quakers, and clergymen of the Roman Catholic church. This was felt to be an intolerable grievance, because it excluded all dissenters, so called, that is to say, all who were not in communion with the Church of England, with the Kirk of Scotland, or with the Roman Catholic church. Methodists, Baptists, and all Presbyterians, except those connected with the Church of Scotland, were excluded from the operation of this marriage law. The agitation for a change in this system commenced at an early period, and as early as 1821 a bill passed the House of Assembly, authorizing all ministers of the gospel to solemnize marriage. The vote by which this bill was finally passed was a narrow

one, thirteen "yeas" to eleven "nays," all the ancient
Tories being, as was to be expected, ranged against the
so called innovation. It may be interesting to note that
among those who opposed this just measure were Hugh
Johnston, Harry Peters and Ward Chipman, jr., of St.
John, and John Allen, of the County of York, while John
Wilmot, Charles Simonds and Andrew S. Ritchie, of St.
John, and Peter Fraser, John Dow and Stair Agnew, of
the County of York, were on the side of reform. The
two members for Kings County of that day, John C.
Vail and David B. Whitmore, were against the bill,
while of the Queens County members one, William
Peters, was for it, and the other, Samuel Scovil, was
against it. This bill was defeated in the Council, a fate
that befel many subsequent bills of the same kind in that
body. For several years the House of Assembly continued to pass the dissenters' marriage bill, and the
Council as steadily to reject it. The opposition to this
measure in the House gradually died away, until in 1830
there was no division taken on its passage, but that made
no difference in regard to the attitude of the Council
towards it, and the bill was rejected, as it had been so
many times before. In 1831 a dissenters' marriage bill
was again passed by the new House of Assembly, which
met that year, and when a committee was appointed to
search the journals of the Council to learn what had
become of their bill, they found the following entry, the
like of which will be found repeated hundreds of times
in the published journals of the Legislative Council. It

is republished here for the purpose of showing how the business of the Province was done by the Council half a century ago:

"COUNCIL CHAMBER, 21st March, 1831.

PRESENT.

The Honorable Mr. Chief Justice Saunders, President.

Mr. Justice Bliss,	Mr. Shore,
Mr. Justice Botsford,	Mr. Justice Chipman,
Mr. Peters,	Mr. Robinson,

Mr. Hurd.

"Read a second time, the bill to authorize the ministers of congregations dissenting from the Church of England to solemnize marriage in the Province.

"On motion resolved, That the further consideration of this bill be put off for three months."

This was the kind of satisfaction the House of Assembly received when they wished to discover why this salutary measure, and others of a similar character, were rejected. Eight old men, sitting in a Council with closed doors, were able to defeat the best intentions of the popular branch of the Legislature, and to block the wheels of progress. Their action in this case was the more absurd because by an act passed on the 8th of March, 1830, at the request of the British Government, the Imperial Act 10, George IV., chapter VII, entitled, "An act for the relief of His Majesty's Roman Catholic subjects," was made applicable to the Province of New Brunswick, and all disabilities of every kind removed from persons of

that faith. The House of Assembly concluded that
nothing would serve to bring about the reform asked for
but to petition the King, and accordingly in 1831, a
petition was prepared in which the grievance with regard
to dissenting Protestant clergymen was duly set forth,
and it was stated that for several years in succession the
House of Assembly had passed a bill to extend the
privilege of celebrating marriage to dissenting clergymen,
but that for reasons unknown to the House such bills had
not been concurred in by the other branch of the Legislature. The petitioners, who described themselves as
"Your Majesty's Faithful Commons," asked that the King
" would be pleased graciously to give instructions to the
administrator of the Government to recommend the
Legislature to pass such bill as he may deem proper to
obtain Your Majesty's royal sanction for the purpose of
extending the privilege of celebrating and solemnizing
marriages, to the regularly ordained and settled clergy of
dissenting congregations in Your Majesty's Province of
New Brunswick." At the next meeting of the Legislature, in 1832, the various dissenting religious bodies
showed great activity in presenting petitions in favor of
the passing of the dissenters' marriage bill.   These
petitions came from every part of the Province, and very
largely from the ministers and adherents of the Wesleyan
Methodist Society. The bill was passed by the House
on the 10th of February, apparently without any opposition, and went to the Council, where it passed with a
suspending clause, being reserved for His Majesty's

approval.   It was supposed that this bill would settle the
dissenters' marriage question, and the Lieutenant Governor, Sir Archibald Campbell, seems to have shared in
this belief, for in proroguing the Legislature he said :

"I am particularly gratified to find that the new
marriage act, which has just passed into a law, is
calculated to give a high degree of satisfaction to a large
portion of His Majesty's loyal subjects in this colony."

Nothing more was heard of the act, however, until the
session of 1834, when a despatch was received from His
Majesty's Secretary of State for the Colonies, dated the
1st of January of that year, in which it was announced
that His Majesty had been advised to withhold his
assent from the bill, on the ground that the act was
confined in its operation to four denominations of
Christians, the Wesleyan Methodists, the Baptists, Presbyterian seceeders from the Kirk of Scotland, and Independents, and also because before obtaining a license
from the Governor, the minister who desired to solemnize
such marriages must produce a certificate or letters of
ordination, which must be derived from some British
convention, synod, conference or association.   In other
words, the act was disallowed because it was not liberal
enough, and thus two years of time were lost, no doubt in
consequence of the act having originally been drawn in
a restricted form to enable it to pass the Council.   Thus
the malign influence of that antiquated and illiberal body
was the means of postponing the operation of the
dissenters' marriage act until the year 1834, when on the

22nd of March, a bill which was in the terms suggested by the Colonial Secretary, was passed, and the dissenters' marriage question settled forever on an equitable basis.

The old restrictive system which hindered the trade of New Brunswick for the first forty years of its existence has already been referred to. Grievances which rose from that source were perhaps less felt by the people of this Province than some others, because the policy which created that system was a part of the fashion of the times, and no better arrangement was then understood. The first blow that was dealt to this policy came in 1822, when the acts of the Imperial Parliament 3rd, Geo. IV., chapters 44 and 45 were passed. Under these acts the importation of provisions, lumber, cattle, tobacco and other articles from any foreign country in North and South America and the West Indies, into ports of British North America and the British West Indies, was allowed under a fixed scale of duty, and a free export was allowed to goods going from all our ports to these countries. The importation of the productions of foreign countries in Europe into the ports of British North America was also permitted, and a schedule of duties annexed. Under these acts it was arranged that the duties on both imports and exports were to be collected by the Imperial officers of customs, and the net revenue thus obtained was to be placed at the disposal of the Colonial Treasuries. By these acts duties were placed on wines, varying from 7 to 10 guineas a tun, in addition to $7\frac{1}{2}$ per cent. ad valorem. This arrangement was a decided gain to New Brunswick, because, for the first time, it placed the revenue collected by the Imperial officers under the control of the Legislature. The first intimation that we have of the change that had taken place in the status of these duties, was a message from the Lieutenant Governor to the House of Assembly, dated 18th of February, 1823, in which he informed the House that, owing to a representation made by the Collector of His Majesty's Customs at St. John, he had, with the advice of His Majesty's Council, appointed a number of persons to assist in collecting the duties lately given to the Province by the act of the Imperial Parliament. On the 20th of February of the same year, there appeared in the Provincial Treasurer's accounts, an acknowledgment of the receipt of £422 3s. from Henry Wright, the Collector of Customs, for duties collected by him under the acts of Parliament. During the same session returns were laid before the House of the accounts of the Collector and Controller of His Majesty's Customs in this Province, of the duties received both at St. John and St. Andrews, and thus a new era in the history of our commerce was commenced.

The acts of the Imperial Parliament 6th, Geo. IV., chapters 73 and 114, went still farther in the way of removing restrictions from Colonial trade. These acts provided that the duties imposed under them should be paid by the Collector of Customs into the hands of the Treasurer or Receiver General of the colony, to be applied to such uses as were directed by the Local Legislature of such colony, exception being made in regard to produce of duties payable to His Majesty, under any act passed prior to the 18th year of his late Majesty, George III. This exception is important for the purpose of illustrating the pernicious and absurd system under which duties had been collected. Even so late as the year 1833, Messrs. Simonds and Chandler, our delegates to the Imperial Government, were complaining that duties were collected at the several Custom Houses in New Brunswick upon wine, molasses, coffee and pimento, under the provisions of the acts of Parliament 6th, Geo. II., chapter 13; 4th, Geo. III., chapter 15, and 6th, Geo. III., chapter 52, amounting to upwards of £1000 sterling annually, which duties were not accounted for to the Legislature, and that it was not known to the House of Assembly by whom and to what purpose these duties were applied. The reply to this on the part of the Imperial Government was, that in pursuance of the directions contained in the statutes themselves, the duties levied under them were remitted to the exchequer in England, in aid of the expenses incurred for the defence of the British Colonies in North America. Thus ten years after the British Government had undertaken to remit the duties collected in the colonies to the exchequers of the colonies in which the money was collected, there still remained a considerable revenue, collected under old and obscure acts of Parliament, which was held back, and the destination of which was not known, until disclosed in the manner stated to the delegates sent to England to obtain the redress of New Brunswick grievances.

In the meantime, however, the money collected for duties under the acts 3rd, Geo. IV., and 6, Geo. IV., began to flow into the exchequer, but it was found that the amount thus received was much smaller than the Legislature had a right to expect, in consequence of the large reductions that were made by the Imperial collectors for their own salaries and expenses. The Customs officials of that day were, for the most part, men whose only concern was to fill their own pockets. They were all natives of the British Islands and had been appointed, not because of their merit, but through influence, and a few of them for reasons not fit to be mentioned. Some of them, when in their cups, were accustomed to boast that they had royal blood in their veins, and their boasts derived some probability from a family resemblance, which at least was striking, and from the notoriously immoral conduct of George IV., both as a prince and a king. Such men were not likely to aid the Legislature of New Brunswick in its efforts to keep down the expense of the Customs system. In February, 1827, Mr. Simonds, from the committee appointed to take into consideration all matters affecting the commercial interests of the Province, submitted a report, in which it was shown that, by an abstract of duties received by the several collectors of customs in the Province, it appeared that £18,278 2s. 3½d. sterling had been collected between the 5th of January, 1826, and the 5th of January, 1827, under the act 6th, Geo. IV., chapter 114, which was equal in the currency of the Province to the

sum of £20,309 11s. 5d., but that of the above sum only
£11.613 13s. 8d. had been paid into the hands of the
Provincial Treasurer and his deputies, leaving still in the
hands of the collectors of customs, unaccounted for, the
sum of £8,695 17s. 8½d. The report recommended that
the House take immediate steps to ascertain by what
authority the collectors in this Province have been
induced to retain so large a proportion to the whole
amount of duties collected by them. This report was
accepted and ordered to lie on the table.

This subject had already been one of the matters dealt
with by the committee of correspondence in a letter to the
Province agent in England, and it was a matter in regard
to which our people felt keenly. At that time the
revenue of the Province was small, and it seemed absurd
that the Customs officials should be able to take, in
salaries, about one half the amount of the revenue they
collected. A few days later a message was received from
the Lieutenant Governor, Sir Howard Douglas, laying
before the House a copy of a despatch from Earl Bathurst, dated the 20th of April, 1826, enclosing a copy of a
minute of the Lord Commissioners of the Treasury, on the
subject of the establishment of the Customs in North
America and the West Indies, and the payment of the
expenses of this service out of the produce of the
duties of customs, which they were appointed to collect.

On the 2nd of March, 1827, a series of resolutions were
passed in regard to this message, and others on the same
subject, ending with a humble address to the Lieutenant

Governor, praying that His Excellency would lay the resolutions in question before His Majesty. Sir Howard Douglas, on receiving these resolutions, intimated to the House of Assembly that the proper method of approaching His Majesty on this subject was by way of address, and the House complying with this suggestion, prepared an address, which was adopted on the 6th of March of the same year. This address contains, in a brief form, a statement of the grievances which the House considered the Province was suffering in consequence of the existing arrangements with regard to the disposition of the monies derived from the customs duties. In it the members thanked His Majesty for the relief of the coasting trade, especially in this Province, by the abolition of the Custom House fees, and said that they regard it as an additional proof of that fostering care which His Majesty and Parliament have so often evinced for the welfare of this part of his extended dominions. They say that they cannot for a moment believe that it was ever intended to lessen those benefits by taking from the Colonial Legislature the right of appropriating the whole of the duties levied upon the people of the Province. They add that it was not without feelings of extreme regret that the House heard, just before the close of the last session, that the Custom House officers had received instructions from the Commissioner of Customs to retain for their salaries a large portion of the duties collected by them. As no official communication had been received by His Majesty's Government in the Province relating to these instructions, the House considered this order which so materially affected their dearest interests, and which appeared to them at variance with the acts of Parliament, to have been intended as a temporary arrangement, to continue in operation only until the subject had been submitted to the House, in which they humbly conceived the appropriation of the Provincial revenue for the payment of these salaries or for any other purpose should originate. The address then goes on to say that as the services of the Custom House officers are principally required for carrying into effect the laws of trade and navigation, it is the opinion of the House that the more proper mode of paying for these services would be by charges on shipping. The address recites the fact already stated, that of the £20,000 collected under acts of Parliament for the previous year by the officers of customs, but little more than half had gone into the Provincial Treasury, the balance having been retained by the officers for their salaries. The enormous disproportion of this scale of remuneration, as compared to that of the Provincial officers, was shown by the statement in the address that the Provincial revenue of £30,000 was collected at an expense of about £2,000, and by a further statement that these Imperial duties, which cost so much to collect, could have been collected by the Provincial officers of revenue with little or no additional charge. The address closed by expressing the hope that His Majesty would grant the desired relief by making such reductions as were practical in the customs establishment, and by causing the whole of the revenue, which might hereafter be collected in the Colony, under the provisions of any act of the Imperial Parliament, to be placed at the disposal of the Provincial Assembly.

In 1828 this subject was again before the Legislature, and the chairman of the Committee of Privileges reported, as a result of an inspection of the returns of the customs of St. John and St. Andrews, that the whole of the duties collected at the port of St. John under the acts of the Imperial Parliament, had amounted during the year to £15,231 16s. 10¼d., from which sum the officers of customs had retained £4,135 10s. 9¾d., leaving £11,096 7s. ½d. as the net amount of duties. The whole amount collected in customs duties at St. Andrews in 1827 was £6,007 19s. 2d., of which sum £2,382 was retained for salaries. These sums, it must be remembered, are all in sterling money. It was found by the same report that the salary of the collector at St. John was £1,500 sterling, or considerably more than twice as much as the salary of the present collector of the port of St. John, the revenue of which now approaches $1,000,000 a year. The controller of the port then received £700 sterling, or more than double the salary of the present surveyor of the port of St. John, who is the second officer in the service. The other salaries were in the same proportion; two surveyors and searchers receiving £400 sterling each, the warehouse keeper £300 sterling, and the indoor officers from £270 to £150. The collector at St. Andrews received £800 sterling, the controller £400, and the searcher £300. These salaries were justly considered to be excessive, and would be far too much even at the present day, when the business has so greatly increased. No answer was received during the session of 1828 from the British Government to the address which had been forwarded the previous year, but in 1829 a reply came. This reply, which was a lengthy document, can only be regarded as a piece of special pleading. After reciting the language of the acts, the reply states that it is the opinion of the law officers of the Crown that the salaries of the customs officers in the case of the duties raised, under 6th, Geo. IV., chapter 114, as in that of those received under former acts, are legally payable out of the gross produce, and that the balance alone, after such payment, is to be paid over to the Colonial officers. The reply also pointed out that fees to a large amount, heretofore paid to the Naval officers in the several Colonies had been abolished, and that the compensation to the officers, in lieu of fees, was then paid out of the revenue of Great Britain. It stated also, that His Majesty's Government had consented that the Crown revenues would continue to be charged with the incidental expenses of the collection of the customs, and with the compensation which has been found necessary to assign to the customs officers, whose salaries have been reduced; and if there should be any Colony in which the salaries of the officers exceeded the amount of fees formerly levied, it was not intended that the excess should be borne by the Colony. With these qualifications, however, the reply stated

G

that it appeared to His Majesty's Government as
not unreasonable, that the Colonies should either
acquiesce in the' deduction, from the duties received
in the Colony, of the adequate salaries now fixed
for the officers, or should themselves make a permanent provision for the officers to that amount. The
reply states that by the adoption of either alternative,
the additional expense thrown upon the Mother Country
will not be extravagant, and the Customs officers enjoying
salaries which are considered moderate, will still be placed
in that state of independence which is essential to the due
discharge of their duty.

This reply was accompanied by a detailed statement of
the charge for salaries heretofore defrayed by fees levied
in this Province, and that now proposed to be borne out
of the duties collected in the Colonies, and also the
salaries, compensations and expenses proposed to be borne
by the Crown, or out of the revenue of the United
Kingdom, under the new arrangement which was to take
effect from the 5th of January, 1829. It appeared from
this statement that prior to the year 1826, £9,133 7s. 1d.
sterling, was paid in fees, and £509 paid by the Crown
in the shape of salaries. In 1826, the same amount as
that formerly paid in fees, was paid by the Colony, and
£1,086 3¾d. was paid by the Crown in the shape of
salaries and incidental charges. It was now proposed
that the sum of £6,397 should be paid for salaries out of
the Colonial duties, and the sum of £1,636 3s. 3d. paid
by the Crown for salaries and incidental charges. In a

financial point of view this was a more favorable arrangement for the Province than the one that had previously existed, saving as it did almost £3,000 of the Customs revenues, which were to go into the Provincial exchequer; but as the House of Assembly of New Brunswick was contending for the principle that they alone had the right to dispose of the revenues which were collected in the Province, it was unsatisfactory. Therefore it was resolved unanimously by the House, that this settlement of the matter proposed by the British Government could not be accepted. The House said that in unanimously coming to this determination they did so on the principle that the House of Assembly are the sole constitutional judges of the proper compensation to be afforded public officers when their salaries are to arise from taxation within the Province, and that although the House are well satisfied of the necessity of making proper provision for officers of the Customs, and will be at all times ready to appropriate a reasonable sum for that purpose, when the revenues are left to the disposal of the Legislature, they felt bound to say that the scale proposed was far beyond what the circumstances of the country would admit, and out of all proportion to the allowances made for similar services by the General Assembly.

This manly resolution was a crude expression of the sentiments of a vast majority of the people of New Brunswick, although it must not be forgotten that the Council took no part in these remonstrances against excessive salaries, and declined to stand up for constitutional usage, thus showing themselves to be wholly subservient to the wishes of the officials as they had been in every instance where the interests of the people and those of the official classes came in conflict.

No progress seems to have been made in respect to the matter of Customs salaries during the year 1830, but it appears by the returns that for the year ending 5th of January, 1830, the Customs duties collected in the Province amounted to £16,616 18s. 11d. sterling, from which was deducted for salaries £7,073 6s., leaving a balance of £9,543 12s. 11d. Thus it appears that in that year the salaries of the Customs officials amounted to about 40 per cent. of the whole sum collected by them, a scale of remuneration which would seem very absurd at the present day.

In March, 1831, a series of resolutions was moved by Mr. Partelow in reference to the King's casual revenue and to Customs salaries. These resolutions, which need not be recited, announced the desire of the Legislature to provide for the whole civil list, including the Customs establishment, and asked for returns showing the salaries which had been annually received by the several Custom house establishments in the Province, for the payment of their officers and clerks, since the Imperial acts for the abolition of fees went into operation. These resolutions were carried and ordered to be laid before the President. At a later day, during the same session, an address was adopted by the House upon the subject of the Custom House establishment in this Province, which was ordered to be sent to the Lieutenant Governor, so that it might be forwarded to His Majesty. This address recited the dissatisfaction that so uniformly prevailed at the circumstance of such large sums being annually withheld by the officers of Customs without the consent of the Legislature. It stated that the Provincial officers, such as the Provincial Treasurer, whose duties were far more arduous, received much smaller salaries than those given to the Customs officials. The principal object of the address, however, was to place before His Majesty a scale of salaries which the House deemed sufficient for the service, and to ask that this scale be adopted. The Assembly offered to make a permanent annual grant to His Majesty of £4,250 sterling, for the payment of the Customs officers, either in gross or in such other way as His Majesty might direct. This scale of salaries gave the Collector of the port of St. John £700 sterling a year, which was a larger salary than this official now enjoys; the Controller was to receive £400 sterling, a larger salary than the surveyor of the port now has. The whole cost of the St. John Customs establishment was to be brought down to £1,930. The Miramichi Custom House was to be maintained for £450; that of St. Andrews for £990, the Collector there receiving a salary of £400, while the other salaries were reduced in the same proportion, so that the total sum for salaries and incidentals was brought down to £4,250 sterling, equal to £4,903 16s. 10d. currency, or about $20,000 of the money of the present day.

This proposal brought a favorable reply, which was addressed from Downing street, on the 5th January, 1832, by Lord Howick, who afterwards, as Earl Gray, was Secretary of State for the Colonies, and had a great deal to do with the negotiations between New Brunswick and the Mother Country in the matter of building a line of railway from Halifax to Quebec.

It was fortunate for the people of New Brunswick that a Liberal Government had come into power in England prior to this time, and that the old vested interests which were thought to be superior to the rights of the people, were beginning to be looked upon with less favor than had been the case formerly. Lord Howick, in his despatch, stated that the Lord Commissioners of His Majesty's Treasury were willing at once to accede to the proposal of the Legislative Assembly of New Brunswick to make a permanent grant to His Majesty of £4,250 sterling per annum to the Custom House establishment in New Brunswick. Their Lordships were also of the opinion that the present scale of salaries ought to be reduced, but they were not yet possessed of all the information which they required to enable them to determine on the amount of reduction, either of the number or salaries of the officers, which could be effected without impairing the efficiency of the department. They promised, however, that at an early period they would revise the Customs establishments in all the ports of the North American Colonies, with a view to fix them on a reasonable and moderate scale. This was a very satisfactory despatch, and although the arrangement was not carried out immediately, yet it became operative in due course, in the latter part of the year 1835. An act was passed in March of that year, by the Legislature of New Brunswick which declared that "it is one of the most inherent and unquestionable rights of the General Assembly of this Province to dispose of the whole amount of all duties, taxes and supplies collected within the same." The act then went on to declare that His Majesty's faithful and loyal subjects of the Assembly of New Brunswick have freely and voluntarily resolved to give a grant to the King's most excellent Majesty, his heirs and successors, towards providing for the Custom House establishment in this Province; that the principal officers of the Customs of this Province are authorized to retain the annual sum of £4,250 sterling, out of the monies arising from the duties which they may collect under the acts of the Imperial Parliament, the surplus to be paid over to the Provincial Treasurer quarterly. Thus was vindicated the principle for which our House of Assembly had so steadily contended, and the right of that body to dispose of the entire revenues collected in the Province in whatever manner they saw fit, was freely admitted by the special confirmation and ratification of the act by order of the King in Council, dated 30th of September, 1835.

It is a singular fact that while the House of Assembly contended so strongly for its right to appropriate all the monies collected by the Imperial Custom House officers in this Province, it seems to have ignored or forgotten the still more important question of the right of taxation which was involved in this matter. The contest between the Mother Country and the thirteen Colonies was the result of an attempt on the part of the British Government to impose Customs duties on the Colonists, and the contention of the Colonists, which they successfully maintained as the result of a long and bloody war, was that there should be no taxation without representation. This principle was so far admitted by the British Government, that in 1778 an act was passed declaring that from and after its passing "the King and Parliament of Great Britain will not impose any duty or tax assessment whatever, payable in any of His Majesty's Colonies, excepting only such duties as it may be expedient to impose for the regulation of commerce." In spite of this very plain provision it has already been seen that the Imperial Customs establishment of New Brunswick, and the other North American Colonies of Great Britain, continued to collect duties, which, whether they were necessary for the regulation of commerce, or merely for the purpose of raising a revenue, were entirely in opposition to the principle that there should be no taxation without representation.

The indifference of the House of Assembly of New Brunswick in regard to this particular phase of the question must be ascribed to defects in the political education of the people, who had been so much accustomed to regard the royal prerogative as sacred and the

Imperial Parliament as supreme, that they failed to recognize the fact that the rights of the people of New Brunswick were being seriously interfered with by the Imperial legislation which provided for the maintenance of Customs establishments.

There were indeed many grave abuses and difficulties in connection with the collection of two sets of duties by two sets of officers on the same goods imported into this Province. In general such a condition of things was only made tolerable by the liberal manner in which the tariff of duties was interpreted by the officials, yet there were sometimes collisions between the Provincial and Imperial officers which led to difficulties. An instance of this was presented to the notice of the British Government in 1833 by Messrs. Chandler and Simonds, when they went to England as a deputation on the subject of the grievances of the Province. They stated that, although the revenue laws of the Province and the Imperial acts specified the manner in which the proceeds· of seizures made by the officers of Customs and Provincial officers should be disposed of, collisions had taken place between these officials, and instances had occurred of seizures by the officers of His Majesty's Customs of articles which had been previously seized by the Provincial revenue officers, and condemned and sold by them. The delegates pointed out that unless a remedy was applied to proceedings of this nature, the Provincial revenue laws for the prevention of smuggling, would, so far as they applied to articles which were liable to

Parliamentary duties, become entirely nugatory. This matter was brought to the notice of the proper officers by the British Government, and from that time the complaints on the subject became less frequent.

It was not, however, until the year 1848 that the whole complicated system of collecting double duties by two sets of officers was swept away. The history of the legislation which brought this about and which resulted in England becoming a free trade country, does not properly belong to the narrative which I have in hand. The fall of the Imperial Customs system in the Colonies was due, not so much to any attacks that were made upon it from without, as to its own inherent weakness and inefficiency. The year 1846 was a memorable epoch in the commercial history of the United Kingdom, and from that time the old order of things began to pass away. The Imperial Customs establishments in the Colonies were abolished by legislation, which was passed in 1846, and the officers who had been charged with the duty of collecting the Parliamentary revenue were either pensioned or removed to other positions. The collector of the port of St. John, Mr. H. Bowyer Smith, was at this time placed on a retiring allowance, and the only Imperial officers of that establishment retained here were the Controller of Customs and Navigation Laws and a few other officials whose duty it was to regulate the shipping interests, which was still regarded as an Imperial concern. A few years later even this feature of the old Customs system was abolished, and the interests of the shipping were entrusted to Provincial officers, who from that time to the present, have done their duty in a manner not less efficient than their predecessors.

Mention has already been made of the singular constitution of the Council of this Province, which combined both executive and Legislative functions. The Council was a body wholly irresponsible, but quite powerful enough, with the assistance of the Lieutenant Governor, to defeat the wishes of the popular branch of the Legislature, whenever it chose to stand in the way of progressive Legislation. The arbitrary conduct of this body had always been a subject of complaint, both by the people at large and the members of the House of Assembly, because, while the Council was constituted as it was, it was felt that legislation was wholly at the mercy of an irresponsible body, which had little or no sympathy with the wishes of the people.

A very important change was made in 1833 with respect to the Council, which first came to the knowledge of the House by a message dated 11th of February of that year. The Lieutenant Governor informed the House of Assembly that His Majesty had been pleased by his royal commission to appoint two separate and distinct Councils in the Province, to be respectively called the Legislative Council and the Executive Council, and had vested in the Legislative Council all the powers heretofore given to the Council of the Province as far as regarded the enacting of laws, and in the Executive Council all the other powers heretofore exercised by the Council originally appointed. It is not known by what influence this important change was brought about, but it may be inferred that it came as a result of representations made by the Lieutenant Governor himself, at the instance of one or two of his most trusted advisers. It was stated in a communication to the British Government by Messrs. Simonds and Chandler, in June, 1833, that the change had been advised, determined upon and carried into effect without the knowledge, advice or consent of the late Council, or the concurrence of the Legislature, and it was objected to on that ground. The delegates maintained that the established constitution of the Colony should not have been changed or modified by His Majesty's Government without the concurrence of the Legislature itself. It is a singular proof of the political infancy of our Provincial members of Assembly at that period that a change so obviously necessary in the interests of good Government should have been considered improper, no matter in what manner it may have been brought about. These members ought to have understood very clearly that while the Council continued to exercise both Legislative and Executive functions, no member of the House of Assembly could ever become a member of the Executive Council or take any active part in the administration of the affairs of the Government. The House of Assembly, prior to that time, had been merely a body, free from executive responsibility, charged with the duty of guarding the public purse, and therefore coming into constant collision with the Governor and his advisers, in consequence of their refusal to grant money, which the Governor deemed necessary for the maintenance of the public services of the Province.

On the 23rd of February, 1833, the Lieutenant Governor sent to the House of Assembly the despatch relative to the constitution of the Legislative and Executive Councils. In this document it was declared that the Executive Council should consist of five members, and that three of such members should constitute a quorum, for the transaction of business. The five members appointed Executive Councillors at this time were Thomas Baillie, the Surveyor General, William F. Odell, the Provincial Secretary, Frederick P. Robinson, George Frederick Street, Advocate General, and John Simcoe Saunders. Messrs. Baillie and Robinson had been members of the old Council, but the other members of the Executive named were new men. The document by which these gentlemen were appointed members of the Executive Council declared that in the absence of the Lieutenant Governor or of the officer administering the Government for the time being, the member of the Council whose name should be first on the list should preside in said Council. It was also declared that the members of the Executive Council, as well as of the Legislative Council, should hold their office during His Majesty's pleasure. The new Legislative Council, as constituted on the 11th of February, 1833, consisted of ten members, three of whom, Messrs. Baillie, Robinson and Saunders, were members of the Executive Council, Chief Justice Saunders, who had been originally appointed a member of the Council in 1793, being President. Several members of the old Council were dropped from the list, among them being Judges Bliss, Botsford and Chipman, and the Lord Bishop of Nova Scotia, who had attended but once as a member of the Council seven years before. It is worthy of mention in this connection that, from the time of the first establishment of the Council in 1784 up to the period with which we are now dealing, the public had been wholly without information in regard to the proceedings of that body. Its meetings were held with closed doors ; no member even of the popular branch of the Legislature was allowed to be present at its deliberations, and the only information in regard to its doings that reached the outside world was when a Committee of the House was appointed to search the journals of the Council for the purpose of discovering what had become of some bill, which after being passed by the House of Assembly as a result of much deliberation and long debate, had disappeared in the Council, to be heard of no more.

In 1831, the sum of £500 was granted by the Legislature for the purpose of defraying the expenses, of arranging, compiling and printing the journals of the Legislative Council, from the commencement of its existence to the session of 1830. In 1832 this was supplemented by a further grant of £210 15s. for the payment of the balance due for arranging, compiling and printing the journals of the Legislative Council. The result of this grant was the publication of two volumes containing all the proceedings of the Legislative Council from the beginning, and then the public for the first time learned the manner in which the business of that body had been conducted, and the amount of regard which was paid to their wishes, as expressed by the action of their representatives in the House of Assembly.

CHAPTER IV.

THE CASUAL AND TERRITORIAL REVENUE.

The abuses connected with the Crown Land department naturally attracted a larger amount of attention than any others, in the Legislature of the Province. It has already been explained that the revenues derived from the Crown lands of the Province were not under the control of the Legislature, and were expended without regard to its wishes. This was a very practical grievance, and our ancestors, who were little given to theorizing in regard to systems of Government, made the Crown Land office the main object of attack for many years.

The question of the control and management of the Crown lands was one that involved many features, so that to deal with them fully would require a larger space than is necessary to give to the matter in this volume. One grievance, which was felt to be an important one, was that in connection with the collection of quit rents. The grants of land originally given to the first settlers of this Province provided for the payment of a certain annual sum in the shape of quit rents. It appears that when these grants were made the grantees had no idea that the provision for quit rents would ever be enforced, looking upon it merely as a nominal acknowledgment of the sovereignty of the Crown. But in the year 1830 an attempt was made to collect these rents, and it brought on a very unpleasant state of affairs between the Lieutenant Governor on the one side and the House of Assembly, representing the Province, on the other. The quit rent grievance formed the subject of numerous addresses to His Majesty. It was one of the matters entrusted to Messrs. Chandler and Simonds, who were sent as a deputation to England on the subject of grievances in 1833. The collection of quit rents had at that time been suspended, but the British Government informed the delegates that unless the Assembly should be disposed to enter into some arrangement for a permanent civil list, on the relinquishment by the Crown of quit rents throughout the Province, there would be no alternative but to resume their collection. Finally a bill was passed in 1835, in which the sum of £1,200 currency was granted to His Majesty, in commutation and full discharge of all quit rents and arrears of quit rents then due or to become due, reserved in any grants or letters patent from the Crown, of lands within the Province of New Brunswick. This annual sum of £1,200 currency was to be applied by His Majesty towards making and improving roads and bridges within the Province. This was a solution of the difficulty which gave the Province itself the benefit of the quit rents, and which might have been reached earlier without the amount of negotia-

H

tion and correspondence which was expended upon it.

Under the old system by which the Crown lands were regulated, large areas of the Province of New Brunswick were held as reserved lands for the avowed purpose of supplying masts for His Majesty's navy. It was always felt that the existence of these large reserves was a great hindrance to settlement, because land was thus locked up which was required for actual settlers, and which might have very well been opened without at all interfering with the naval establishment.

In 1819 a Committee of the House of Assembly was appointed for the purpose of inquiring into the subject of reserved lands, in Charlotte and Northumberland Counties. The report of this committee showed that considerable areas of these lands consisted of hardwood land, suitable for settlement, and not in any sense valuable for the purpose of growing masts for His Majesty's navy. The Council was requested to join in an address to His Majesty, asking to have these lands opened up to settlement, but it declined to do so. As the Council would take no part in this movement, the House of Assembly had to proceed on its own responsibility, and during the session of 1820, an address was prepared to be forwarded to His Royal Highness, the Prince Regent, on the subject of these reserved lands. During the session of 1821 a letter was received from Earl Bathurst, acknowledging the receipt of the address from the House of Assembly, and stating that the matter had been referred to the Surveyor General of Woods and Forests in North America, for the purpose of ascertaining from him whether the lands in question abounded with pine so as to make their reservation important in the public interest. The Surveyor General of Woods and Forests in America was ex-Governor Sir John Wentworth, who, at the time Earl Bathurst wrote the communication in question, was dead, although the news of his death had not then reached England. The position of Surveyor General of Woods and Forests, which he held for many years, was a sort of sinecure office and was not filled after his death. As Sir John Wentworth was dead, and therefore unable to give his opinion as to the reserved lands, in March, 1821, a committee was appointed to wait upon the Lieutenant Governor in regard to their reservation, asking him whether any person had been appointed Surveyor of Woods and Forests in North America, and, if any, what steps had been taken to convey to His Majesty's ministers the information relative to the reserves in Charlotte, referred to in Lord Bathurst's letter. In February, 1822, a communication was received from Lord Bathurst, stating that His Majesty had caused inquiries to be made as to the state of the timber on the several reserves in Charlotte County, and as it appeared that they contained a considerable quantity of timber most valuable for naval purposes, His Majesty did not feel that he could accede to the wishes of the Assembly, or abandon the reserves for the purpose of allotting them to settlers. This disposed of the subject for the time being, but it was by no means lost sight of in the subsequent agitation in regard to other branches of the Crown land service.

During the session of 1819, another matter was brought to the attention of the House, which formed the subject of a long and acrimonious dispute with the home Government. On motion of Mr. Colin Campbell, one of the members for Charlotte County, it was resolved that an humble address be presented to the Lieutenant Governor, stating that the House of Assembly had learned with surprise and regret of the bonds which were taken in the office of the Deputy Surveyor of Woods for one shilling a ton on licenses to cut and ship pine timber in this Province. The House of Assembly expressed the opinion that this measure, if persisted in, must prove ruinous to the timber trade of the Province. The resolutions also requested that His Excellency should inform the House, if a recent instruction had been received from His Majesty's ministers, requiring such bonds to be taken, and to what purpose the large sums arising therefrom were to be appropriated.

Lieutenant Governor Smyth, in reply, stated that in consequence of representations made to the Government in England of the great and unwarrantable destruction committed in His Majesty's woods in this Province, positive orders were issued by the Lord Commissioners of the Treasury forbidding any license to be granted for cutting timber, except under the sanction of the Lieutenant Governor, first obtained. He stated that these orders had been communicated to the Council, who, after deliberate consideration, arranged and recommended a system which, in their opinion, might effectually prevent the recurrence of similar mischiefs in future. The shilling a ton, he said, formed a part of that system which had been transmitted for the consideration of His Majesty, and bonds had been taken to secure the payment of that sum in case it should eventually be demanded. The money which might arise from the permission to cut timber, as well as all other sums of money which might accrue to His Majesty from the sale, or other disposition of property belonging to the Crown in this Province, was to be appropriated to such uses as His Majesty might be pleased to direct.

This reply involved a declaration to the members, that the King could do what he pleased with the Crown lands of New Brunswick, and that such a rate of taxation might be imposed upon those who desired to cut timber in this Province as would effectually put an end to the trade. It also involved the proposition that the money arising from the sale or rents of the Crown land in New Brunswick belonged to the King alone, and might be disposed of by him in any manner he saw fit, without any regard whatever to the wishes of the Legislature. The House of Assembly was not disposed to submit meekly to this rebuff, and, a few days later, it was resolved that the system which required bonds to be taken for the payment of one shilling a ton on all pine timber manufactured in the Province, was a measure highly injurious to its trade, and in the opinion of the House, not contemplated by the instructions of His Majesty's ministers, communicated to the House in the message of the Lieutenant Governor. The House of Assembly also expressed the opinion that the instructions referred to were only intended to prevent the destruction of pine trees fit for naval purposes, and that this object could have been carried into effect without injury to the numerous classes of His Majesty's subjects employed in manufacturing and shipping timber to the mother country.

This resolution appears to have greatly annoyed Lieutenant Governor Smyth, who was a gentleman who seems to have had no small opinion of himself and of the office which he held. In a message which he communicated to the House of Assembly a few days later, he said that he had read with surprise and concern the resolution of the House, animadverting upon the conduct of His Majesty's Executive Government in the Province. He expressed his belief that the resolution had been passed without due consideration, and stated that, as the business in question was a matter belonging exclusively to the Executive, the House should rescind the resolution, which was the subject of his complaint. This message was taken into consideration by the House on the same day, and Mr. Humbert, of St. John, who appears to have been one of the Lieutenant Governor's friends, moved a resolution that, as the system adopted by His Majesty's Government in this Province, for the payment of one shilling a ton on pine timber, was not necessarily within the consideration of the House of

Assembly, any resolve of the House on the said system may be deemed an improper interference with His Majesty's prerogative. The resolution ended by declaring that the resolve, of which the Lieutenant Governor complained, should not be retained on the journals of the House.

Fortunately there was enough manliness in the House of Assembly to reject this absurd resolution, which was defeated by a vote of 19 to 4; the four members who voted for it being Mr. Humbert, of St. John, Mr. Myles and Mr. Wilmot, of Sunbury, and Mr. Allen of York. The Lieutenant Governor seems to have been greatly annoyed at the refusal of the House of Assembly to comply with his request, and on the following day he came down and dissolved the House with the following words. " It was with great concern that I noticed your proceedings in a measure to which your attention has been very recently called, which conduct I cannot suffer to pass unnoticed, consistent with the duty I owe to my Sovereign. The only mode which you have now left me to do is by dissolving this general assembly." The House thus dissolved so peremptorily had only sat three sessions, and had still four more sessions to sit, under the septennial arrangement, which ' was then the law of the Province.

The subject of bonds on timber licenses does not seem to have been discussed by the Legislature during the session of 1820, but in 1821 a resolution was passed that an address be presented to His Excellency, the

Lieutenant Governor, expressing the anxiety of the people of the Province with regard to these bonds, and asking whether any further instruction had been received from His Majesty, in regard to them, since the message of the 11th of March, 1819.   In reply to this the Lieutenant Governor informed the House that he had not received any instructions from His Majesty's ministers on the subject.

The same session the House passed a resolution that an address be presented to the King, praying that His Majesty would be graciously pleased to direct that the duty of one shilling a ton on all timber be discontinued, and that His Majesty's subjects in this Province, who had entered into bonds for the payment of said duty, might be relieved from the payment of the same.   A few days later a resolve was passed that an humble address be presented to His Excellency, praying that he would be pleased to take steps to have the timber bonds cancelled.   On the following day, Governor Smyth informed the House of Assembly that under all the circumstances of the case, and remembering the embarrassed state of the timber trade, he would recommend to the favorable consideration of His Majesty's ministers the cancellation of such bonds as had already been taken for securing payment of that money.   The matter was again brought up at the session of 1822 by a resolution asking the Governor if he had received any instruction from His Majesty's Government relative to the timber bonds or their cancellation.   In reply, he submitted to the House a letter from Mr. Goulburn, stating that although Lord Bathurst had every disposition to recommend a compliance with the requisition to cancel the timber bonds, he was desirous of previously ascertaining the total amount of the bonds in question, in order that he might be able to judge how far the depression in the timber trade had been occasioned by an excessive issue of licenses. A few days later an address was ordered by the House, asking His Excellency to direct that a statement be furnished of the total amounts of bonds taken for pine timber cut on lands in this Province. Governor Smyth declined to comply with this request on the ground that the matter was then under the consideration of His Majesty's ministers. The House of Assembly was determined that this subject should not be allowed to rest, and a day or two later, on motion of Mr. Allen of York, it was resolved that a dutiful and humble address be prepared and laid before the King, praying that His Majesty take into consideration the depressed state of the timber trade of the Province, and that he direct that the bonds taken for pine timber cut on the Crown lands be cancelled.

The subject of the timber bonds still continued to engage the attention of the House. On the 15th March, 1822, on motion of Mr. R. Simonds, it was resolved that His Excellency be asked to inform the House whether any regulation had been adopted with regard to the issuing of licenses for cutting pine timber on Crown lands, by which none was to be granted until a shilling a

ton on the whole be first paid.   On the 19th March
the Governor returned for an answer to this question,
that a new regulation had been adopted in Council
respecting the cutting of pine timber, by which a shilling
per ton was to be paid for the quantities applied for.   On
the 21st March, a draft address was reported to the
House by a committee which had been appointed to
prepare it, asking the King to take into consideration the
depressed state of the timber trade of the Province, and
to direct that the bonds taken for the pine timber cut on
Crown lands be cancelled.   The Governor was asked to
lay this address at the foot of the throne, and he replied
that, although he considered the address irregular, not
having received the sanction of the Legislative Council,
yet he would, as requested by the House, transmit it to
His Majesty's ministers.   He added that at the same
time, he should consider it his duty to accompany it with
his own observations and those of His Majesty's Council
on the subject.   On the same day, Lieutenant Governor
Smyth prorogued the Legislature, accompanying his
closing observations with some advice to the House of
Assembly, in regard to what he conceived to be their
errors as to the constitution of the Province. He directed
their attention to the expediency of amending these
errors as early as possible, and declared that the best
method of discovering them was to compare the working
of the constitution with the parliamentary forms and
usages of the mother country.   The modern reader will
appreciate the absurdity involved in such a statement on

the part of Lieutenant Governor Smyth, when it is remembered that at this period about one-third of the representatives in the British Parliament were elected from rotten boroughs which either had no population at all, or had so small a constituency that they were virtually under the control of the rich land owners, who held the territory in which they were situated. That was the system which the Lieutenant Governor of New Brunswick, seventy years ago, desired the free people of this Province to imitate.

During the session of 1823 the House of Assembly inquired of the Lieutenant Governor whether any answer had been received in regard to their address, in reference to the duty on pine timber. In reply Governor Smyth laid before them a letter from Lord Bathurst, in which he stated that the matter had been referred to the Lords Commissioners of the Treasury, to whose department it more particularly belonged. He stated that in the meantime he concurred generally in the opinion put forth in the report of the Council. This opinion, it is hardly necessary to remark, was entirely opposed to the claims of the House of Assembly interfering with the regulation of the cutting of timber, which was held to be a subject belonging exclusively to the Executive.

Lieutenant Governor Smyth took ill during this session of the Legislature, and died on the 27th March, 1823, so that the Province was relieved from the malign influence which he had exercised in England, on all matters where the House sought to limit the royal prerogative or the authority of the Council.

In 1824 the House addressed President Chipman, who was administering the Government, for the purpose of ascertaining the amount of money paid to the Receiver General of His Majesty's casual revenue, or his deputy in this Province, between February 1822, and January 1824. This reasonable request was refused by President Chipman on the ground that he could not give the information without instructions from the Lords Commissioners of His Majesty's Treasury, under whose control the casual revenues of the Province were held. President Chipman died just fifteen days after he gave the House of Assembly this answer, and was succeeded as president by John Murray Bliss.

The session of 1825 was opened by Sir Howard Douglas, the new Lieutenant Governor, but the timber duties did not come up for discussion in the House at that session. The following session, however, on motion of Mr. Slason, of York, it was resolved to ask His Excellency to take such steps as he might deem expedient and proper to have the timber bonds taken for licenses in the years 1819, 1820 and 1821 cancelled. When this message was received by His Excellency, he replied that he would not fail to recommend to His Majesty's Government that the bonds referred to be cancelled. Sir Howard Douglas was a man of a different spirit from the narrow-minded, prejudiced person who was his predecessor in the office of Lieutenant Governor, and he was much more disposed to favor the interests of the people of New Brunswick than some of the natives of the Province, who got themselves placed in permanent public positions, which they used mainly for the purpose of promoting their own private fortunes, rather than for the benefit of the country.

It was not, however, until February 9th, 1827, that Sir Howard Douglas was able to lay before the House of Assembly a message acquainting that body with the important fact that he had been duly authorized to comply with the address of the House and cancel the timber bonds. This good news was further confirmed by a message on the 7th March of the same year, when Sir Howard Douglas was able to inform the House of Assembly that the timber bonds taken between the years 1818 and 1821 inclusive, amounting to £8,210 13s. 4d. had been cancelled agreeably to the directions of Earl Bathurst, of the 31st July previous. Thus one episode of the controversy between the House of Assembly and the home authorities, in regard to the timber revenues of the Province, was brought to a satisfactory conclusion. The same conclusion might have been reached years before had the Council of the Province displayed a more patriotic spirit, and been imbued with a stronger desire to advance the material interests of their fellow-subjects in the Province. It was the curse of this time that persons who considered themselves to belong to the upper classes, held themselves aloof from the people and professed to believe that their interests and those of the rest of the inhabitants of the

Province, were entirely separate and distinct from each other. They forgot that the general prosperity of the Province could only be promoted by the prosperity of each individual in it, and that any regulation which imposed burdens on a leading industry, such as the timber trade, must necessarily be injurious to the entire community.

The settlement of the timber bond business by no means closed the controversy with respect to the casual and territorial revenues. The fact that the House of Assembly had no control whatever over these revenues was a standing grievance which would continue to be the subject of agitation until it was removed. Prior to this time a new system of selling and disposing of the Crown lands of the Province had been introduced, and during the session of 1829 it came under the notice of the House of Assembly. On motion of Mr. Chandler, a series of resolutions was carried, praying His Majesty to annul the orders recently issued, in regard to the granting of Crown lands, which the House considered to be based on a system, which if persevered in, would be productive of great loss and damage to the Crown, and an irreparable injury to the colony. It seems that these regulations permitted the lands to be sold in large blocks, frequently without being sufficiently advertised, so that large areas were locked up which otherwise would have been opened to settlement.

The Council of the Province joined the House on this occasion in an address to the King on the subject, showing that between the 30th of June, 1827, and the 31st of December, 1828, 187,336 acres of Crown lands had been sold, for which there had been received in payment only the sum of £965 16s. 4d., from which sum the incidental expenses attending the sales amounted to £503 18s. 8d., which being deducted, left the sum of £461 17s. 7d. as the net amount of the purchase money for these enormous areas of land. A very slight calculation will show that the land thus sold realized something less than a cent an an acre. Under these circumstances it need occasion no surprise that even the Council became alarmed at a condition of affairs, which threatened to denude the public domain of its best lands without any suitable equivalent. ·Even this sum, inadequate as it was, was not available for any public purposes, because considerably larger amounts had been expended by the Surveyor General's department on the surveys, so that the land went for absolutely nothing.

The question of the casual and territorial revenue of the Province was one which was not to be allowed to rest. In March, 1831, on motion of Mr. Partelow, it was resolved that an humble address be presented to His Honor the President, praying that he would cause to be laid before the House a detailed account, showing the amount paid into the casual revenues from the 1st of January, 1824, to the 1st of January, 1831, particularizing the sums in each year respectively, and from what source or sources the revenue was derived; also a statement of the expenditure from the casual revenue for the

same period, and for what purposes, and under what
authority the respective payments had been made ; also
the amount of salaries enjoyed respectively by all heads
of departments, and from what fund or funds their
emoluments were derived. The committee appointed to
present this address consisted of Mr. Partelow, Mr.
Simonds, and Mr. Clinch, and they reported four days
later that they had waited upon His Honor the President
with the address of the House, relative to the civil list,
and that he had replied, that consistently with such
instructions as had been hitherto received respecting the
King's casual revenue and the civil list of the Province
he could not now comply with the prayer of the address
but that he would transmit it for the consideration of His
Majesty's ministers, and their orders thereon.

The answer of His Honor the President was taken into
consideration by the House on the 16th March, about a
week after it had been received. Mr. Partelow moved a
resolution, which was passed by the House, in which the
former resolution of the House was recited, and it was
resolved that, as the information sought for had not been
obtained, the subject referred to in the address should be
brought under the consideration of His Majesty's Government by an address from the House, and that a
committee be appointed to prepare the same. Messrs.
Partelow, Simonds and Chandler were appointed a
committee to prepare this address, which was laid before
the House of Assembly on the 31st March, and passed by
a vote of 14 to 8. As this address was the basis of the

demand made upon the Imperial Government for a change in the system of disposing of the casual and territorial revenues of the Province, I quote the major part of it. It was as follows :

"Deeply sensible of the paternal affection entertained by Your Majesty for the welfare of all Your Majesty's subjects, however remote their situation from the parent state, the Assembly most humbly venture to bring under Your Majesty's notice the grievances which Your Majesty's loyal subjects residing in this colony endure from the office established here, called the office of Department of Crown Lands and Forests.

"By the operation of the system practised in this office, very large sums are taken from the people of this Province for licenses to cut timber on Crown Lands, and although the Assembly do not question the right Your Majesty undoubtedly has to the lands in question, they think the tremendous powers with which the Commissioner is vested, with regard to impositions of tonnage money and the enormous exactions for fees, to be incompatible with a free government, and to require redress.

"It is generally understood, as well as universally believed, that the Commissioner in question is under no control in this Province, and to this may be ascribed the mode in which licenses to cut timber are issued in very many cases, in quantities less than 100 tons, subject to a duty of 1s. 3d. per ton, and the excessive fee on each of 45s. By this mode, a large part of the receipts is paid

I

in the shape of fees, at once injuring the subject without benefitting the revenue ; and the Assembly feel convinced if the office were under Colonial management, that while the oppressions would be removed, the revenues would be more productive ; and besides, the Assembly cannot but view with just alarm that the day may possibly come when, by a single mandate from the office, exactions of such magnitude may be made, as literally to stop the export trade of the country, a power which no person should have even the shadow of authority to exercise.

"The Assembly, at an early day the present session, by an address to the administrator of the Government, sought for documents regarding this office, to enable them officially to bring the subject more in detail under the consideration of Your Majesty, but this information, so highly desirable and necessary, has been withheld from them; and the Assembly, therefore, with great submission, lay before Your Majesty herewith, a copy of the said address, with the reply thereto, for Your Majesty's gracious consideration.

"It will by that be seen the objects contemplated by the Assembly ; no less than relieving Your Majesty's Government permanently from the burthen of the whole civil list of the Province, a subject which the Assembly humbly conceive to be of great advantage to the parent state, and only requiring that the revenues, from whatever source or sources derived in or collected within the Province, should be placed under the control of its Legislature.

"The Assembly have so often brought under the notice of Your Majesty's royal predecessors, the privations endured by your loyal subjects, the first settlers of the country, and the unswerving attachment to the British constitution that induced them to abandon their homes and seek an asylum under British protection in a wilderness, that they deem it unnecessary to dwell upon that interesting topic on the present occasion.

"But they humbly beg leave to represent to Your Majesty that although, as before expressed, they do not deny the unquestionable sovereignty of Your Majesty to the wild lands in this colony, they most humbly conceive that the revenues derived from them, when the trying circumstances under which this Province was originally settled are duly considered, should be under the control of the Legislature, although from the comparatively small value of the ungranted lands, with those granted, but little can be anticipated after the grant fees are first paid, and it will, therefore, be from the timber duties almost alone, the Assembly may expect any addition of revenue in part provision for the civil list.

"The House of Assembly, therefore, most humbly pray that this, their representation, may meet from Your Majesty a gracious reception, and that Your Majesty will be pleased to give such directions to the administrator of the Government as will enable the Assembly to carry these important objects into effect."

When the House met again in January, 1832, Sir Archibald Campbell was Governor. Sir Archibald

Campbell was a soldier who had received his military education mainly in India and Burmah. He was therefore very ill-suited to be the Chief Magistrate of a free people, especially in a Province like New Brunswick. Why the British Government persisted in sending men of the stamp of Sir Archibald Campbell to govern the free colonies of Great Britain in America, is something that is impossible now to understand. Bitter experience and the fatal results of their system of administration in the case of the old thirteen colonies ought surely to have taught the Government that better men were required for such service, but it would seem it did not have this effect. Whatever may have been Sir Archibald Campbell's merits as a soldier, he took a stand in the Province of New Brunswick as an enemy to liberty, and to all good Government, and he will be remembered as an upholder of an ancient despotic system which was falling to pieces, and as a man who endeavored, and for some time successfully, to stand in the way of the political progress of the country.

A few days after the opening of the Legislature in 1832, Lieutenant Governor Campbell laid before the House a despatch which he had received from Lord Goderich, referring to the address of the House, which had been passed the previous session. In regard to supplying information as to the amount of expenditure of the casual revenue, Lord Goderich said that he had not received any commands from His Majesty on the subject, and that, as the resolutions of the Assembly were grounded altogether on erroneous information, it was not in his power to authorize the Lieutenant Governor to comply with the request of the House.

The preamble to the resolutions seemed to express the belief that His Majesty, in a speech from the throne in opening the Imperial Parliament, had announced his intention of surrendering all Provincial revenues, and placing them under the control of the Provincial Legislature, and it seems this was the error to which Lord Goderich so pointedly directed their attention.

This curt reply did not prevent the House of Assembly from again dealing with this important matter of revenue. A few days after Lord Goderich's reply had been received, a resolution was passed that an humble address be presented to His Excellency, praying that he would lay before the House an account of the monies received by all persons employed in collecting the casual and other Crown revenues, between the first day of January, 1830, and the 31st of December, 1831, inclusive, and that he would lay before the House a statement of the amount of the incomes of all officers in the civil departments of the Province. This resolution was passed by a vote of 18 to 8, there being at that period in the Legislature an element unfriendly to liberty and progress, which was content to let the Crown lands revenues remain in the hands of the Imperial authorities. In reply to this address, Sir Archibald Campbell expressed his regret that with Lord Goderich's despatch before the House, they should have placed him under the necessity of declining to comply with this request.

The House of Assembly was not deterred by the obnoxious and improper attitude of the Lieutenant Governor in regard to the casual and territorial revenues. It returned to the subject, and on motion of Mr. Simonds, resolved that it was reasonable and proper that His Majesty should be relieved from the payment of the civil list of the Province, and it was necessary that information should be obtained as to the amount of the Crown revenues, and the annual charges thereon. It was also resolved that an address be presented to His Excellency, praying that he would cause to be laid before the House an account of the receipts and expenditure of His Majesty's casual and all other Crown revenues levied, collected, and expended in the year 1831. Messrs. Simonds, Kinnear and Chandler were appointed a committee to wait upon the Lieutenant Governor with this address. They reported his reply as follows :—
"Gentlemen, the specific and loyal purposes for which information is asked in this address, respecting the amount and expenditure of His Majesty's casual revenue for the last year, enables me to give a willing compliance to the request of the House of Assembly, by directing the necessary documents to be laid before you."

As there was nothing in the last address of the House different in any respect from its predecessors, it must be assumed that the ready compliance of the Lieutenant Governor was due to information received from England, in regard to the intentions of the British Government with respect to the casual and territorial revenue. It appeared from the returns then furnished that the Crown land receipts of the Province for the year 1831 amounted to £14,913 18s. 5¼d., out of which was taken £1,750 for the salary of the Surveyor General, £909 for his clerks, £2,750 1s. for the expenses of preparing and issuing patents for lands sold and for timber licences, £1,932 10s. 2d. for survey money, and £150 for the annuity of Mr. Lockwood. The rest of the revenue went to defray the salary of the Commander-in-Chief, the Chief Justice, three Assistant Judges, the Attorney General, the Secretary and Clerk of the Council, Immigration Agent, the Archdeacon, the Presbyterian minister of St. John, a donation to King's College, and a donation to the Indians.

A few days later, on motion of Mr. Simonds, it was resolved that, in the opinion of the House, a proposition should immediately be made to His Majesty's Government, that upon the condition that all the Crown revenues, levied and collected in this Province, which might arise from the sale of Crown lands therein by His Majesty's Government, be placed under the control and management of the Provincial Legislature, this House will then make proper provision for the whole civil list in the Province; and further resolved, that a committee be appointed to prepare a petition to His Majesty upon the subject of the Crown revenues and civil list of the Province.

The address, which was the result of this resolution,

was as follows: "The House of Assembly of Your
Majesty's loyal Province of New Brunswick, humbly beg
leave to call the attention of Your Majesty to the situation of the Crown revenues, and the mauagement of the
Crown lands and forests in this Province, sensible that
the paternal affection of your Majesty for the welfare of
all your subjects, wherever situated, will induce your
Majesty to give to this address that consideration which
its importance to the prosperity of New Brunswick
demands.

"The House of Assembly having received such information from the Lieutenant Governor of the Province as
His Excellency was authorized to give upon the subject
of your Majesty's casual revenues, by which it appears
large sums are received from the people of the Province,
at a charge far greater than would be necessary under
proper management, are convinced of the justice and
propriety of relieving your Majesty from the payment of
any part of the civil list of the Province, and beg leave
to submit this, their proposition, to take upon themselves
the payment of all the necessary expenses of the civil
government of the Province, by making such permanent
and other grants as may be necessary for this purpose.

"In making this proposition, the Assembly do it in
the full assurance that previous to this measure being
carried into effect, your Majesty will accede to the
reasonable condition that all the Crown revenues levied
and collected in the Province, or which may arise from
the sale of Crown lands by your Majesty's government,

shall be placed under the management and control of the Provincial Legislature.

"The Assembly are satisfied that no measure could more conduce to the true interests of your Majesty and to the prosperity of this Province, than the proposed one of placing the management and control of your royal revenues in the Legislature of the Province, by which the complaints of the people of the Province against the system adopted for collection of the casual revenues would be removed, and a large saving in the collection of said revenues effected.

"The Assembly are well assured that under a proper system of management, the expense of collecting the Crown revenues in the Province could be reduced to less than half the amount of the present charges, and that the saving to be effected would be of incalculable advantage to the Province, in opening roads and making bridges, to facilitate the improvement of the country, and the settlement of emigrants from the United Kingdom.

"The Assembly will not further urge the necessity of correcting the present system of collecting the Crown revenues in the Province, as they hope they have made it sufficiently apparent to your Majesty; and they therefore beg leave to suggest for your Majesty's consideration, that for carrying the proposition made in this address into effect, they will make such provision for the salaries of all officers in the civil department, as is consistent with the resources and condition of the Province, and which, in addition to the sums required as a provision for the ordinary services, would leave but a small surplus of the Crown and ordinary Provincial revenues to be applied to general purposes of improvement ; and in adopting hereafter a scale of salaries, the Assembly are of the opinion that the sums named for each officer should be in full of all fees and emoluments of every nature and kind whatever ; and that the usual fees should be collected and accounted for quarterly, and become a part of the revenues to be placed under the control of the Legislature.

" The Assembly cannot think that the Crown revenues, even under a judicious and economical system of management will, for a long period, be sufficiently productive to pay the annual expenses of the civil list, and they are persuaded that in a few years a large proportion of those expenses must be provided for out of the ordinary revenues of the Province.

" The Assembly cannot refrain from remarking how desirable it would be that a final arrangement should be made of all questions of revenue which have arisen or might arise between your Majesty's government and the Legislature of this Province, and they therefore most earnestly pray that your Majesty would give to this address an early and favorable consideration."

A committee was appointed to wait on the Lieutenant Governor and ask him to transmit this address to His Majesty. Sir Archibald Campbell replied that he should do so, but he would consider it his imperative duty to accompany it with such explanations as he might deem necessary, and particularly to rebut the charges made against the public departments. Thus the Lieutenant Governor assumed an attitude of direct hostility to the House of Assembly in regard to this highly important matter.

The Crown land difficulty was not lost sight of during the session of 1833. Early in that session, on motion of Mr. Partelow, a resolution was carried, that an humble address be presented to His Excellency, praying that he would cause to be laid before the House, at as early a date as possible, a detailed account, showing the amount of the Crown revenues from the 1st of January, 1829, to the 1st of January, 1833, particularizing the amount received each year; also a statement of the salaries of all the public officers paid from the Crown revenues. To this the Lieutenant Governor replied, expressing his regret that he did not consider himself authorized to furnish accounts embracing a period so long elapsed, but that he would furnish the House of Assembly with returns of the receipts and expenditures for the year 1832 as he had done for the year 1831. A day or two later a despatch from Lord Goderich was laid before the House of Assembly by the Lieutenant Governor, in which he acknowledged the receipt of their despatch, proposing to assume the expenses of the civil list of the Province on the relinquishment by the Crown of the territorial revenues. The reply to this was, that His Majesty did not consider it necessary at present to call upon the House for a grant of the nature proposed, as he did not anticipate such a falling off of the revenue at his disposal as the House appeared to have apprehended. This was a sarcastic way of informing the House of Assembly that no change was to be made in the management of the casual and territorial revenues of the Province.

Sir Archibald Campbell, at a later day during this session, laid before the House an account of the casual and territorial revenue for 1832. From this account it appeared that there was a balance on hand in favor of the revenue, on the 1st of January, 1832, amounting to £4,617 12s. 8d., and that the receipts for the year brought up the total to £20,421 12s. 6½d., against which warrants had been drawn for £11,764 6s. 8d., leaving a balance of £8,657 5s. 10½d. at the end of the year. This account was referred to a committee, who called attention to "the tremendous expenses attendant upon the Crown land department, the enormous salary of the Commissioner and the large amount swallowed up in the collection and protection of this revenue." They expressed the opinion that under proper management an immense saving could be effected. The reply of the Lieutenant Governor to their address for information in regard to the Crown lands was considered by a committee of the House of Assembly, and resulted in the passing of the following series of resolution :

1. Resolved, As the opinion of this Committee that the powers exercised by the Commissioner of Crown Lands and Forests in this Province are far greater than ought to be possessed by any subject, and that these powers have been too frequently used in a manner

exceedingly detrimental to the general interests of this Province, as well as to the invasion of private rights.

2. Resolved, As the opinion of this Committee, that the abuse of these powers has disturbed that tranquillity which every subject ought to enjoy, and which can only result from a consciousness that his rights cannot be invaded with impunity by the rich and powerful.

3. Resolved, As the opinion of this Committee, that the timber and extensive mill reserves which have been made to individuals, are highly injurious to the commercial prosperity of this Province, by preventing fair and honorable competition and the introduction of capital, discouraging the industry and enterprise of the lumbermen and new settlers, and creating great dissatisfaction throughout the country.

4. Resolved, As the opinion of this Committee, that the want of control by the Legislature over the Commissioner of Crown Lands and Forests and the revenues collected by him, and the refusal of His Excellency, the Lieutenant Governor, to furnish the Assembly with particular accounts of the receipts and expenditure of these revenues, to the extent prayed for by the House, have given just reason to believe that great abuses exist in that department.

5. Resolved, As the opinion of this Committee that the majority of the present Executive Council of the Province cannot have the confidence of the country, inasmuch as the first named on the list holds the situation of Commissioner of Crown Lands and Forests in this

Province, an office of such great power and authority as renders it incompatible with the administration of the government of the Province, to which such Councillor would immediately succeed, in the event of the death or absence of the Lieutenent Governor, and that the persons second and third named on the said list hold public situations in this Province also inconsistent with the administration of the government, to which they might hereafter succeed; and it is the further opinion of this Committee that the composition of the said Executive Council is highly unsatisfactory, by the exclusion therefrom of old and faithful councillors who were entitled by the former Constitution to succeed to the government of the Province, prior to any of those placed on the list of the Executive Council.

A Committee on Grievances consisting of Messrs. Kinnear, Simonds, Chandler, Partelow, Taylor, Weldon and Wyer had been previously appointed for the purpose of taking into consideration and investigating all matters in connection with the Crown lands, which were the subject of complaint. After hearing the evidence of a number of witnesses and reporting to the House, this Committee prepared an address to His Majesty which recited the difficulties in connection with the Crown lands of the Province, in very similar terms to the resolution already quoted. The House resolved to send a deputation to England with the petition which had been prepared by the Committee on Grievances, and they asked the Lieutenant Governor to give to the deputation such

letters to the Secretary of the State for the colonies as
would enable them with as little delay as possible to
enter upon the important matters entrusted to them. Sir
Archibald Campbell replied that he could not comply
with the prayer in the address, and that, even if he considered himself authorized to do so, the well known
accessability of the Colonial Secretary would render such
letters unnecessary. The deputies appointed to proceed
to England and lay the grievances of the Province at the
' foot of the throne, were Charles Simonds and Edward B.
Chandler, both men of wealth, influence and position, and
well qualified for the performance of the work with which
they were entrusted. Messrs. Chandler and Simonds
arrived in England in June, 1833, and immediately placed
themselves in communication with the Right Honorable
E. G. Stanley, who was then Colonial Secretary. Their
report was laid before the Legislature in February, 1834,
and the result was highly satisfactory to the House of
Assembly. A few days later a despatch from Mr. Stanley
to Sir Archibald Campbell was laid before the House, in
which he stated the terms on which he should feel that
His Majesty might properly be advised to place the proceeds of the casual and territorial revenue under the
control of the Assembly of New Brunswick. He would,
he said, be prepared to advise His Majesty to accept a
permanent appropriation by the Legislature, duly secured,
to the amount of £14,000 per annum, and that the Crown
should undertake to charge on any such permanent grant
the salaries of the Lieutenant Governor, his Private

Secretary, the Commissioner of Crown Lands, Provincial
Secretary, Chief Justice, three puisne Judges, the Attorney General, Auditor, Receiver General, the expenses of
the indoor establishment of the Crown Land department,
and a grant of £1,000 to the College. It would be
necessary, Mr. Stanley stated, that any bill passed in
consequence of the proposal contained in this despatch,
should contain a suspending clause in order that it might
be submitted to His Majesty before it was finally assented
to. It was also stated, in order to prevent misunder-
standing or delay, that the House should be apprised that,
unless some other fully equivalent and sufficient security
could be devised, it would be expected that the act should
provide that the stipulated annual commutation should
be payable out of the first receipts in each year, and that
in case of any default in such payment that the whole of
the revenue surrendered should revert to the Crown. A
Committee was appointed to prepare the bill on the subject of the surrender, by His Majesty, of his casual and
territorial revenues of the Province. The House of
Assembly had previously passed a resolution that the sum
of £14,000, required by His Majesty's government as
a permanent grant for the surrender of the casual and
territorial revenues of the Province, was greater than the
charges contemplated to be thereon required, yet that the
great desire of the House of Assembly to have this
important subject finally settled, should induce them to
accept the proposal contained in Mr. Stanley's despatch.
On the day after this a resolution was passed and a

Committee appointed; the Lieutenant Governor communicated to the House of Assembly an extract from a despatch, received the previous day by him from the Right Honorable Mr. Stanley, dated the 4th January, 1834. This extract was as follows:

"In your message communicating to the Assembly the proposal contained in my despatch of the 30th September, you will take care distinctly to explain that the payments expected from the New Brunswick Land Company are not included in the revenue which is offered to the acceptance of the Assembly." It is with great regret that an historian of this period must record the receipt of such a despatch from an Imperial head of department to a Colonial Governor, for the spirit displayed in the message was not that of an enlightened statesman, but such as might have been expected from a peddler, or an old clothesman, who was endeavoring to drive the hardest possible bargain with the Province of New Brunswick, and to grind down the House of Assembly as much as possible, in order that a number of bloated officials, swollen with pride and enjoying enormous salaries, might not suffer.

A few days after the receipt of this despatch a resolution was passed by the House in Committee, regretting that the additional condition contained in Mr. Stanley's last despatch would prevent the Committee recommending to the House further action in the matter of preparing a civil list bill. Thus ended the attempt to settle this vexed question in the year 1834. The House of Assem-

J

bly, however, still continued to agitate the matter, and to make Sir Archibald Campbell's life a burden to him. On the 7th March they addressed him, asking for accounts in detail of the casual and territorial revenues, and calling for a number of statements which they had not received except in such a shape that they could not be properly understood. They also addressed His Excellency, requesting him to lay before them copies of all official despatches transmitted to him by the Secretary of State for the Colonies since he assumed the administration of the government, relating to the subject of the casual and territorial revenues. The reply of His Excellency to the request for more detailed accounts was a courteous one; but while he consented to furnish the accounts requested in detail, it was with the understanding that his compliance was not to be considered as a precedent. He declined, however, to give the names of the parties who had their timber seized or forfeited, or the names of the petitioners for Crown land. He also refused to furnish the accounts of the Receiver General and Commissioner of Crown Lands on the ground that they were accounts exclusively between these officers and the Crown.

With regard to the request for his correspondence with the Colonial Secretary, Sir Archibald Campbell, in another message, gave a tart refusal, stating that such a request was subversive of the principles and spirit of the British Constitution, and that he would ill deserve the confidence put in him by His Majesty were he to hesitate in meeting so dangerous an encroachment, not only on the independence of the Executive, but the prerogatives of the British Crown, with a most decided and unqualified refusal. This old military tyrant considered himself a proper exponent of the principles and spirit of the British Constitution. He failed to understand that the British Constitution rests upon the support of the people, while his system of government was intended to ignore the people altogether.

A few days after the receipt of this message, a resolution was passed by the House of Assembly, declaring that the language used by the Lieutenant Governor, in his reply to the address of the House, was at variance with all Parliamentary precedent and usage, and such as was not called forth by the address. Some of the Governor's friends attempted to weaken the force of this resolution by an amendment of a milder nature, but their amendment was defeated, and the resolution carried by a vote of 15 to 8. Another address on the subject of the casual and territorial revenues and civil list was prepared and passed by the Assembly for the purpose of being forwarded to His Majesty. It recited the proceedings in regard to the matter which had taken place already, and the desire of the House of Assembly to accept the proposition contained in Mr. Stanley's despatch, and expressed the regret of the House at the new condition imposed with regard to the New Brunswick Land Company, which made it impossible to accept the settlement as amended. The House concluded by expressing the hope that the terms proposed in the original despatch might yet be considered definitive, and that the proviso with regard to the New Brunswick Land Company might be withdrawn. This was transmitted to England; but before the year ended Sir Archibald Campbell concluded to rid himself of the House of Assembly, which had given him so much annoyance, and accordingly it was dissolved early in November, so that when the Legislature met again in January, 1835, the House of Assembly was a new one, although largely composed of the old members. The answer to the address of the House to the King of the previous session was not laid before the House of Assembly until that body had been sitting about a month. It consisted of an extract from a despatch of the Earl of Aberdeen, dated Downing street, 24th December, 1834. This despatch is so curious a document that it is well worth being quoted. The portion of it laid before the House of Assembly was as follows:

"I have had under my serious consideration your despatch No. 17, of the 24th March last, accompanied by an address to His Majesty from the House of Assembly, respecting the recent offer which has been made to them of the proceeds of the Crown revenues in New Brunswick.

"From various parts of the address I infer that the proposal conveyed to the Assembly, through my predecessors, must have been misapprehended in more than one important particular; and I have especially remarked the erroneous assumption that, in offering to surrender the proceeds of the Crown lands, it was intended also to give up their management, and to place them under the control of the Legislature.

"From the course of their proceedings, as well as the tenor of the present expression of their sentiments, the Assembly must be understood to consider it an indispensable condition that the payments of the Land Company should be comprised among the objects to be surrendered to them. This is a condition to which His Majesty's government cannot agree. His Majesty's government would also be unable to recognize the interpretation which was placed on their former offer, so far as regards the control over the lands belonging to the Crown in New Brunswick. Under these circumstances I can only desire you to convey to the Assembly His Majesty's regrets that the objects of their address cannot be complied with; and adverting to the wide difference between the views entertained by the government and those manifested by the Assembly on this subject, it seems to me that no advantage could be anticipated from making any further proposals at present respecting the cession of the territorial revenue."

This despatch, which brought a sudden close to the negotiations with regard to the casual and territorial revenues of the Province, did not emanate from the government with which the House of Assembly had been previously negotiating, but from a new administration which had just been formed under the premiership of Sir Robert Peel, and which lasted just one hundred and thirteen days. The creation of this administration was due to the action of King William IV., in dismissing his advisers on the death of Earl Gray. The King had grown to detest his Cabinet for their reforming spirit, but fortunately for Great Britain and for New Brunswick, the King's designs were thwarted by the failure of Sir Robert Peel to form an administration capable of facing the House of Commons. As a consequence, Viscount Melbourne became premier, and a renewal of the negotiations with the government in regard to the casual and territorial revenues was rendered possible. During the same session that this despatch was received, another address was prepared by the House of Assembly, to be laid before His Majesty, on the subject of the casual and territorial revenues. In this address the grievances with regard to the management of the Crown Lands of New Brunswick were recited, and the willingness of the Legislature to provide for the civil establishment of the Province was stated. The address urged the benefits that would result to the people of New Brunswick by placing the net proceeds of the Crown land revenues under the control of the Legislature. Attached to this address was a schedule of salaries paid out of the casual and territorial revenues, amounting in all to £10,500 currency. The address was transmitted to the Governor to be forwarded to His Majesty.

This session was remarkable from the fact that it closed without the passage of any appropriation bill. This was due to the action of the Legislative Council, who rejected the appropriation bill, because it did not contain any provision for the payment of the expenses of the President and the members of that body. The Legislature was prorogued on the 19th March, and called together again on the 15th June, when a short session was held for the purpose of passing the appropriation bill. At this session the bill for collecting Quit Rents, which has been already referred to, was passed, but no further steps were taken in regard to the casual and territorial revenue.

At the Legislative session of 1836, the House of Assembly again passed an address to the King on the subject of the grievances of the Province, with regard to the casual and territorial revenues, and Messrs. L. A. Wilmot and William Crane were appointed a deputation to proceed to England, for the purpose of concluding arrangements in regard to these matters. They arrived in England in June of that year, and immediately placed themselves in communication with Lord Glenelg, with whom they had many interviews. The result of their work was that an arrangement was made satisfactory both to the British Government and to the delegates representing the House of Assembly, by which the casual and territorial revenues were to be transferred to the Province, in consideration of the Legislature undertaking to provide for a civil list of £14,500 currency annually, for the payment of certain salaries chargeable to that fund. A draft of a civil list bill was prepared and agreed to by the Lords of the Treasury, and the understanding was that this bill should be passed by the Legislature, and receive the assent of the Lieutenant Governor, when it would immediately become operative.

The first clause of this bill transferred the proceeds of the territorial and casual revenues, and of all woods, mines and royalties which had been collected, and were then in hand, or which should thereafter be collected to the Provincial Treasurer; he was authorized to receive them for the use of the Province, while the act remained in force. The second clause charged the revenues with the payment of £14,500 for a civil list. The third clause enacted that all the surplus over and above the sum of £14,500 currency, should remain in the Treasury of the Province, until appropriated or disposed of by an act or acts of the General Assembly. The fourth clause gave the Lieutenant Governor, with the advice of his Executive Council, power to expend such sums as they might deem necessary for the prudent management, protection and collection of the said revenues, a detailed account of which was to be laid before the Legislature within fourteen days of the commencement of each session, with all vouchers for the same. It was also enacted that all grants or sales of Crown lands should be void unless the land had been sold at public auction, after due notice in the "Royal Gazette." By this arrangement the House of Assembly had obtained the boon for which they had so long been contending, but there was still one more obstacle to be overcome, the opposition of the Lieutenant Governor, Sir Archibald Campbell, who had entered into a plot with some of the enemies of freedom in the Province for the purpose of thwarting not only the wishes of the House of Assembly, but also the intentions of the

Home Government. As soon as Sir Archibald Campbell was apprised of the intention of His Majesty's advisers in England to transfer the casual and territorial revenues to the Provincial Legislature, he commenced a correspondence with the Colonial office, pointing out what he deemed to be imperfections in the scheme which they had prepared for the management of the public lands. He pretended to have discovered that there was some error in the calculation of the Lords of the Treasury with regard to the sum to be paid in lieu of the Civil List, and that the amount of £14,500 currency would not be sufficient to defray all the expenditures chargeable on the Civil List. Sir Archibald Campbell, soon after the opening of the session of the Legislature in December, 1836, requested the House of Assembly to add a suspending clause to any Civil List bill they might pass, so that he might forward it to the home government for their approval. As this was entirely contrary to the understanding which had been reached between Messrs. Wilmot and Crane and the Colonial Secretary, it being understood that the Civil List bill if passed in the form agreed upon would be immediately assented to by the Lieutenant Governor, the House of Assembly very naturally refused to comply with Sir Archibald Campbell's wishes. The old military tyrant, however, held firm in his resolution, and the Civil List bill which had been agreed to by the home authorities, after being passed by both houses, did not receive his assent. At the close of the session, while the matter was under discussion, at the instigation of the

Lieutenant Governor, one of the Executive Council, Solicitor General Street, was sent on a secret mission to Downing street. The object of this mission was to make such representations to the home authorities as would induce them to delay in giving their assent to the Civil List bill. The truth of the matter seems to have been that Sir Archibald Campbell and his advisers in New Brunswick thought if they could only gain time, the Imperial Government of England, which had granted such favorable terms to the Province might be defeated, and a Tory Government would come into power which would speedily undo all their predecessors had done, and refuse to grant any concessions to the Legislature of New Brunswick. There was great excitement in the Province in consequence of the action of the Lieutenant Governor, and this excitement was fairly voiced in the House of Assembly, where an address was prepared representing the condition of affairs to His Majesty, and detailing the manner in which the Lieutenant Governor had sought to thwart the intentions of the Imperial Government. This address was passed by a vote of 27 to 2, the only members of the House who ventured to stand in with the man who occupied Government House being John Ambrose Street and William End.

Messrs. Crane and Wilmot were again appointed a deputation to proceed to England with this address of the House of Assembly, and took their departure two days after it was passed, amidst great popular demonstrations of the citizens of Fredericton. The Legislature was

prorogued on March 1st, on which day the House of
Assembly again requested the Lieutenant Governor to
pass the Civil List bill, pointing out that under the
arrangements made with the Colonial Office it was his
duty to do so, but their request fell upon deaf ears. In
the speech proroguing the Legislature, Sir Archibald
Campbell stated that he had withheld his assent from this
bill because a suspending clause had not been appended
to it. These were the last words that Sir Archibald
Campbell was destined to speak before a New Brunswick
Legislature. Finding that all his hopes of impeding the
progress of the Province in the direction of liberty were
in vain, he tendered his resignation to save himself from
being removed, as he would have been, for his direct
disobedience to the commands of his superiors in England.
Sir John Harvey, a real soldier, and a man of a very
different spirit, was appointed to succeed him as Lieutenant Governor. The Civil List bill was again passed by
the Legislature and received the royal assent, becoming
law on July 17, 1837, and from that time to the present
the Province of New Brunswick has controlled the
revenues which it derives from its Crown Lands and
similar sources, and whether wisely expended or not, the
people of this Province have at least the satisfaction of
knowing that the money is appropriated by their own
representatives, and by a Government which is responsible
to them for its actions.

The manner in which the money granted by the Province as a consideration for the surrender of the Casual

and Territorial Revenue was to be appropriated, was specified in the despatch of Lord Glenelg and was as follows :—

Salary of the Lieutenant Governor,	£3,500
Chief Justice,	950
Three Puisne Judges,	1,950
Attorney General,	550
Solicitor General,	200
Private Secretary,	200
Commissioner of Crown Lands,	1,750
Establishment of Crown Lands,	909
Provincial Secretary,	1,430
Auditor,	300
Receiver General,	300
Scotch Minister,	50
Emigrant Agent at St. John,	100
Annuity to late Surveyor General,	150
College,	1,000
Indians,	54
Total, in Sterling money,	£13,393

It will be observed from the above figures that the salaries were arranged on a sufficiently liberal scale, the Surveyor General alone receiving as large a sum as the three principal heads of department in the present Government of New Brunswick are now paid. The Lieutenant Governor received about double the present salary of that official, and the Secretary of the Province was paid almost three times as much as the present incumbent of that office. Those were the days when officers enjoyed enormous incomes and performed but little service for them.

CHAPTER V.

The transfer of the Casual and Territorial Revenues of
the Province placed a very large sum, amounting to
£150,000, at the disposal of the Legislature and made
the Government, for the time being, rich. This, however,
was by no means an unmixed benefit, because it introduced a spirit of extravagance into the Legislature, which
was not calculated to be advantageous to the Province.
Having so much money at their disposal the members of
the House of Assembly expended it freely, frequently for
objects that were not at all essential to the public welfare.
This, however, is a matter which has no necessary place
in this work, except for the purpose of illustrating the
faulty system of appropriating the public money, which
prevailed at the time. It has already been explained in
previous pages that there was no executive control of the
expenditure. The initiation of money grants being in the
House of Assembly, any private member had it in his
power to move an appropriation of money for any object
that he deemed proper. In this way a system of "log
rolling" was inaugurated in the Legislature which resulted

in extravagant expenditures, and the appropriation of
money for objects which, under a better system, would
not have received it. As a result of this evil system the
surplus of the Casual and Territorial Revenue was very
speedily dissipated and in the year 1842, when Sir
William Colebrooke became Lieutenant Governor of the
Province, its finances were in an embarrassed condition.
Towards the close of 1841 a despatch was received from
Lord Stanley, the Colonial Secretary, suggesting that it
was desirable that a better system of appropriating the
funds of the Province should be inaugurated. This
brought up a discussion in the Legislature during the
session of 1842 in regard to the propriety of adopting the
principle of placing the initiation of money grants in the
Executive Council. Mr. L. A. Wilmot moved a resolution in a committee of the whole House that no appropriation of public money should be made at any future
session in supply, for any purpose whatever, until there
be a particular account of the income and expenditure of
the previous year, together with an estimate of the sums
required to be expended, as well for ordinary as extraordinary services, respectively, and also a particular
estimate of the principal amount of Revenue for the ensuing year. To this an amendment was moved by Mr.
Partelow as follows: "Whereas the present mode of
appropriation, tested by an experience of more than fifty
years, has not only given satisfaction to the people of this
Province, but repeatedly attracted the deserved approbation of the Colonial Ministers, as securing its constitu-

tional position to every branch of the Legislature; therefore resolved, as the opinion of this committee, that it is
not expedient to make any alteration in the same." This
amendment was carried by a vote of 18 to 12, the minority including Mr. Charles Fisher of York, who afterwards
became prominent as a reformer and did good service to
the cause of liberalism in connection with his colleague,
Mr. L. A. Wilmot. Such an amendment as that passed
by the House of Assembly of New Brunswick in 1842
would now only be an object of ridicule, because as a
matter of fact the financial condition of the Province
showed that the system of appropriation which prevailed
was based on false principles, while the approval of
the Colonial Ministers, of which so much account was
made, had been equally extended to the most illiberal
features of the constitution. There was, however, some
excuse for the reluctance of the members of the House
of Assembly to surrender the initiation of money votes
to the Executive, because the Executive of that day was
not a body properly under the control of the Legislature,
or in sympathy with the people.

The session of 1842 terminated the existence of the
twelfth Legislature of New Brunswick, and a general
election was held in December, 1842. At this election
the question of Responsible Government, which was the
term applied to the new system, was a prominent factor
in determining the fate of the candidates. On the hustings all the aspirants for the Legislature were expected
to give their views on this important matter, but the

result of the election showed that the public mind was in a very unsettled condition in regard to it. For the city of St. John, Mr. R. L. Hazen, who was certainly not a person who favored Responsible Government, and Mr. W. H. Street, who favored the initiation of money grants being placed in the Executive, were elected. The successful candidates for the County were Mr. John R. Partelow, who was wholly opposed to any change in the Constitution, Mr. Robert Paine, Mr. John Jordan, and the Hon. Charles Simonds. The three latter were in favor of Responsible Government, so that the voice of St. John in regard to this vital and important political question was divided. In York County two anti-reformers, Messrs. Allen and Taylor, and the two great reformers of the Legislature, Mr. L. A. Wilmot and Charles Fisher, were elected, but the anti-reformers led the poll. When the House of Assembly met on the last day of January, 1843, it was seen that the friends of Responsible Government were still in the minority, and Mr. John W. Weldon, as a representative of the old system, was elected speaker without any opposition. Still the friends of reform brought up the subject of the appropriation of the public monies by a resolution which sought to fix the responsibility of the expenditures on the Government. This was met by an amendment, moved by Mr. J. W. Weldon, that the House would not surrender the initiation of the money votes. The amendment was carried by a vote of 24 to 7, which showed that the friends of reform had still much leeway to make up before they could hope to impress their views upon the Legislature.

As it was hopeless to expect that the House of Assembly, as thus constituted, would vote in favor of the transfer of the initiation of money grants to the Executive, the subject does not seem to have been discussed again during the remainder of its term ; but by the operation of the Quadrennial Act, which came in force in 1846, a new House was elected in that year, and at the first session of this House, held early in 1847, Mr. Fisher again brought forward resolutions requiring the Government to prepare and bring before the Legislature such measures as might be required for the development of the provincial resources and the general advancement of the public interests.

The debate on this resolution assumed the character of an attack on the Government, and the resolution was treated as one of want of confidence and defeated, the vote being 23 to 12. In the following year there was another discussion on the initiation of money grants, arising out of a despatch which had been received from Earl Grey, then Colonial Minister, in which he referred to the laxity of the system by which money was voted in the New Brunswick Legislature without any estimate, and suggested that the initiation of money grants should be surrendered to the Executive.

This proposal was fiercely opposed and all the forces of ancient Toryism were rallied against it, one member from Queens County, Mr. Thomas Gilbert, going so far as to apply to the advocacy of the old rotten system the soul-stirring words contained in Nelson's last signal at

K

Trafalgar, "England expects that every man this day will do his duty." Finally the following resolution, which was moved by Mr. Fisher, was carried by a vote of 24 to 11 :—"Resolved, as the opinion of this committee, that the House should approve of the principles of Colonial Government contained in the despatch of the Right Honorable Earl Grey, Her Majesty's principal Secretary of State for the Colonies, of the 31st March, 1847, and for their application to this Province." This resolution was the first unequivocal admission by both parties that Responsible Government had obtained a foot-hold in New Brunswick. The passage of this resolution, however, made no difference in the practice of the Government during the term of the Legislature elected in 1846, and it was not until the year 1851, after the subject of this biography had become a member of the Legislature, that a resolution was finally carried in the House of Assembly in favor of surrendering the initiation of money grants into the hands of the Executive Government.

The arrangement by which the Executive and Legislative Councils were separated, which came in force in 1833, although it was a decided improvement on the old state of affairs, did not produce universal satisfaction. The constitution of the Legislative Council was complained of, and it was described as an obstructive body which disregarded the wishes of the people. The complaints against the Legislative Council that the House of Assembly had to make were embodied in an address to the

Queen, which was passed at the session of 1843. In this address it was stated that in the opinion of the House the Legislative Council should be composed of persons not only representing all the leading interests of the Province, but so independent in respect to property and so free from the official control, as to form a constitutional check on the Executive as well as a branch of the Legislature. Although by the laws that existed then members of the Assembly were required to be possessed of real estate to the value of £300, over and above all encumbrance, there was no property qualification whatever required for members of the Legislative Council. The address of the House expressed the opinion that members of the Council should be required to possess a certain amount of real estate, and that their seats should be vacant on the loss of this qualification, or on their being bankrupt or a public defaulter, or from neglect to give their attendance for a given time without leave of the Lieutenant Governor. The address also stated that the constitution of the Legislative Council was defective and objectionable in other respects, because of the eighteen members who composed it a great proportion held offices at the pleasure of the Crown, and the principal officers of the Government usually formed a majority of the members present. It was also complained that members of the Church of England had too great a preponderance in the Council, the only members not of that communion being one Presbyterian and one Baptist, while there was not a single member in the Council who, in the opinion of the House, could be classed as a reformer. At the next session of the Legislature despatches were laid before the House of Assembly in which it was stated that the Council would be increased in number to twenty-one, and four new members of the Council were to be appointed. The new members then appointed were T. H. Peters, Admiral Owen, William Crane and George Minchin, while the Honorable Thomas Baillie, the Surveyor General, the Honorable Mr. Lee, the Receiver General, the Honorable Mr. Allanshaw, of St. Andrews, and the Honorable Harry Peters, of Gagetown, retired from the body. No doubt the retirement of two officials who received large salaries was some improvement, but the Council required much remodelling before it could be said to be an efficient body, or one in sympathy with the inhabitants of the Province.

The Legislative Council has now ceased to exist and it may be said of it that it was never a very satisfactory body for legislative purposes. Perhaps the original composition of it created a prejudice against Legislative Councils so as to hamper its activities, and from having been at first merely the echo of the wishes of the Governor, it became latterly, to a large extent, the echo of the wishes of the Government. Gradually it became relieved of its official members and in its latter years no head of a department ever occupied a seat in the Legislative Council, for it was thought, and rightly, that the power ought to be in the House where the responsibility to the people was most felt, and that it was not wise to place a departmental official, whose department expended large sums of money, in a body which properly had no control over the public expenditure. The Legislative Council had undoubtedly from time to time many able and useful members, and at certain periods in the history of the Province, particularly during the confederation discussions, it took a firm stand in favor of measures which seemed essential to the prosperity of the British North American Provinces. No one can deny that at that time it exercised an authority fully equal to that of the lower House, but it cannot be doubted that some of this work was done at the expense of the proper balance of the constitution. Such an exercise of unusual authority on the part of a body not elected by the people may serve the purpose at a particular crisis, but cannot be commended, and if frequently repeated would end in the destruction of the constitution. The Legislative Council lost a considerable proportion of its able men at the time of confederation by the removal of twelve of its members to the Senate of Canada, although one or two remained with it who were not inferior to any of those who then took their departure. The new members who came in as their successors were naturally inferior to the old in practical experience and ability, and this had no doubt an influence on the future of the House. The example of Ontario, which was able to conduct its affairs with one House, showed that two independent branches of the Legislature were by no means necessary, and that the Council might be abolished with safety. No doubt

it was difficult to bring this about among a people who
had been trained to believe that there was something
essential to legislation in the balance of king, lords and
commons making up one legislative body. But in the
course of time people began to think that the Council
was not exactly the proper representative of the House
of Lords, and the Lieutenant Governor was very far from
standing in the position of a king. Old prejudices in
favor of a constitution framed after a particular model
are difficult to remove, but in the case of New Brunswick
these prejudices have been finally overcome, and it is safe
to say that in the course of time all the provincial legislatures of Canada will consist of but a single chamber.
It is equally safe to assert that under the new system
the work of legislation will be as well or better done than
it was under the old.

It has been already stated that the Governor of the
Province made such appointments to office as he pleased,
usually without the advice of his Council. He was supposed to have power to do this as the representative of
Her Majesty, and in the exercise of what was termed the
Royal Prerogative. In this way persons were frequently
appointed to offices who were not residents of the Province, and in all other cases appointments were given to
the members of certain favored families. In 1834 a
vacancy was created on the Supreme Court Bench by the
death of Chief Justice Saunders. Ward Chipman was
appointed Chief Justice in place of Mr. Saunders, and
the vacant puisne judgeship was given to James Carter,

who afterwards became Chief Justice of the Province.
James Carter was a young Englishman and was certainly
no better qualified to fill the position of judge that many
natives of the Province, so that it was undoubtedly a
gross insult to the members of the New Brunswick bar
to give such an appointment to a stranger. Yet so slow
was public opinion to make itself felt in regard to the
evil of the appointing power being given to the Governor
without qualification, that ten years later the House of
Assembly presented an address to Sir Charles Metcalf,
Governor General of Canada, expressing the high sense
entertained by them as representatives of the people of
New Brunswick, of the "constitutional stand" taken by
him in maintaining the Prerogative of the Crown in the
then recent memorable conflict. The city of St. John
also, to show its loyalty, presented a similar address, and
one signed by one thousand persons was sent from the
County of York. Yet nothing can be more clear than that
the stand taken by Sir Charles Metcalf was wholly wrong,
for it consisted in refusing to consult with his Council in
regard to appointments, and in making appointments contrary to their advice. What would the people of Canada
say to-day to a Governor General who insisted on appointing men to offices against the advice of his Cabinet?
Yet it was for doing this that the New Brunswick House
of Assembly, the City and County of St. John and the
County of York actually grovelled in the dust before this
despotic Governor, thus approving of all his detestable
acts. Such abasement and subserviency to an unconsti-

tutional Governor was certain to bring its own punish-
ment, and it came much sooner than any one could have
anticipated. On Christmas day of the same year the
Hon. William Franklin Odell, who had been Provincial
Secretary for thirty-two years, died at Fredericton. Mr.
Odell's father had been Secretary before him from the
foundation of the Province, so that the Odell family had
held that important and highly lucrative office for sixty
years.

The Governor at this time was Sir William Colebrooke,
and on the 1st of January, 1845, just one week after the
death of Mr. Odell, he appointed his son-in-law, Alfred
Reade, who was a native of England and a stranger to
the Province, to the vacant office. The gentlemen who
had been most prominent in shouting their approval of
the " constitutional stand" taken by Sir Charles Metcalf
now suddenly discovered that Sir William Colebrooke's
conduct in making this appointment, without consulting
his Council, was a fearful outrage, and their distress was
pitiable to behold. Several members of the Government,
including such strong upholders of the Prerogative as the
Hon. Robert L. Hazen, of St. John, at once resigned their
positions. A communication from three of them, Hugh
Johnson, E. B. Chandler and R. L. Hazen, addressed to
His Excellency, gave as their reasons for resigning that
they could not justify the exercise of the Prerogative of
the Crown in respect to Mr. Reade's appointment, because
they felt that the "elevation to the highest offices of trust
and emolument of individuals whose character, services

. and claims to preferment, however appreciated elsewhere, are entirely unknown to the country generally, is prejudicial to the best interests of the Province." They did not, however, make it a ground of objection that the appointment of Mr. Reade was forwarded for the royal approbation without the advice or concurrence of the Council. These gentlemen evidently thought it was too early for them to eat the words in regard to the Prerogative of the Crown of which they had been so free a few months before, but they showed their true character by deserting the Governor because he had been foolish enough to believe that their profuse expressions in favor of the Royal Prerogative were sincere.

Hon. L. A. Wilmot, who also resigned, sent a separate communication to the Lieutenant Governor, in which he stated that such appointments should be given to inhabitants of the Province and not to a comparative stranger and a transient person like Mr. Reade. He also expressed the opinion that the principles of Responsible Government should be put in operation in New Brunswick, and that the Provincial Secretary should be brought into the Executive and should hold a seat in one of the Houses of the Legislature, his tenure of office being contingent upon the successful administration of the Government. When the House met, in the latter part of January, the Reade appointment immediately became the subject of discussion, and by the vote of 24 to 6, an address was passed to Her Majesty the Queen, condemning the appointment, not, as the members said, because they questioned "in the remotest degree the Prerogative in its undoubted right to make such appointments," but because they thought that the right of appointment had been improperly or unjustly exercised. In other words the members of the House of Assembly surrendered the principle that appointments should be made by the Governor, with the advice of his Executive, and only objected to the Reade appointment because in their opinion some one else should have been chosen. It is easy to see that in subscribing to this address the members of the House stultified themselves, and cut the ground from under their feet; for if it was a part of the Prerogative of the Crown to make appointments without the advice of the Council, surely the exercise of that prerogative in the appointment of a particular individual could not be fairly questioned. The result of the difficulty, however, was the cancelling of Mr. Reade's appointment by the home government. This decision was communicated to the House of Assembly by message on the 3rd of February, 1846. The despatch from the Colonial office, upon which the Lieutenant Governor acted, was written on the 31st of March, 1845, and must have been received by him at Fredericton not later than the last of April. But notwithstanding this despatch Mr. Reade held office until the 17th of July, so it will be seen that Sir William Colebrooke was in no hurry to carry out the wishes of the home government. Lord Stanley, the writer of the despatch in question, expressed the opinion that public employment should be bestowed on the natives or settled inhabitants of the Province, and he thought that Mr. Reade did not come under this description. He closed his despatch with the following singular statement: " I observe with satisfaction that the House of Assembly have not only abstained from complicating the subject with any abstract questions of government, but have rejected every proposal for laying down formal principles upon such questions. The House has, I think, in this course done justice to the earnest desire of Her Majesty, that the Colonial administration generally should be conducted in harmony with the wishes of her people, whatever may be the variations arising out of local considerations and the state of society in various Colonies, subject to which that principle may be carried into practice ; and it is anxiously hoped that the same wise forbearance which has led the House of Assembly to decline the unnecessary discussion of sub-jects of so much delicacy, may lead them also to regard the practical decision now announced as the final close of the controversy, and to unite in the promotion, not of objects of party strife and rivalry, but of the more sub-stantial and enduring interests of the Colony which they represent." If these words have any meaning they seem to show that at that date the British Government believed the right of appointment to be in the Crown, without reference to the Council, and that they were unwilling any general principle should be laid down by the Legis-ture of the Province which conflicted with this view. Even so late as the year 1851 the Colonial Secretary

ordered the Lieutenant Governor to appoint Mr. Justice
Carter to be Chief Justice of the Province and Mr. L. A.
Wilmot a puisne judge, without any reference whatever
to the wishes of the Council on the subject, and this order
was obeyed.   Such an easy acquiescence in claims which
could not be defended on constitutional grounds showed
that even at the period when Mr. Tilley entered public
life neither the British Government nor the people of
this Province had grasped the true meaning of the constitution which was supposed to be in force in the
Province.   It was absurd to pretend that Responsible
Government really existed in New Brunswick, if the
Crown could make appointments to the most important
offices on its mere motion, and without consulting the
wishes of the people or their representatives.

There were many people in New Brunswick at that
time who had been ready to support constitutional
improvements which directly affected their own interests,
but who became very lukewarm advocates for reform
when this spur to their activity was removed.   They
desired changes in the law relative to matters which
directly touched themselves, but with respect to constitutional questions which were of more general interest, they
held sometimes very conservative views.   We can trace
in the old system of family compact elements and
conditions which afterwards arose in this Province and
affected its politics.   New Brunswick has always been
slow to adopt constitutional changes, even when these
changes were based on sound principles, and there has

often been a great disposition on the part of our people to judge the merits of a question rather by its effect upon individuals than by its relation to the public interests. No person who has studied the political history of this Province in recent times will deny that this spirit still prevails, and it is one which has a continual tendency to make our people backward in political matters. Yet it is difficult now to understand how the people of New Brunswick so long endured the system by which they were governed, where a few powerful families controlled all the offices and all the influence, and legislated largely to suit themselves. Such a state of affairs could only have been tolerated by persons who had been trained to regard these influential families as their political superiors, and to accept with meekness whatever they might choose to impose upon them.

I have now traced step by step the progress of the principal reforms in the constitution of this Province which were brought about between the year 1818, when Mr. Tilley was born, and 1850, when he became a member of the Legislature. These reforms were not brought about suddenly, nor were they achieved without difficulty, for there is in the human mind a strong inclination to cling to old customs and to old methods in politics as in other matters, which in itself is sufficient to prevent the accomplishment of any great change at once. This conservative spirit was very powerful in New Brunswick, and there were large classes of people within the Province to whom all changes were objectionable, because they had a strong interest in permitting matters to remain as they were. Under these circumstances, and considering that these people had the ear of the Colonial office, we need not be so much surprised that the changes were resisted so long, as that they were at length accomplished. The British Government, naturally conservative in its views, and paying but little heed to the Colonies, notwithstanding the lessons furnished by the revolution which separated the thirteen colonies from the mother country, was not disposed to proceed fast in the work of reform when so large a class in the colonies were so firmly opposed to all reform. Thus the Liberals who sought to bring about a better state of affairs were on every side surrounded with difficulties, and their work could never have been accomplished successfully had it not been that the other Colonies of the British empire were at the same time struggling for similar changes, and pressing upon the British government those reforms in the Colonial system which were necessary to make the Provincial Governments popular and efficient. Having thus cleared the ground for the main feature of the story, and explained the condition of the Province at the time of his entrance into public life, the hour has come in which to bring the man himself upon the stage, and hereafter the story of political progress in this Province will be the story of Mr. Tilley's own life.

CHAPTER VI.

In the United States, and particularly in the New England States, the fact that a man's ancestors came over in the "Mayflower" is regarded as almost as clear a proof of good family as in England the legend that the head of a family came over with William the Conqueror. To have been descended from one of the earliest English settlers of this continent is certainly a distinction, and at all events stamps the wearer of it as being an American to the fullest extent, and one "to the manner born." This distinction Sir Leonard Tilley enjoys, for among those who came over in the "Mayflower" in 1620, and landed at Plymouth, were two brothers, Edward and John Tilley. History does not preserve any very full record of these two persons, because they both died at an early period in the settlement of the Colony. But there is no doubt that Sir Leonard Tilley is a lineal descendant of John Tilley, who came over in company with Winslow, Brewster and Miles Standish two hundred and seventy-three years ago. The origin of the Tilley family is probably to be found in France or Germany, there having been several eminent persons of that name on the continent of Europe. This, however, is a matter which I leave to the antiquarian, and which does not greatly concern the present history. The great grandfather of Sir Leonard Tilley was Samuel Tilley, who was a farmer on Long Island at the time of the Revolutionary war. His farm was then within the boundaries of the present city of Brooklyn, and the curious in such matters can find the very lot upon which he resided laid down upon some of the ancient maps of that locality. At the time the British occupied Long Island, after the battle which took place there in the autumn of 1776 and the defeat of the Americans, the Brooklyn farmers were called upon to provide cattle for the sustenence of the troops. Samuel Tilley, being a loyal man and a friend of the government complied, and for this he was made the subject of an attack by the disloyal element among his neighbors, and in the course of time was compelled to seek shelter within the British lines. The occupation of Long Island by the British during the whole period of the war made it secure enough for Samuel Tilley, as well as for loyal men who lived in the vicinity of Brooklyn, but when the war was over it became necessary for him to seek shelter in Nova Scotia, the acts of confiscation and banishment against the Loyalists being of the most severe character. Samuel Tilley came to this Province in the spring fleet, which arrived in St. John in May, 1783, and was a grantee of Parrtown. He erected a house and store on King street, on the south side, just to the east of Germain, on the lot now occupied by the store of George Robertson & Co., and there commenced a business which he continued for several years. He died at St. John in the year 1815. His wife was Elizabeth Morgan, who survived him for many years and died in the North end in 1835, aged eighty-four years. Sir Leonard Tilley was not born when his great grandfather died, but has a clear recollection of his great grandmother, who lived for about four years after he came to reside at St. John. James Tilley, the grandfather of Sir Leonard, was also a grantee of Parrtown, he having purchased for a trifling sum when a boy a lot on Princess street, which had been drawn by some person who was anxious to dispose of it. This lot, after lying uncared for and unthought of for a great many years, was finally sold to the late Charles Patton for the sum of $400, and the house in which he died, erected after the great fire, is built upon it. James Tilley was a resident of Sunbury County and a magistrate there for a great many years, dying in the year 1851.

Sir Leonard Tilley's father, Thomas Morgan Tilley, was born in 1790, and served his time with Israel Gove, who was a house joiner and builder. He spent his early days as a lumberman getting out ship timber, his operations being carried on mainly at Tautiwanty, in the rear of Upper Gagetown. He afterwards went into business at Gagetown and kept a store there up to the time of his death, which took place in 1870. Sir Leonard's grandmother, on his father's side, was Mary Chase, of the Chase family of Massachusetts, she having come from

L

Freetown, in that state. Sir Leonard's mother was Susan
Ann Peters, daughter of William Peters, who was for
many years a prominent farmer in Queens County, and
a member of the Legislative Assembly. William Peters
owned a large property and had one of the finest tracts
of land possessed by any man in the Province in his day.
But he was unwise enough to sell it for the purpose of
obtaining money with which to enter into lumbering with
William Wilmot, the father of the late Governor Wilmot,
and being unsuccessful in his operations, his whole
fortune was swept away. The ancestors of William
Peters were from New York state, from which they came
with the rest of the Loyalists in 1783. The future
Finance Minister of Canada and Governor of New
Brunswick was born at Gagetown in May, 1818, in the
house to which his father had removed after his marriage
to Susan Ann Peters in 1817. This house is now
Simpson's Hotel. It was originally built by a Dr.
Stickles, a German who settled in Gagetown soon after
the Loyalist immigration, and who resided in it for some
years. It was purchased from Dr. Stickles by Samuel
Tilley, the great grandfather of Sir Leonard, and sold by
him to his father, Thomas Morgan Tilley, together with
the three acres of land attached to it. Gagetown was
at that period and still is, one of the most beautiful country places in New Brunswick, for the river St. John flows
in front of it and Gagetown Creek, which is almost as
wide as the river, laves its shores. The land in the
vicinity is fertile and productive, and fine old trees line

the streets, giving an air of beauty and refinement to the
locality.   Not many facts in connection with Sir Leonard
Tilley's infancy are preserved, nor would they be of much
interest to the reader of a political biography. It is
proper, however, to mention that he was named after
his uncle, Samuel Leonard Peters, and that the latter was
named after an English school master named Samuel
Leonard, who was a great favorite with William Peters,
the grandfather of the subject of this biography.   Samuel
Leonard, after leaving Gagetown, appears to have removed
to Nova Scotia, and probably died in that Province.
When Sir Leonard was five years old he commenced
going to the Madras school in Gagetown, of which Samuel
Babbitt was teacher.   He attended this school from 1823
until 1827, when the Grammar school was started in
Gagetown.   The Madras school system was at that time
in high favor with the people of the Province, and these
schools received large grants from the government, it
being thought that this system was more advantageous
than any other for the instruction of youth.   This
idea, however, did not prove to be universally correct, for
in the course of a few years we find the Legislature
declaring that while they believed the Madras system
suitable to towns and populous places, it did not answer
so well in rural districts.   Samuel Babbitt, the teacher
of the Madras school, was an uncle of Samuel Babbitt,
who was afterwards cashier of the Peoples Bank, and
whom many of our citizens remember.   Samuel Babbitt,
the elder, was Clerk of the Parish, and according to the

custom of that day, led the responses in church. The rector of Gagetown at this period was Rev. Samuel Clark. The teacher of the Grammar school to which Sir Leonard Tilley went from 1827 to 1831 was William Jenkins, a graduate of Dublin University. He was an uncle of Dr. Hea, who was for a short period president of the University of New Brunswick. Jenkins was a very severe man, and believed in the doctrine that he who spares the rod spoils the child, and Sir Leonard has a very vivid recollection of the vigor with which he applied the birch. He removed from Gagetown shortly after the year 1831, and took up his residence in Quebec, where he conducted a large school for many years, dying about the year 1863. Sir Leonard, after he had become a well known political character and a member of the government of New Brunswick, had the pleasure of paying him a visit some time in the year 1858. Among the boys who were with young Tilley at the Grammar school were Dr. George Peters, H. S. Peters, Edward Peters and Dr. Murray Peters, sons of the then Attorney General of this Province; the Rev. James Disbrow and Robert Disbrow, sons of Noah Disbrow; Dr. Harry Peters, son of the late Hon. Harry Peters; also Richard and Nelson DeVeber, sons of L. H. DeVeber and Gabriel DeVeber, son of the late Sheriff DeVeber. There were also Robertson Bayard, LeBaron Drury, Thomas Hanford, Rev. H. Jarvis and Gustavus Jarvis. All these mentioned above are now dead. Among the living persons who went to Gagetown Grammar school at that time were Henry, Thomas and

James Gilbert, sons of Henry Gilbert, Dr. William Bayard, of this city, and John Emery Doe, of Portland, Maine
who is now about eighty years of age, and who was then
the oldest boy in the school. An interesting incident
occurred in 1827, at the time young Tilley commenced to
attend the Grammar school. Sir Howard Douglas, who
was then Governor of New Brunswick, paid a visit to
Gagetown, and was the guest of Colonel Harry Peters,
then the Speaker of the House of Assembly. While the
Governor and his host were walking through Gagetown
they met young Tilley and a son of Harry Peters returning from school, and the boys were introduced to His
Excellency, who presented each of them with a Spanish
quarter dollar. Sir Leonard can still remember as well
as if it had taken place yesterday the appearance of Sir
Howard Douglas, dressed in a blue coat and brass buttons,
a fine, erect looking gentleman, with a pleasant face and
a kindly smile. Little thought the then Governor of New
Brunswick that the boy to whom he was speaking, a lad
of nine years of age, would fifty years later, sit in his
own chair in the Government House.

Young Tilley was not one of those home staying youths
who was likely to be satisfied to reside all his life in
Gagetown. Other boys of less ambition might be content
to settle down on the farm and to fulfil their destinies
within the comparatively limited sphere of action which
that little town in Queens County afforded, but Samuel
Leonard Tilley had within him longings for a higher
destiny, and a desire to reach more elevated heights than

he was likely to attain as a mere resident of a rural district. In those days ambitious boys went early as apprentices to the line of business which they had elected to follow. This was a necessity because the years of apprenticeship were long. Full fledged journeymen were not manufactured in those days in three or four years, but it took seven years at least to give a boy a trade, and to make him a free man, competent to stand with his fellows in the line of industry which he had chosen.

Young Tilley came to St. John in May, 1831, he then having reached the age of thirteen. He at once entered as a clerk in the drug store of the late Dr. Henry Cook, it being the fashion of those times for medical men to have a drug store in connection with their professional practice, so that they could give advice, prescribe and dispense medicines with equal facility. At that period St. John was a very different town from what it is at the present day, and although some people are disposed to regret the old days, it is quite certain that if we could have the St. John of 1831 restored to us we should be very ill-content to reside in it, or to put up with the inconveniences which a residence in it involved.

We have a contemporary account of St. John, written by a stranger, a British officer, who visited it in 1832. He reached this city by way of River DuLoup, Grand Falls and Fredericton, and he describes, in a book which he published giving an account of his travels, the position and prospects of the city very intelligently and clearly.

The town, containing nearly 11,000 inhabitants, is built upon a rocky and irregular promontory, formed by the harbour and the river which here empties itself into the Bay of Fundy. The principal streets are broad, well paved, and neatly laid out, with excellent private dwellings, and some elegant stone public edifices. The corporation in a most spirited manner are laying out large sums of money in beautifying and levelling the streets, though much to the inconvenience of private individuals, whose houses at the bottom of some hills have been blocked up by these improvements to the attic windows, so that a passer by may peep into the first or second story. On the summit of the hill again 20 feet of solid rock have been cut away, leaving the dwellings perched on high, and allowing the occupants a view of little else save sky and the occasional roof of a lofty house. The barracks, a fine extensive range of buildings, with some small batteries overlooking the sea and commanding the entrance to the harbour, occupy an elevated and pleasant situation in front of the town, whence in clear weather the opposite coast of Nova Scotia can be seen across the Bay of Fundy.

Everything about St. John presented the air of a flourishing place, and numerous vessels were upon the stocks in the upper part of the bay, where the tide rises to the height of 30 feet. In point of commercial importance it is the capital of New Brunswick, and upwards of 400 square rigged vessels enter the port annually, exporting more than 100,000 tons of square timber.

Young Tilley continued as a clerk with Dr. Cook until February, 1835, when he entered the service of the late W. O. Smith, who, from 1857 to 1860, was Mayor of this city. Mr. Smith, at that time, had his drug store on the north side of Market Square, at the corner of Prince William street, a locality which is still dedicated to the same use, although now in different hands. It was while a clerk with William O. Smith that Tilley became a member of the St. John Young Men's Debating Society, an organization which, if it has no other claim to the remembrance of posterity, at least has the merit of giving one distinguished statesman to British America, and a Governor to this Province. It was in this society that young Tilley made his first attempt at public speaking, and it may be said that from the very beginning he showed a remarkable aptitude for debate and public discussions. The surviving members of the Society besides Sir. S. L. Tilley, are James H. Delancey and Robert Smith. The late Sheriff, James A. Harding, and Joseph W. Lawrence also belonged to it, so that it will be seen that at least three of the members of the society entered public life.

In December, 1837, our future Governor took one of the most important steps of his life by espousing the cause of total abstinence. Having taken up this movement he threw his whole energy into it, and from that time down to the present he has been a consistent temperance man, and a strong advocate of the principle of total abstinence. It was, perhaps, this strong advocacy of the cause of temperance more than any other reason that brought him before the public as a suitable person to become a candidate for the House of Assembly, and led to his first election as a representative for the city of St. John in the Local Legislature thirteen years later. Certainly the fact that Mr. Tilley, from that time until the close of his public career, had always the support of the temperance bodies, gave him a strength which he hardly would have obtained otherwise, and rallied around him a phalanx of friends, who for fidelity to his interests and zeal for his political advancement, could hardly have been surpassed.

Mr. Tilley commenced business on his own account in 1838, before he had attained the age of twenty years, as a member of the firm of Peters & Tilley, and he continued a successful business career until 1855, when he transferred his business to Mr. T. B. Barker, senior member of the present firm of T. B. Barker & Sons. It is unnecessary to say anything more in regard to Mr. Tilley's career as a business man, further than that it was a highly prosperous one. Mr. Tilley showed so much energy and enterprise in business matters that when he entered political life he was comparatively wealthy. There is no doubt that if he had continued in business instead of devoting his energies to the services of the Province and Dominion, he would have made far more money than he has done as a politician. I have the authority of Mr. Tilley for stating that his private means have not been increased by his political career, and that any wealth he possesses at present is the result of his success in business early in life, and the accumulations from his private property.

At a meeting of the electors of the city of St. John in favor of protection, which was held at the office of Barzilla Ansley previous to the general election of 1850, Mr. Tilley was nominated as one of the candidates for the city of St. John. He was not present at the meeting and had no knowledge whatever of the intention of the electors to make such a nomination.   A meeting of the electors was called a few nights later in Carleton to confirm the nomination made at Mr. Ansley's office, and at that meeting Mr. Tilley was present.   He then made the strongest possible protest against the nomination, but the electors present would not take no for an answer, and he eventually consented to stand as a candidate, informing them at the same time that he had an engagement to be in Boston on the day fixed for the nomination, and could not therefore be at the hustings on that day.   Notwithstanding this statement they still persisted in his nomination, and, as Mr. Tilley was absent in the United States, his nomination speech on that occasion was made by Mr. Joseph W. Lawrence, who was afterwards found among his strongest opponents.   At the general election of 1850 all of the candidates elected for the City and County and for the City of St. John were avowed opponents of the Government.   The constituency of St. John did not contain so many voters at that time as it does at present. Mr. Tilley, who was at the head of the poll, received on that occasion 943 votes, while Mr. W. H. Needham, who came next and who was likewise elected, had 752 votes. Mr. Ansley, who was defeated, received 724 votes, and Mr. Isaac Woodward, 336.   The members elected for the County were R. D. Wilmot, William J. Ritchie, John H. Gray and Charles Simonds; while J. R. Partelow, Charles Watters and John Jordan were the three defeated candidates.   The list of candidates for the City and County of

St. John included two future Governors, a future Chief
Justice of the Supreme Court of Canada, and two other
Judges, to say nothing of the ex-Provincial Secretary,
Mr. Partelow, a Speaker of the House of Assembly and
a future Mayor of St. John.   It must be admitted that
few elections that have ever been held in any part of
British North America have had so many candidates
presented to the electors who were afterwards eminent in
public life.

Of the forty-one members of the House of Assembly
elected in 1850 only one, Sir Leonard Tilley, is now living.   He was elected at an important epoch in the history
of the Province, when the old order was passing away and
men's minds were prepared for the great change that was
to take place in the political aspect of affairs.   It was a
reform House of Assembly, and although all the members
elected for the purpose of upholding reform principles did
not prove true to their trust, still it contained a larger
number of men of Liberal views than any of its
predecessors.

Among the members of this House were several who
had taken a very important part in public affairs, or who
afterwards became members of the Executive.   The
County of York sent among its representatives Lemuel
A. Wilmot, who had been a member of the House for
twenty-five years, and who had taken a leading part in
many measures of importance for the improvement of the
system by which the country was governed.   Mr. Wilmot
was a man of tall and commanding presence, a natural

orator with a fine flow of language and abundance of
action.   As a stump speaker he could hardly be surpassed,
and while his mind was not of great force, he was acute
and well fitted for the work to which he had to apply
himself.   Mr. Wilmot was not a great man because he
lacked thoroughness, and also was somewhat deficient in
courage ; but after all deductions have been made, it
cannot be denied that he performed great services to his
native Province, and that he was one who is worthy to be
remembered with honor and respect among her distinguished sons.   He became a Judge of the Supreme
Court of the Province, and was its first native Governor.

Mr. Charles Fisher, who had been a colleague of Mr.
Wilmot in the County of York, was defeated at the
general election, but soon afterwards became a member of
the House.   Mr. Fisher had not the oratorical gifts
possessed by Mr. Wilmot, but he was even stronger in
his Liberal views, and as a constitutional lawyer he had
no equal, at that time, in the Province.   Although his
manners were somewhat uncouth and his address far from
polished, Mr. Fisher had strong individuality and a
singularly clear intellect.   His services in the cause of
Liberalism in New Brunswick can hardly be overesti-
mated, and these services were rendered at a time when
to be a Liberal was to be, to a large extent, ostracized by
the great and powerful, who looked upon any interference
with their vested rights as little short of treason.

Mr. Tilley's colleague from St. John city was Mr.
William H. Needham, who afterwards represented the

County of York in the Legislature. Mr. Needham was
of short and stout figure, and so bald and round that his
appearance almost involuntarily suggested low comedy;
yet he had some remarkable gifts as a speaker and a
public man, and he might have risen to a much higher
position than he ever attained had it not been that his
principles were somewhat uncertain. In truth Mr.
Needham never succeeded in getting sufficiently clear of
the world to be quite independent, and this misfortune
hampered him greatly in his political career.

One of the members from St. John County was
William J. Ritchie, a lawyer who had risen by his own
efforts to a commanding position at the bar. Mr. Ritchie
had been a member of the House of Assembly for several
years, and always a useful one. He possessed, what few
members at that time had, a clear knowledge of the true
principles of Responsible Government. Mr. Ritchie had
an eminently practical mind; he was a forcible and
impressive speaker, and he was bold in the enunciation of
those Liberal principles to which he held. It was a great
misfortune to the Province that at a comparatively early
age he was transferred to the Bench, so that his great
abilities were lost at a critical period when they might
have been useful to New Brunswick in many ways.

John H. Gray, a new member, also sat in this House
for the County of St. John. Mr. Gray was a man of fine
presence, handsome appearance, and had a style of oratory
that was very captivating and impressive. His fluency,
however, was greater than his ability, and he injured

himself greatly by deserting the Liberal party, which he
had been elected to uphold. Mr. Gray never quite
recovered from the unpopularity connected with this
action, and he never became in any sense a real leader.
The party he had deserted soon obtained the control of
the Province, and his final appearance in the Legislature
was as a supporter of Mr. Tilley, content to play a secon-
dary part during the great Confederation conflict.

Robert Duncan Wilmot, another of the St. John County
members, was not new to the Legislature, and his mind
being naturally conservative, it is in connexion with the
Conservative party that he is best known in the history
of the Province. He was elected as a Liberal, however,
in 1850, but seemed to have forgotten that fact as soon
as he reached the House of Assembly. This was not the
only occasion on which Mr. Wilmot contrived to change
his principles, for he performed a similar feat during the
time of Confederation, and left the anti-Confederate Government in the lurch at a moment when its existence
almost depended on his fidelity. Mr. Wilmot never was
an eloquent man and he entertained some highly visionary
views in regard to an irredeemable paper currency, but
he was a useful public servant, and he afterwards became
a member of the government of Canada and eventually
Lieutenant Governor of New Brunswick.

Hon. John R. Partelow, who was now defeated in St.
John but elected for Victoria, and whose name occurs
frequently in these pages, was a man who might have
acquired a great political reputation had the stage on

which he appeared been a larger one. Mr. Partelow's qualifications for high public position did not depend upon his oratory, which was not of a high order, but upon his moderation and good sense. Mr. Partelow was not born in high life, his origin was lowly, and his early days were spent as a clerk in a store on the North wharf, St. John. Even in that humble position, he made himself so useful and displayed so much ability that he was marked for higher preferment. The idea which resulted in his nomination as a candidate for the city of St. John seems to have originated with his employers, but when he got to the Legislature he speedily made his influence felt. Mr. Partelow spoke but seldom, but when he did address the Legislature it was generally with good effect, and after the debate had been to a large extent exhausted by previous speakers. He then had a faculty of drafting a resolution which seemed to express the general sense of all, and which was usually accepted as a solution of the matter. Mr. Partelow was a good business man, understood accounts thoroughly, and therefore had a great advantage in legislative work over those who were not so well equipped in this respect. New Brunswick may have produced greater men than he in public life, but none whose talents were more useful to the Province, or better fitted to serve its interests at a critical period in its constitutional history.

Shortly after the general election Chief Justice Chipman, who had been in infirm health, resigned his office and a vacancy was thus left on the bench of the Supreme

Court of the Province.   In the natural course this office
ought to have gone to the Attorney General, Mr. L. A.
Wilmot, but this appointment was not made. The
responsibility for the result which followed is not very
easy to fix; certainly if the government had insisted on
Mr. Wilmot's appointment to the Chief Justiceship it
must have taken place, but they seem to have been unde-
cided in opinion, and perhaps were not willing to lose the
services of Mr. Wilmot in the Government.   Instead of
making the appointment, as they had a right to do, they
commenced a correspondence with the Colonial office,
which resulted in the receipt of a despatch from Downing
street, ordering the government to give the Chief Justiceship to Judge Carter and to offer the puisne judgeship to
Mr. Wilmot, or if he should refuse it, to Mr. Kinnear,
the Solicitor General.   The Executive Council complained
that the appointment of Mr. Wilmot to a seat on the
Bench, by the authority of the Secretary of State without
the advice or recommendation of the responsible executive
within the Province, was at variance with the principles
of Responsible Government which were understood to
be in force.   They, however, had only themselves to
thank for this, for they were continually appealing to
Downing street, and seemed unable to act without advice
from that quarter.   The government at that time was a
composite affair, supposed to be a coalition government,
but the only Liberals in it were Mr. Wilmot and Mr.
Fisher, so that it was virtually a Tory administration, for
Mr. Wilmot was now going to the Bench and Mr. Fisher

was a defeated candidate for York. As a majority of the House had been elected as opponents of the Government, it was supposed there would be no difficulty in bringing about a change of administration. Mr. Simonds, of St. John, who was reputed to be a Liberal, was elected Speaker without opposition, and at an early day in the session Mr. Ritchie, of St. John, moved as an amendment to the address a want of confidence resolution. This resolution, instead of being carried by a large majority as was expected, was lost by a vote of 22 to 15, Messrs. Alexander Rankine and John T. Williston of Northumberland, Messrs. Robert Gordon and Joseph Reed of Gloucester, Mr. A. Barbarie of Restigouche, and Mr. Francis McPhelim of Kent, having deserted their Liberal allies and sold themselves to the Tory government. Had they proved faithful as they were faithless the government would have been defeated, and the Province would have been spared another three years of an incompetent Tory administration.

In this division Mr. Tilley and Mr. Needham, who represented the City of St. John, voted for Mr. Ritchie's amendment, and Messrs. R. D. Wilmot and Gray, two of the County members, also voted with Mr. Ritchie, the mover of the amendment, on the same side. As Mr. Wilmot and Mr. Gray showed by their votes that they had no confidence in the government in February, 1851, it was with much surprise that the people of St. John, in the August following, learned that they had become members of the administration which they had so warmly

M

condemned a few months before. Their secession from
the Liberal party destroyed whatever chance had before
existed of ousting the government. Mr. Fisher seceded
from the government in consequence of their action in
reference to the judicial appointments, and Mr. John
Ambrose Street, who was a member for Northumberland,
became Attorney General. Mr. Street was a ready
debater and a strong Conservative, and his entrance into
the government at that time showed that a Conservative
policy was to be maintained.

Mr. Street presented a long programme of measures for
the consideration of the legislature, none of which proved
to be of any particular value. The municipal corporations
bill was passed, but it was a permissive measure, and was
not taken advantage of by any of the counties. A bill
to make the Legislative Council elective, which was also
passed in the lower House at the instance of the government, was defeated in the upper chamber. The bill
appointing commissioners on law reform was carried and
resulted in the production of the three volumes of the
Revised Statutes, issued in 1854, with which the gentlemen of the legal profession are familiar. The most
important bill of the session, introduced by the government, was one in aid of the construction of a railroad
from St. John to Shediac. This bill provided that the
government should give a company £250,000 Sterling, to
assist in the construction of the line referred to. There
was also a bill to assist the St. Andrews and Quebec
Railroad to the extent of £50,000, and a bonus or sub-

vention to the Shediac line amounting to upwards of
$11,000 a mile, for which sum a very good railway could
be constructed at the present time. It may be stated
here, that although the company was formed and undertook to build a railway to Shediac under the terms
offered by the government, the Province had eventually
to construct the road at a cost of $40,000 a mile, or fully
double what a similar road could be constructed for now.

One of the measures brought forward by the government at this session was with reference to the schools of
the Province. Mention has already been made of the
inefficient character of the provincial schools in 1818, and
they had improved but little at the period when Mr.
Tilley entered public life. The idea of taxing the property
of the country for the support of public schools had not
then found any general acceptance in this Province;
indeed it was not till the year 1872 that the measure
embodying this principle was passed by the Legislature.
The government school bill of 1851 provided that the
teachers were to be paid in money, or board and lodging,
by the district to the amount of £10 for six months, in
addition to the government allowance. This bill was
a very slight improvement on the act then in force,
and as the government left it to the House to deal with,
and did not press it as a government measure, it was not
passed. A private member, Mr. Gilbert, of Queens, at
this session proposed to convert Kings College into an
agricultural school, with a model farm in connection.
Kings College had been established by an act passed in

1829, and had received a large endowment from the Province, but it never was a popular institution, because of its connection with a single church. The charter of the college made the Bishop of the diocese the Visitor, and required the President to be always a clergyman of of the Church of England. The number of students who attended it was always small, and it was shown, in the course of the debate on Mr. Gilbert's bill, that it had failed to fulfil the object for which it was created. The college council contsisted of fifteen members, of whom ten were Episcopalians ; and the Visitor, the Chancellor, the President, the Principal, five out of seven of the professors and teachers, and the two examiners were members of the Church of England. The services in the college chapel were required to be attended by all resident students, and of the eighteen students then in the college sixteen were Episcopalians. It was felt that this college required to be placed on a different footing, and Mr. Gilbert's bill, although it provoked much comment at the time, certainly would have been more beneficial to the educational interests of the country, if it had passed, than the state of affairs which resulted from the continuance of the old system. An agricultural school was the very thing the Province required, while, judging from the limited attendance at the college from its foundation to the present time, the people of this Province are not greatly impressed with the value of a classical education. In 1851, however, anyone who proposed to replace the college for the teaching of Greek and Latin with a college of agriculture, and the

sciences allied to it, was looked upon as a Philistine.
Then youths were taught to compose Latin and to read
Greek who never to the day of their death had a competent knowledge of their own language; and agricultural
studies, which were of the highest importance to more
than one-half of the people of the Province, were totally
neglected. Mr. Gilbert's bill was defeated, as it was
certain to be in a Legislature which was still under the
domination of old ideas. Had it passed, New Brunswick
might at this time have had a large body of scientific
farmers, capable of cultivating the soil in the most
efficient manner, and increasing its productiveness to an
extent hardly dreamed of by those who only consider it
in the light of the present system of cultivation.

During this session Mr. Ritchie, of St. John, moved
another series of resolutions condemning the government,
and complaining of the Colonial office and of the conduct
of the Governor. These resolutions declared first that
the House was entitled to full copies of all despatches
addressed to or received from the Colonial office, and that
it was not enough merely to send extracts from a despatch
which had been received by the Governor. They declared
that the appointments to offices were invested in the
Governor by and with the advice of the Executive Council, and that the appointment of the Chief Justice and of
a puisne judge by the Governor, contrary to the advice
of his Council, was inconsistent with the principles of
Responsible Government. They complained that the
salaries were excessive, and condemned the refusal of the

British Government to allow the Colonies to grant bounties for the development of their resources. These resolutions, after being debated for about a week, were rejected by a vote of 19 to 21, which at the time was looked upon as virtually a Liberal victory. If the nineteen had been made up of men who could be relied on to stand by their colors, in all emergencies, it would have been a Liberal triumph, but unfortunately among the nineteen there were some who afterwards basely deserted their party for the sake of offices and power.

Early in August it was announced that John H. Gray and R. D. Wilmot, two of the Liberal members for the County of St. John, had abandoned their party and their principles and become members of the government. The people of St. John, who had elected these gentlemen by a substantial majority, were naturally chagrined at such a proof of their faithlessness, and their colleagues were likewise greatly annoyed. Messrs. Gray and Wilmot made the usual excuses of all deserters for their conduct, the principal one being that they thought they could serve the interests of the constituency and of the Province better by being in the government than out of it. The friends of the four members who still remained faithful, Messrs. Tilley, Simonds, Ritchie and Needham, held a meeting at which these gentlemen were present, and at which it was agreed that they should join in an address to their constituents, condemning the course of Messrs. Wilmot and Gray, and calling on the constituency to pronounce judgment upon it. As Mr. Wilmot, who had been appointed to the office of Surveyor General, had to return to his constituency for re-election, the voice of the constituency could only be ascertained by placing a candidate in the field in opposition to him. This was done, and Allan McLean, Esq., was selected to oppose Mr. Wilmot. The result seemed to show that the people of St. John had condoned the offence, for Mr. Wilmot was re-elected by a majority of 273. As this appeared to be a proof that they had lost the confidence of their constituents, Messrs. Simonds, Ritchie and Tilley at once resigned their seats. This act was at the time thought by many to indicate an excess of sensitiveness, and Mr. Needham absolutely refused to follow their example, thereby forfeiting the regard of those who had formerly supported him. The sequel proved that the three resigning members were right, for they won much more in public respect by their conduct than they lost by their temporary exclusion from the House of Assembly.

The gentlemen returned for the three seats in St. John, which had been vacated by the resigning members, were James A. Harding, John Goddard and John Johnson. Mr. Harding, who ran for the City, was opposed by S. K. Foster. Mr. Harding was a Liberal, but this fact does not seem to have been kept in view when he was elected. The net result of the whole affair was that the constituency of St. John could not be relied upon to support a Liberal principle, or any kind of principle as against men. That has always been a peculiarity of the St. John constituencies, men being more important than measures, and frequently a mere transient feeling being set off against the most important considerations of policy.

Mr. Tilley was not in the House of Assembly during the sessions of 1852, 1853 and 1854; that period was one, however, of development in political matters and of substantial progress. The Governor's speech, at the opening of the session of 1852, was largely devoted to railways, and it expressed the opinion that a railroad connecting Canada and Nova Scotia, and a connection with a line to the United States would produce an abundant return to the Province, and that by means of such a line millions of tons of timber, then standing worthless in the forest, would find a profitable market. It was during this session that Messrs. Peto, Brassy and Betts proposed to construct the European and North American railroad on certain conditions. The subsidies offered by the Province at this time were £20,000 a year for twenty years, and a million acres of land for the European and North American line, as the line to the United States was termed; and for the Quebec line £20,000 Sterling, for twenty years and two millions acres of land. A new company, which included Mr. Jackson, M. P., offered to build the New Brunswick section of both railroads, upon the Province granting them a subsidy of £20,000 a year for twenty years, and four millions acres of land. Attorney General Street introduced a series of railway resolutions favoring the building of the Intercolonial Railway jointly by the three Provinces, according to terms which had been agreed upon by the delegates of each. This arrangement was that the Intercolonial Railroad should be built through the valley of the St. John, and for favoring resolutions in the House confirming this arrangement, Mr. Street's Northumberland constituency called upon him to resign his seat, a step which he refused to take.

The government railway resolutions were carried by a large majority. During the recess Mr. Chandler, as a representative of New Brunswick, and Mr. Hincks, a representative of Canada, went to London to endeavor to obtain from the British Government a sum sufficient to build the Intercolonial Railway. The request of the delegates was refused on the ground that such a work had to be one of military necessity, and that the route which had been selected, by the valley of the St. John, was not a proper one for military purposes. The British Government then and for long afterwards, took but little interest in Canadian affairs, except to interfere with the distribution of patronage, and certainly these Provinces cannot claim to have received any large amount of favor from the British Government, either in sympathy or love, as compared with nations alien in blood to the British race, for whose sake enormous expenditures have been incurred with but little advantage to the British people. As Mr. Chandler could not obtain what he wished from the British Government, he applied to Messrs. Peto, Brassy and Betts, who said they were prepared to build all the railroads that New Brunswick might require, upon the most · advantageous terms. Mr. Jackson visited the

Province in September of the same year, and it was agreed that his company would build a railway from St. John to Amherst, and from St. John to the United States frontier, the distance being then estimated at 214 miles, for the sum of £6,500 Sterling per mile. The Province was to take stock to the extent of £1,200 per mile, and to loan its bonds to the company for £1,800 additional per mile. The completion of this arrangement caused great rejoicing in the Province, especially in St. John ; a special session of the Legislature being called on the 21st of October for the express purpose of amending the Railway Act so that it might conform to the new conditions. As both branches of the Legislature were strongly in favor of the railway policy of the government the necessary bills were speedily passed and the Legislature was prorogued after a session of eight days.

The meeting of the Legislature in 1853 derived its principal importance from the fact that much of its time was taken up with the discussion on the question of a reciprocity treaty with the United States of America. The discussion disclosed a strong disinclination on the part of many members to any arrangement by which the fisheries should be surrendered. The tone of the discussions on this subject, both in 1853 and 1854, shows that reciprocity with the United States was not generally regarded as being an equivalent for the surrender of the fisheries to our neighbors, and it is quite clear that so far as New Brunswick is concerned, the reciprocity treaty would not have been agreed to had it not been that the matter was in the hands of the British Government, and that the Legislature of this Province was not disposed to resist strenuously any arrangement that the British Government had made. At that time our Legislature had been so much accustomed to defer to the wishes of the Colonial office that it was impossible to bring public opinion to bear solidly against any British treaty, however unfavorable to Colonial interests. No important legislation was passed during the session of 1853, but a curious illustration of the undeveloped political condition of the Province was furnished by the discussion which took place in regard to the new election bill brought in by the Attorney General. This bill did not provide for vote by ballot, which many members of the House desired, and when the subject came to be discussed it was found that some members of the government spoke and voted in favor of the ballot and others against it. The Executive of 1853 did not appear to regard itself as a unit, nor did its members consider it necessary that they should be in accord with each other.

The session of 1854 was the last in which the old order of things controlled the Legislature. The people of New Brunswick had been a long time in emancipating themselves from the control of the British Government and the Colonial office, because they were not united, there always being a large element in the Province interested in the continuance of the old order of things. Nevertheless the time had come when men with family influence and loud professions of loyalty could no longer exclusively control affairs in the Province. New men were coming upon the political stage and bringing with them new ideas and new influences. It was felt that hereafter New Brunswick must be governed for the benefit of its people generally, and not merely of a few favored individuals. It was also felt that it was impossible that the Province could longer endure to be treated like a spoiled child, and its members harangued and lectured by some second-rate placeman, who had succeeded in obtaining the Governorship. When it is remembered that Colonial Governors were looked upon by the British people as almost an inferior set of beings, the political wrecks of the time, it is astonishing with what readiness our people were willing to accept their advice, and to regard it with almost as much awe as if it had been a mandate from the Most High. Sir Edmund Head, who seems to have been a person utterly unsuited to govern a Colony, had the assurance to forward a despatch to the Colonial Secretary in 1853, in which he denounced all the legislative methods then in existence in the Provinces, and reproved the gentlemen who were by courtesy regarded as his official advisers for their neglect of duty. It is quite possible that the remarks of the Governor were true enough, but there was a gross impropriety in him communicating with the Colonial office in secret, to the detriment of the Executive, for the purpose of weakening the influence of the very men that he had called to his Council, and in whom he professed to have perfect confidence.

The House, which had been elected in 1850, was dissolved shortly after the prorogation, and the election came on in the month of July. It was a memorable occasion because it was certain that the topics discussed by the House then to be elected would be of the very highest importance. One of these subjects was the reciprocity treaty, which at that time had been arranged with the United States through the British Government. This treaty provided for the free interchange of certain natural products between the great republic and the several Provinces which now form the Dominion of Canada, and it had been brought about through the efforts of Lord Elgin, who at that time was Her Majesty's representative in the United States. The treaty was agreed on the 5th of June, and was subject to ratification by the Imperial Parliament and the Legislatures of these British North American Colonies which were affected by it. In the St. John constituencies there was at that time a strong feeling in favor of the protection policy, but this did not interfere with the desire to effect the interchange of raw material with the United States on advantageous terms. Mr. Tilley had been originally nominated as a protectionist, and still held views favorable to the encouragement and protection of native industries by means of the tariff, but he was also favorable to reciprocity with the United States, if it could be obtained in such a manner as to be beneficial to this Province. At the general election he led the poll in the City of St. John, his colleague being the late James A. Harding, for many

years High Sheriff of the County, who had been elected
at a bye-election to the previous House.   For the County
Mr. William J. Ritchie was one of the successful candi-
dates and the only Liberal returned for that constituency.
The other members for the County were the Hon. John
R. Partelow, Robert D. Wilmot and John H. Gray.

The new House was called together on the 19th of
October, for the purpose of ratifying the reciprocity
treaty, and Hon. D. L. Hannington was elected Speaker
by a vote of 23 to 13.   This gave the Opposition an
earlier opportunity of defeating the Street–Partelow
administration than would under ordinary circumstances
have been possible.   The amendment to the address was
moved by the Hon. Charles Fisher, and was an indictment
of the government for their various shortcomings and
offences.   The amendment was to expunge the whole of
the fifth paragraph and substitute for it the following :—
" It is with feelings of loyalty and attachment to Her
Majesty's person and government that we recognize in
that provision of the treaty which requires the concurrence of this Legislature, a distinct avowal by the Imperial
Government of their determination to preserve inviolate
the principles of self government, and to regard the
constitution of the Province as sacred as that of the
parent state.   We regret that the conduct of the administration, during the last few years, has not been in
accordance with these principles, and we feel constrained
thus early to state to your Excellency that your constitutional advisers have not conducted the government of the

Province in the true spirit of our Colonial constitution."

This amendment was offered on the 23rd of October, and debated on the 24th, 25th, 26th, 27th and 28th. On the latter of these days the vote was taken and the amendment was carried by the following vote :—

Yeas—Charles Fisher, William J. Ritchie, Albert J. Smith, James A. Harding, John M. Johnston, Abner R. McClelan, James Steadman, P. McNaughton, William End, Charles MacPherson, George L. Hatheway, Charles Connell, S. L. Tilley, A. H. Gillmor, John McAdam, James Brown, Francis McPhelim, R. B. Cutler, R. Sutton, C. Botsford, John Farris, R. English, J. Tibbits, A. Landry, G. Ryan, E. Lunt and E. Stevens.

Nays—Hon. Street, Partelow, Montgomery, Wilmot, Gray, Hayward, and James Boyd, F. Rice, J. Taylor, H. W. Purdy, M. McLeod, S. H. Gilbert.

The general ground of accusation against the government, and the one most strongly insisted upon, was that it had yielded to the influence of the Colonial office in the appointment of Judge Wilmot. It was well known that the government at that time did not consider it necessary to appoint another judge ; at all events they took no steps to bring about another appointment ; but they yielded to the Colonial office, and the pressure put upon them by Sir Edmund Head, the Lieutenant Governor, so far as to acquiesce in the appointment of Judge Carter as Chief Justice, and the elevation of Mr. Wilmot to the Bench. This was a fair ground of attack, because it was clear that if the Executive Council of New Brunswick was under the orders of the home government, representative institutions and Responsible Government in this Province did not exist. A strange thing happened in connection with this vote, one which, perhaps, has never been paralleled in any Legislature. The mover of the address was James Brown, a member from the County of Charlotte, and the seconder was Enoch Lunt, who was one of the members from the County of Sunbury; yet when the vote was taken on Mr. Fisher's amendment, both Mr. Brown and Mr. Lunt voted for it, thus assisting to defeat the government, which, it was to be presumed by their moving and seconding the address, they were willing to support. This incident alone illustrates the state of political infancy in which the people of 1854 in this Province still were. For Mr. Brown, who was an honest man, said that he did not know when he was moving the address that there was any politics in it, and he thought he must vote for the motion affirming the right of New Brunswick to make its own appointments.

Thus the Street–Partelow government fell, and with it disappeared at once and forever the old Conservative regime which had existed in the Province from its foundation, and which had hindered and stifled the development of our free institutions, and deprived the people of New Brunswick of the best fruits of representative government. It was a great triumph for the cause of Liberalism that the Conservatives of that period were not only defeated, but swept altogether out of existence. After that a government of men who called themselves

Conservatives might go into power, but the old state of affairs under which the Lieutenant Governor could exercise despotic powers had departed forever, and could no more be revived than the heptarchy could be galvanized into life. All that a Conservative government could do after that was to fall into line with the policy they had displaced and proceed; less rapidly perhaps, but none the less surely along the path of political progress.

The new government which was formed as the result of this vote had for its Premier the Hon. Charles Fisher, who took the office of Attorney General; Mr. Tilley became Provincial Secretary; Mr. James Brown, a few weeks later, received the office of Surveyor General; J. M. Johnston, one of the members for Northumberland, became Solicitor General, and William J. Ritchie, Albert J. Smith and William H. Steeves were members of the government without offices.

On the 1st of November writs were ordered to be issued for a new election to fill the vacancy caused by the acceptance of office by Messrs. Tilley, Fisher and Johnston. The bill to give effect to the reciprocity treaty passed its third reading on the 2nd of November, only Ryan, Purdy, Gilbert, McPhelim and Cutler voting against it. On motion of the Hon. Mr. Ritchie, one of the members of the new government, it was resolved that it was desirable and expedient that the Surveyor General, who was a political officer, should hold a seat in the House of Assembly, and that the government should carry out the wishes of the House in this respect. Before

N

the House again met the wishes of the House had been complied with and Mr. Brown, of Charlotte, became Surveyor General.

The House met again on the 1st of February, 1855, and then the real reform of the legislation of the government began. In the speech from the throne it was stated that the Customs Act would expire in the course of a year, and that it was necessary that a new act should be passed. A better system of auditing the public accounts was also recommended, and a better system of electing members to the Legislature. On the 5th of March correspondence was brought down, dated the 15th of August previous, announcing on the part of the Imperial Government the withdrawal of the Imperial Customs establishment, which was considered to be no longer necessary, and stating that as the duties of these offices were now mainly in connection with the registration of vessels in the Colonies, and the granting of certificates of the origin of Colonial products, this work would hereafter be performed by the Colonial officers. A letter addressed to the comptrollers and other Customs officers, had informed them that their services would be discontinued after the 5th of January, 1855. So disappeared the last remnant of the old Imperial Custom House system, which had been the cause of so many difficulties in all the Colonies, which was the real occasion of the revolution which separated the thirteen Colonies from the mother country, and which in the other American colonies which were left to England, had always been regarded as a grievance.

The new government resolved to make Responsible Government a reality, and to at once bring about a condition of affairs which would end the waste and extravagance which had prevailed under the old system of appropriation. One of their first measures was to vest in themselves the initiation of all money grants, so that no private member hereafter could move the appropriation of money for public purposes, except by the consent or through the action of the government. This was a change which had long been demanded but had been steadily resisted by private members, because their self interest was concerned in the old order of things. It has already been explained how under the old system " log rolling " prevailed, one man voting for an appropriation in some distant county of the merits of which he knew nothing, on condition that the member from that county would vote for an appropriation which he desired to have, although it might not be at all in the general interest. The government also undertook to frame a new tariff, and therefore about in a double sense to grasp the control of the finances of the Province.

CHAPTER VII.

The great measure of the session of 1855 was the law to prevent the importation, manufacture, or selling of liquor. This bill was brought in by Mr. Tilley as a private member, and not on behalf of the government. It was introduced on the 3rd of March. Considering its great importance and the fact that it led to a crisis in the affairs of the government and the temporary defeat of the Liberal party, this measure went through the House with comparatively little difficulty. It was first considered on the 19th of March, and a motion to postpone its further consideration for three months was lost by a vote of 17 to 21. Amongst those who voted for the postponement were Messrs. Ritchie, Gray and Harding of St. John, Mr. Smith of Westmorland, and Mr. Johnston of Northumberland. The final division of the third reading was taken on the 27th of March, and the vote was 21 to 18, so that every member of the House, with one exception, voted yea or nay. The closeness of this last division should have warned the advocates of the measure that it was likely to produce difficulty, for it is clear that all sumptuary laws which are intended to regulate human affairs must be ineffectual unless they have the support of a large majority of the people affected by them. That this was not the case with the prohibition liquor law was shown by the vote in the Legislature, and it was still more clearly shown after the law came into operation on the 1st of January, 1856.

The passage of the prohibitory law was a bold experiment, and as the sequel showed, more bold than wise. The temperance movement in New Brunswick at that time was hardly more than twenty years old, and New Brunswick had always been a Province in which the consumption of liquor was large in proportion to its population. When it was first settled by the Loyalists, and for many years afterwards, the use of liquor was considered necessary to happiness, if not to actual existence. Every person consumed spirits, which generally came to the Province in the form of Jamaica rum from the West Indies, and as this rum was supposed to be an infallible cure for nearly every ill that flesh is heir to, nothing could be done at that time without its use. Large quantities of rum were taken into the woods for the lumbermen to give them sufficient strength to perform the laborious work in which they 'were engaged, and if it had been suggested that a time would come when the same work would be done without any more powerful stimulant than tea, the person who ventured to make such a suggestion would have been regarded as absolutely insane. Experience has shown them that more and better work can be done, not only in the woods, but everywhere else, without the use of stimulants than with them ; but no one could be got to believe this fifty or sixty years ago. Every. kind of work connected with the farm then had to be performed by the aid of liquor. Every house raising, every ploughing match, every meeting at which farmers congregated, had unlimited quantities of rum as one of its leading features. It was also used by almost every man as a part of his regular diet ; the old stagers had their eleven o'clock and their nip before dinner; their regular series of drinks in the afternoon and evening, and they actually believed that without them life would not be worth living. Some idea of the extent of the spirit drinking of the Province may be gathered from the fact that in 1838, when the population did not exceed 120,000, 312,298 gallons of rum, gin and whiskey, and 64,579 gallons of brandy were consumed in New Brunswick. Spirits, especially rum, was very cheap, and the duty being only thirty cents a gallon, everyone could afford to drink it if disposed to do so.

In 1855, it must be remembered also, that some of the original Loyalists, who had gone to New Brunswick in 1783 were still living, and that the men and women of the second generation were numerous. These people had been brought up under the conditions described as to the use of liquor, and had not been educated out of the views which they had imbibed in their youth. That is why the prohibition experiment made in 1856 was so much open to the charge of being a rash one. Man cannot be edu-

cated into a new state of ideas in a single day and hardly
in a single generation. When the total abstinence movement commenced in New Brunswick, those who advocated
it were looked upon as mere fanatics, and even when it
had obtained a sufficient amount of political strength to
influence the Legislature, the great bulk of the people
regarded it with unfavorable eyes, and were ready to
resist any attempt to apply such principles to themselves.
I remember as a boy the hour and the day when prohibition went into effect in New Brunswick, and I took
note of the time that the change came. It was at mid-
night on the 31st of December, 1855, when the bells rang
out a merry peal to announce the advent of the new year,
that this law went in force. The placing of it in operation meant little less than a revolution in the views,
feelings and ideas of the people of the Province, and to a
large extent in their business relations. The liquor trade,
both wholesale and retail, employed large numbers of
men, and occupied many buildings, which brought in
large rents to their owners. The number of taverns in
St. John and Portland was not less than two hundred,
and every one of these establishments had to be closed.
There were probably at least twenty men who sold liquor
at wholesale, and who extended their business to every
section of the Province, as well as all parts of Nova
Scotia, and their operations also had to come to an end.
It was not to be supposed that these people would consent to be deprived suddenly of their means of living,
especially in view of the fact that it was by no means

certain that the sentiment in favor of prohibition was as strong in the country as it appeared to be in the Legislature. It has always been understood that many men voted for prohibition in the House of Assembly who themselves were not total abstainers, but who thought they might make political capital by taking that course, and who relied on the Legislative Council to throw out the bill. No men were more disgusted and disappointed than they when the Council passed the bill.

The result of the attempt to enforce prohibition was what might have been expected. The law was resisted, liquor continued to be sold, and when attempts were made to prevent the violation of the law, and the violators of the law were brought before the courts, able lawyers were employed to defend them, while the sale of liquor by the same parties was continued, thus setting the law at defiance. This state of confusion and conflict lasted for several months, but it is unnecessary to go into details. In the city of St. John especially the conflict became bitter to the last degree, and it was evident that however admirable prohibition might be of itself the people of the city were not then prepared to accept it. At this juncture came the astounding news that the Lieutenant Governor, the Hon. H. T. Manners-Sutton, had dissolved the House of Assembly without the advice of his Council. This Governor, who had been appointed the year previous, was a member of an old Conservative family, one of whom was Speaker of the British House of Commons for a great many years. The traditions of

this family were all opposed to such a radical measure
as the prohibitory law, and therefore it was not to be
expected that Manners-Sutton, who used liquor at his
own table, and who considered that its use was proper and
necessary, would be favorable to the law. But even if
he had been disposed to favor it originally, or to regard it
without prejudice, the confusion which it caused in the
Province, when the attempt was made to enforce it, would
naturally incline him to look upon it as an evil. At all
events he came to the conclusion that the people should
have another opportunity of pronouncing upon it, and as
the result of this view of the situation, resolved to dissolve
the Legislature which had only been elected little more
than a year, and had still three years to run.

The election, which followed in July, 1856, was perhaps the most hotly contested that has ever taken place
in the Province. In St. John especially the conflict was
fierce and bitter, because it was in this city that the
liquor interest was strongest and most influential. All
over the Province, however, the people became interested
in the struggle as they had not been in any previous
campaign. To the Liberals and the friends of the government the action of Governor Sutton was denounced
as tyrannical, unjust, and entirely contrary to the principles of Responsible Government. On the other hand
the friends of the Governor and of the liquor interest
declared that his action was right, and the cry of " Support the Governor," was raised in every county. The
Liberals at this time found a new name for their oppon-

ents, whom they described as " Rummies," while the Tories retorted by designating the Liberals as "Smashers," and these names continued to be used long after the prohibition question was settled. At this day it is easy enough to discern that there was a good deal of unnecessary violence injected into the campaign, and that neither party was inclined to do full justice to the other.

The result of the election was the defeat of the government. Mr. Tilley lost his seat for St. John City, and Hon. James Brown, the Surveyor General, was rejected by the County of Charlotte ; so that two of the principal members of the Executive were not in their places when the House was called together in July. The City of St. John, and the City and County of St. John sent a solid phalanx of six members opposed to prohibition, and the resignation of the government and the passage of an act repealing the prohibitory liquor law speedily followed. The new government which was formed had for its principal members Hon. John H. Gray, who became Attorney General ; Hon. John C. Allen, Solicitor General ; Hon. R. D. Wilmot, Provincial Secretary ; Hon. John Montgomery, Surveyor General ; Hon. Francis McPhelim, Postmaster General. The other members of the Executive Council were Hon. Edward B. Chandler, Hon. Robert L. Hazen and the Hon. Charles McPherson.

When the House met in July, Hon. Charles Simonds of St. John, was elected Speaker, and it was soon discovered, after the liquor bill had been disposed of, that the majority supporting the government was so small as to make it impossible for them to accomplish any useful legislation. When the Legislature again met, in the early part of 1857, it was seen that in a House of forty-one members, twenty were arrayed against the government, and that the only way in which government business could be done was by the casting vote of the Speaker. This condition of affairs speedily became intolerable, because it practically made legislation impossible, but it was brought to an end by Mr. McMonagle, one of the members for the County of Kings, withdrawing his support from the government. No other course was left for them but to tender their resignations, or advise the dissolution of the Legislature, and this was accordingly done. The House of Assembly was dissolved by proclamation on the 1st of April, 1857, and the writs for the election were made returnable on the 16th of May.

The excitement attending this second election was, if possible, even greater than during the election of 1856, for the public mind had been wrought up to a high state of tension by the proceedings in the House and the numerous divisions, in which it was only supported by the casting vote of the Speaker. The result of the election was so unfavorable to the Gray–Wilmot government that they at once tendered their resignations to the Lieutenant Governor, agreeing to hold office only until their successors were appointed. The most bitter contest of the election centered in the city of St. John, and it resulted in the election of Mr. Tilley, with Mr. James A. Harding for his colleague, the latter having changed his

views in regard to the question at issue since the previous
election, when he was chosen as an opponent of the
government of which Mr. Tilley had been a member.
When the Gray-Wilmot government resigned the
Lieutenant Governor sent for Mr. Fisher, and entrusted
to him the business of forming a new government. The
government thus formed comprised the Hons. James
Brown, S. L. Tilley, William Henry Steeves, John M.
Johnston, Albert J. Smith, David Wark and Charles
Watters. The Hon. Charles Fisher became Attorney
General, and resigning his seat, was re-elected for the
County of York, prior to the meeting of the Legislature,
on the 24th of June, 1857. This session only lasted
until the 1st of July, being merely held for the purpose
of disposing of the necessary business. James A. Harding was elected Speaker of the House, and the legislation
was confined to the passage of the supply bills, and a few
other measures regarding subjects which required immediate attention. Mr. Tilley took no part in the legislation
of this session, for his seat immediately became vacant by
his appointment as Provincial Secretary. The other
departments were filled by the appointment of Mr. Brown
to the office of Surveyor General; Mr. Charles Watters
to the office of Solicitor General, and of John M. Johnston
as Postmaster General.

The Legislature met again on the 10th of February,
1858, and the speech from the throne dealt mainly with
the financial crisis which had affected the mercantile
interest of the Province, the Intercolonial Railway, and

the progress that was being made in the construction of
the line between St. John and Shediac as a part of what
was termed the European & North American Railway.
The speech also referred to the fact that the surplus civil
list fund had been, by arrangement with the British
government, made the previous year, placed at the disposal
of the House of Assembly.   It was soon seen that the
government was strong in the House, the first test vote
being that taken on the passage of the address in reply to
the speech from the throne.   This came in the form of an
amendment, which was moved by Mr. McIntosh of York,
regretting that the arrangement in regard to the surplus
civil list fund had been acceded to without the consent of
the House.   This amendment to the address only received
the support of six members.   A return brought down at
an early period in the session showed that the revenue of
the Province for the fiscal year ending October 31st, 1857,
amounted to $668,252, an increase of $86,528 over the
previous year.   Of this sum upwards of $540,000 came
from import duties and what were termed railway impost,
which was simply the duties levied on impost for the
purpose of defraying the cost of the railways then building.   The casual and territorial revenue only yielded
$18,000, but the export duties reached almost $80,000.

The Intercolonial still continued to engage the attention
of the Legislature, and correspondence with the Secretary
of State, with the government of Canada, and with the
government of Nova Scotia in regard to this great work
was laid before the House soon after the session opened.

The government of New Brunswick consulted with the governments of Canada and Nova Scotia as to what assistance should be given by the Imperial Government towards the construction of the Intercolonial from Halifax to Quebec, in the form of a guarantee of interest. The British Government, through the Colonial Secretary, Mr. Labouchere, replied, on January 15th, 1856, that while the British Government felt a strong sense of the importance of the object, they would not feel themselves justified in applying to parliament for the required guarantee, because they felt that the heavy expenditure to which Great Britain had been subjected did not leave them at liberty to pledge its revenue for the purpose of assisting in the construction of public works of this description, however desirable in themselves. In other words, the British Government had so exhausted its resources in fighting useless battles in the Crimea and elsewhere, for the sake of the degraded and effete Mahomedan power, that it was unable to give any assistance to a necessary work of a peaceable character for the consolidation of the Empire. The Intercolonial Railway has now been constructed without the British treasury being drawn upon to the extent of one penny, and the British Government is now glad to use it and its kindred work, the Canadian Pacific, for the purpose of forwarding its soldiers from the Atlantic to the Pacific. These two great works remain as monuments of the spirit and courage of the people of the British Provinces of North America, but they redound nothing to the credit of any British Government or any Imperial statesmen, it apparently being impossible for any one brought up under the shadow of Downing street to discern any good thing in the Colonies. The correspondence on the subject of the Intercolonial extended over a period of more than twenty years and grew to enormous proportions, but it is entirely safe to assert that this line of railway would not have been constructed in our own time but for the fact that it was undertaken by the Canadian Dominion as a work which had to be built for the purpose of carrying out the terms of confederation as set out in the British North America Act.

Correspondence was also brought down during this session on the subject of emigration to New Brunswick. Mr. Moses H. Perley, the immigration agent, had visited the United Kingdom for the purpose of promoting the movement to induce people to emigrate to this country, but he did not find the British Government disposed to lend any assistance in relieving their cities of the unemployed who might have been able to make a good living in this Province if brought to it. At this time there was a considerable amount of competition on the part of the Australian Colonies for immigrants, and New Brunswick was not looked upon favorably as a field of immigration. It does not appear that the result of Mr. Perley's mission to England was very fruitful, the principal difficulty being that he had no authority to expend much money for the purpose of promoting the object in view. There has always been a certain small movement towards this

Province on the part of the people of the British Islands desiring to change their residence, but the condition of the Province is such, both as to its labor markets and its resources, that it would be unwise to bring people here in large numbers, unless arrangements had previously been made for settling them comfortably. British immigrants now prefer to go to those lands where there is no forest to be felled, or where the cities are large and the chance of employment in various lines of industry are greater.

The financial statement brought down by Mr. Tilley showed that the public debt of the Province at the end of the fiscal year, 1857, amounted to $2,050,000, of which $1,376,000 was funded and bearing interest at the rate of six per cent. This debt had been largely incurred in railway construction or in stock taken in railways. The ordinary revenue was estimated at nearly $650,000, and the ordinary expenditure at about $2,000 less. These figures do not greatly differ from those of the present time, notwithstanding the fact that confederation has relieved us of many items of expenditure which the Province formerly had to bear. Everything, however, was on a small scale in those days. A committee was appointed at this session of the Legislature to inquire into the manner in which the work of railway construction to Shediac was being carried on. The committee reported later in the session. Their report seemed hostile to the government and censured the manner in which the contracts had been given out and work done in many places without tenders. The people of this Province were then quite ignorant of railway building, and there is no doubt that the line to Shediac cost far more money than it ought to have done. The committee reported that according to the Engineer's statement the line would cost, when completed, £930,702, or £8,460 a mile; but the cost was considerably more, and exceeded four million dollars, and may be roughly put down at forty thousand dollars a mile, or twice the sum for which a similar railway could be constructed now. This report was received by the House, but was not adopted, although the vote upon it was a close one.

The railway to Shediac was finally completed and opened for traffic on August 5th, 1860, its length being 108 miles. The nineteen miles between Point du Chene and Moncton had been open as early as August, 1857, and the nine miles from St. John to Rothesay on June 1st, 1858. The railway was opened from St. John to Hampton in June, 1859, and to Sussex in November of the same year. Although the people of the Province had abated something of their enthusiasm for railways by the time the St. John and Shediac line was finished, still its opening was a great event, because it was the commencement of a new era in transportation in this Province, and gave St. John access to the North Shore, from which it had been practically shut out previously. Goods could now be sent by means of railway and steamer to Prince Edward Island, and to the New Brunswick ports on the Gulf of St. Lawrence, and a community of interest was

o

thus created between the most remote sections of the
Province which did not exist before.   The traffic receipts
of the complete line were thought to be highly satisfactory ; the business for the first three months amounted to
about $45,000, and yielded a revenue of $18,000.   This
was a good showing and gave promise of still better
things for the future.   It may be interesting to state
that in the last year that the railway was operated by the
government of this Province the gross receipts amounted
to $148,330, and the net receipts to $51,760.   The gross
and net revenue of the road had shown a steady increase
from the first, and although it had been a costly public
work, the people of the Province considered it a good
investment.   It was only after it had passed into the
hands of the government of Canada, and become a part of
the Intercolonial Railway, that any color was given to
the accusation that it was an unprofitable line.   The
railway from St. John to Shediac has always paid well,
and probably, if disassociated from its connecting lines,
would at this day pay three or four per cent. upon its
original cost.

The legislation of the Province between 1858 and
1861, although it included many useful measures, evolved
nothing that calls for particular mention, with the exception of the law which provided for voting by ballot. This
was an innovation to which many were opposed, but
which the Liberal party very properly considered necessary to the protection of the voter, who was liable to be
coerced by his employer, or by those who had financial

relations with him. The ballot system introduced by the government was quite imperfect and did not insure absolute secrecy, because it did not provide for an official ballot such as is required in the system of election which now prevails in connexion with the choice of members to our Canadian parliament. Yet it was a vast improvement on open voting, not only because it gave the voter a certain degree of protection, but also from the fact that it tended to promote order at elections, and to do away with that riotous spirit which was characteristic of the earlier elections in the Province.

In 1859 an important step was taken for the re-organization of Kings College, which by an act passed in that year was changed into the University of New Brunswick. There had always been a great deal of dissatisfaction with the college in consequence of its denominational character, and in 1854 an act was passed empowering the Lieutenant Governor to appoint a commission to inquire into the state of Kings College, its management and utility, with a view to improving it. The commissioners appointed were the Hon. John H. Gray, Rev. Egerton Ryerson, J. W. Dawson, Hon. John S. Saunders and Hon. James Brown. The report, which was dated Dec. 28th, 1854, was laid before both branches of the Legislature in 1855. In 1857 the college council appointed a committee and prepared a draft of a bill, which was laid before the Legislature. This with a few slight alterations was the bill which was passed in 1859, for the establishment of the University of New Brunswick, and in this bill were embodied the principal recommendations of the commissioners appointed in 1854 to inquire into the state of the college. This act transferred to the University of New Brunswick all the property of Kings College and its endowment, and made the university liable for the payment of the debts and the performance of the contracts of Kings College. It created a new governing body for the college to be styled the Senate, to be appointed by the governor in council, and the President of the council was required to be a member of that body and also to be a layman. It conferred upon the Senate the power of appointing the professors and other officers of the university, except the President, and also the power of removing them from office, subject to the approval of the governor in council. It also authorized the Senate to fix their salaries. It abolished the professorship of theology and provided for the affiliation of other institutions with the university, and also for a number of free scholars. This act, which was passed in April, 1859, was specially approved by Her Majesty in council on January 25th, 1860. Thus a new era in the higher education of New Brunswick was commenced, and a long step was taken in advance towards making the college more acceptable to the people of this Province. Great hopes were entertained at the time that this change in the constitution of the college would lead to a large increase in the number of its students, and a more general interest in its work, but unfortunately, as the sequel showed, these hopes were only partially realized.

During the spring of 1860 circumstances occurred which led to the resignation of the Post Master General, Hon. Charles Connell. The Legislature having adopted the decimal system of currency in the place of the pounds, shillings and pence which had been the currency of the Province since its foundation, in March, 1860, Mr. Connell was authorized to obtain a new set of postage stamps of the denominations required for use in the postal service of the Province. No person at that time thought that a political crisis would arise out of this order, but it appears that Mr. Connell, guided by the example of Presidents and Post Masters General of the United States, had made up his mind that instead of the likeness of the Queen, which had been upon all the old postage stamps of the Province, the five cent stamp, the one which would be most in use, should bear the impress of his own countenance. Accordingly the Connell postage stamp, which is now one of the rarest and most costly of all in the lists of collectors, was procured and was ready to be used, when Mr. Connell's colleagues in the government discovered what was going on and took steps to prevent the new five cent stamp from being issued. The correspondence on the subject, which will be found in the journals of 1861, is curious and interesting, but it ended in the withdrawal of the objectionable stamps and in the resignation of Mr. Connell, who complained that he had lost the confidence of his colleagues, and who in resigning, charged them with neglecting the affairs of the Province. Only a few of the Connell stamps got into circulation, the remainder of the issue being destroyed. If anyone could have foreseen the enormous value which they would attain at a future day a fortune might have been made by the lucky individual who succeeded in getting possession of them. Mr. Connell's place as Post Master General was filled by the appointment of James Steadman to that office.

In the early part of 1861 a very important event occurred in connection with the government which produced a lasting effect on Provincial politics. Charges were made by a St. John Conservative paper, "The Colonial Empire," in which it was stated that members of the Government and Crown Land officials had been purchasing the most desirable and valuable Crown Lands of the Province for speculative purposes, and that in bringing these lands to sale the government regulations had been violated and the public treasury had thereby suffered. A committee of the House was appointed to investigate these charges and inquiry established the fact that an official of the Crown Land Department had purchased a large quantity of Crown Land, and that the then Attorney General and leader of the Government had purchased some 800 acres. These lands were all bought at public sale, but in the forms of application, other names were used, which was a violation of the rules of the Department. A portion of the press at the time created a widespread excitement upon this subject, and the services of the official referred to were dispensed with. Some of the supporters of the Government also took such ground in reference to the Attorney General, Mr. Fisher, that his retirement from the Government became necessary. It was felt at the time that the penalty that was paid by the Attorney General was excessive for the offence, but, under the excitement of the public mind then existing, it was the only course that could be taken to avoid the defeat of the Government. At the general election that followed a few months later, Mr. Fisher was re-elected for the County of York, and later on, after the excitement had passed over, the Crown Land official was reinstated. At the general election, that took place in 1861, the Government was handsomely sustained, after one of the warmest contests that had ever taken place in New Brunswick. Probably the most effective nomination speech ever made by Mr. Tilley, during his long political career, was the one then delivered at the Court House, St. John, in his own defense, and in the vindication of his government against the charges made by the opposition candidates and press.

CHAPTER VIII.

The successful running of the railway from St. John
to Shediac, and the opening of a portion of the St. Andrews railway from that port northward towards Woodstock, stimulated a desire for additional railway connection, particularly with Quebec and the United States.   It
may be safely said that from the formation of the Liberal
Government in 1854 to the time of Confederation the
principal policy of the government was always a railway
policy, and numberless communications were exchanged
with the British government, and the other Colonies
which now form the Dominion of Canada, for the purpose
of agreeing upon some common policy with the object of
completing what is now known as the Intercolonial Railway.   All previous applications to the Imperal Government for pecuniary aid to secure the construction of this
railway having failed, the governments of Canada, Nova
Scotia and New Brunswick concluded, in 1861, to make
one more effort before abandoning an undertaking of such
national and provincial interest, and to that end decided
upon a meeting of representatives from the three govern-

ments at Quebec. At a meeting held in the Executive
Council Chamber at Quebec, on the 30th September,
1861, there were present :—

FROM NEW BRUNSWICK.	FROM NOVA SCOTIA.
Hon. Mr. Tilley,	Hon. Joseph Howe,
Hon. Mr. Smith,	Hon. Mr. Archibald,
Hon. Mr. Mitchell,	Hon. Mr. McCully.
Hon. Mr. Watters.	

FROM CANADA.

Hon. Mr. Cartier,
Hon. Mr. Macdonald,
Hon. Mr. Ross,
Hon. Mr. Vankoughnet,
Hon. Mr. Alleyn,
Hon. Mr. N. Belleau,
Hon. Mr. Galt,
Hon. Mr. Cauchon.

It was then unanimously

Resolved, "That the three governments of Canada,
New Brunswick and Nova Scotia do renew the offers
made to the Imperial Government on the 26th day of
October, 1858, to aid in the construction of an Intercolonial Railway, to connect Halifax with Quebec; and
that a delegation from each Province shall immediately
proceed to England, with the object of pressing the project
upon the attention of the Home Government; giving
the assurance that the governments of the respective
Provinces will endeavor to procure the necessary legislation at the next ensuing sessions of their respective
Parliaments; and it was further

Resolved, "That the route to be adopted be decided by the Imperial Government."

The following gentlemen were appointed delegates to confer with the Imperial Government upon the subject above referred to : Hon. P. M. Vankoughnet, by the Canadian Government, Hon. Joseph Howe, by the Government of Nova Scotia, and Hon. S. L. Tilley, by the Government of New Brunswick.

While the delegates were in England engaged in submitting their proposition to the Colonial Secretary, news of the Trent affair reached that country. This was the seizure of Messrs. Mason and Slidell, two representatives of the southern confederacy on board the British mail steamer "Trent," in the Bahama Channel, in December, 1861, by Capt. Wilkes, who was in command of the United States war-ship "San Jacinto." This flagrant violation of international law was disapproved by the government of the United States, and Messrs. Mason and Slidell were given up to the British government; but for a time it met with popular applause, and it seemed likely to lead to a war between Great Britain and the United States. Troops were sent out hastily to Canada for the purpose of defending that Province in the event of a war occurring, and as many of these troops had to be taken over land through the wilderness between St. John and Quebec, it brought to the attention of the British government in a very emphatic manner the imperfection of the existing means of communication between the several

Provinces.   Such an object lesson coming at such a time
was calculated to assist the delegates in placing their case
before the British government.   They were able to show
that the frontier of Canada was unprotected, and that a
large hostile force might be thrown against it during the
winter long before any assistance could reach that Province from England.

The following extract from a letter from Hon. Mr.
Joseph Howe to the Lieutenant Governor of Nova
Scotia, the Earl of Mulgrave, describes in detail the
proceedings of the delegates in England :—

HALIFAX, 5th April, 1862.

MY LORD,—

. In obedience to Your Excellency's commands I proceeded to England in the steamship "Arabia," leaving Halifax
on the 1st November, landing on the 11th, and returning in the
" Europa " on the 25th January. The Hon. S. L. Tilley, Provincial
Secretary of New Brunswick, went over with me, but the Hon. P.
M. Vankoughnet, the delegate from Canada, was wrecked on his
passage down the St. Lawrence, and did not reach England until
late in November.

A few days after our arrival Mr. Tilley and I waited upon the
Duke of Newcastle, presented our credentials, and discussed with
His Grace the objects of our mission.   We were gratified to find
that His Grace viewed most favorably the enterprise which we
had been sent to England to advocate.   His opinions were frankly
avowed, but, while he promised us his aid, he did not conceal
from us his opinion that there were difficulties in the way that
would probably require all our skill and industry to overcome.
His Grace advised us to see Lord Palmerston and such other
members of the Cabinet as might be in town from time to time,
and left us free to take any steps that we might consider
judicious in order to rouse and combine public opinion in aid of
the project; that the decision of the Cabinet, if it were favorable,
might be fortified and sustained by memorials from the large
towns and principal centres of commerce in the three kingdoms.

On the arrival of Mr. Vankoughnet we saw in succession the Prime Minister, the Chancellor of the Exchequer, the Secretary of War, and the President of the Board of Trade, and explained to them the nature of the enterprize and the views of the respective governments. Though the subject had been almost exhausted by previous delegations it appeared prudent to construct an argument based upon the latest information, and it was in point of form indispensible that we should place in the hands of the Colonial Secretary some written paper upon which he could invite the deliberation of the Cabinet. We had nearly completed this task when the news arrived in England of the arrest of the southern commissioners. The determination of Her Majesty's government to demand reparation was almost instantly known. The moment that a war in winter with the United States became imminent we could not but feel that our mission was suddenly invested with a dignity and importance that could only be measured by the difficulties and the cost of protecting our Canadian frontier in case reparation should be refused. It was clear that circumstances favored our exertions in proportion as they confirmed the anticipations and the arguments of those who had preceded us. We lost no time in addressing the following letter to His Grace, the Colonial Secretary :—

"LONDON, December 2nd, 1861.

" MAY IT PLEASE YOUR GRACE,—

"The undersigned, having presented credentials and discussed informally with Your Grace, and with some other members of the Cabinet, the objects of our mission, were about to forward to Your Grace a communication on the subject of the Intercolonial Railway (the draft of which they enclose), when the startling events of the last week rendered that task superorogatory.

"These events so completely vindicate the forethought and patriotism of the Colonial Legislatures—of the gentlemen who from time to time have represented their views in this country, and of the British statesmen who have given them countenance and aid, that the undersigned deem it unnecessary to do more than to present to Your Grace a list of the papers in which their arguments are embodied, and a copy of the minute of council by which they have been empowered to make, as they now do in terms of that minute, a renewed offer to Her Majesty's government.

"The war which in the Provinces we have long seen as likely to arise out of the complications between the mother country and the United States of America is now imminent. The frontier which would have been defended by means of rapid communication is unprotected and exposed to the concentration of troops upon the termini of at least seven railroads. Winter is upon us and a hundred thousand men are to be thrown by the enemy upon the frontier with more ease than a single battery can be transported to Canada or a single barrel of flour can be brought down to the seaboard Provinces which, cut off by war from the United States, and by ice from Canada, must depend upon Europe for breadstuffs with the granaries of half a continent in their rear.

" If those events and strategic contrasts now patent to all the world do not plead the cause of British America and finally settle this question the undersigned feel that anything that they could add would be a needless instrument upon the patience of the Cabinet. The undersigned do not believe that in the presence of the perils which all Her Majesty's subjects are called upon to confront, an hour should be lost in deciding upon a question which lies at the very basis of national defence. If the Provinces are to be plunged into a war without the cheap defence which they have urged was indispensable to their protection, let them have at least the satisfaction of reflecting that it is for the last time; and if our commerce is to be imperilled and our cities exposed to pillage and conflagration, let us not have to defend both with the depressing conviction on our minds that Her Majesty's Ministers are indifferent to our position and care less for the security of our frontier than they do for that of their island homes.

" Whatever the answer is to be the undersigned would respectfully urge that it should not be delayed. War will find all the Provinces in many ways unprepared, and the undersigned, upon whom will rest heavy responsibilities, will require every hour of time to meet the exigencies of the period as they ought. They will not permit themselves to believe that any but one answer will be given, but whatever the answer is it should, if possible, be prompt and decisive, that their minds may be freed from other thoughts than those which the stern duties of the hour imperatively demand.

"We have the honor to be

Your Grace's most obedient servants,

P. M. Vankoughnet,

For Canada.

Joseph Howe,

For Nova Scotia.

S. L. Tilley,

For New Brunswick.

To His Grace

The Duke of Newcastle, &c."

MEMORANDUM.

The undersigned have been deputed by the governments of Canada, Nova Scotia and New Brunswick to submit a renewed proposition for the completion of the Intercolonial Railroad, connecting the harbor of Halifax—which is open all the year round—with the railway on the St. Lawrence. Having delivered our credentials and discussed the subject of our mission with His Grace the Duke of Newcastle, and with some other members of the Cabinet, we now proceed to submit in a more formal shape a recapitulation of the grounds upon which we think that the proposition we have been sent to make ought to be favorably and speedily entertained. These naturally divide themselves under three heads :—

First.—To what extent previous communications with the Imperial Government have justly led the Provinces to rely upon Imperial assistance in the construction of that which has been admitted to be an Imperial work.

Second.—The reasons of public policy which render its construction at the present time a measure of wise precaution indispensable to our national defence, and

Third.—The financial aspect of the question.

We beg, in the first place, to refer to the Memorandum dated August, 1857, and signed by Messrs. Macdonald and Rose, together with the letter of Messrs. Johnston and Archibald, of August 20th, 1857; and also to the Memorandum dated October 26th, 1858, and signed by Messrs. Cartier, Ross, Galt, Fisher, Smith, Tupper, Henry and Dickie, which contain the history of the question so far as respects the general argument. These papers are enclosed.

To the Memorandum and letter of August, 1857, a reply is contained in the despatch of the Right Honorable H. Labouchere, addressed to the Governor General of Canada, and dated May 15th, 1858. That despatch states:

"Although participating with the members of the several Local Governments, and with their own predecessors in office, in a strong sense of the importance of this object, Her Majesty's advisers cannot feel themselves justified in applying to parliament for the required guarantee. Their reasons for declining to take this step are solely of a financial description. They feel that the heavy expenditure to which this country has been subjected of late years, and the calls upon the resources of the Empire for pressing emergencies, do not leave them at liberty, for the present at least, to pledge its revenue to so considerable an extent, for the purpose of assisting in the construction of public works of this character, however in themselves desirable."

In answer to the Memorandum of October 26th, 1858, a despatch from the Right Honorable Sir E. B. Lytton to the Governor General of Canada, and the Lieutenants of New Brunswick and Nova Scotia, and dated December 24th, 1858, states that:

"Independently of any military advantages which might attend the existence of an uninterrupted communication by rail over British territory, in the event of any disturbance of the existing friendly relations of Great Britain with all other countries, some benefits of an Imperial kind would at once accrue from the completion of the Intercolonial Railway. The letters from England would pass over a shorter and cheaper route, and the movement of the troops would gain in point of convenience and economy."

The despatch, however, postpones Imperial assistance for reasons analogous to those given in the despatch of Sir. H. Labouchere. This despatch closes the official correspondence on the subject.

We submit, therefore, appealing to past communications, that the Provinces have full justification for relying upon Imperial co-operation, to be rendered at least when the position of Great Britain warranted her in undertaking the responsibility of the completion of the Intercolonial Railway.

The undersigned feel that here they might rest their case, as they do not believe that Her Majesty's advisers will forget the hopes held out by previous governments, or press a literal construction of any bargain or understanding with the Colonies, where, especially as in this case, it can be shown that in a measure of common interest and mutual defence the Colonies have already done more than their share ; but they are desirous to meet every argument by which the proposition for Imperial aid may be opposed.

Those who in this country fear the cost of Colonial garrisons in the west, should remember that the British Provinces lost more during the last war than those garrisons have ever cost, and that in a single year of war with the United States, they would again lose more than the value of all the military expenditure for half a century to come.

We are content, however, with our present position and with the affectionate and honorable relations with the mother country, which it is clearly our mutual interest to maintain, and which were never more firmly based in thorough loyalty than at this moment. But the question always arises : How can the connection be best cemented and the frontier be put in the best attitude of defence ?

The Colonial Secretary, who has recently visited America, does not require to be informed that since the war of 1812 the United States have covered their country with a network of railways, and that seven of these lines run directly in upon the Canadian frontier; while others traverse or reach the shores of the great lakes, commanding the chief entreports of Canadian commerce, and others again extend to the seaboard cities directly fronting the Province of Nova Scotia, or through the State of Maine to within eighty miles of the borders of New Brunswick. If these railroads did not exist the Colonial militia, with slight aid from the Imperial government, could defend our frontiers in case of war, as they did in 1812. But by the aid of these railroads it is obvious that the United States could at any time within a week concentrate upon their termini a hundred thousand men or more, a force that we might in the end successfully oppose, but one so formidable as to enable them to capture, if they were so disposed, or to destroy our chief cities before, by any means at our disposal, we could concentrate our domestic forces, or receive effective aid from England. While the United States maintained an army of only 10,000 men, the danger of a surprise did not appear to be very imminent. A few British regiments would have been sufficient to cope with such a force, and our volunteers with such instructors could have been disciplined as fast as theirs.

But all this has been changed within a year. The Northern States have now at least a quarter of a million of embodied troops upon the Potomac, considerable numbers under arms in various States, and 50,000 three months men, who have returned to their homes with some degree of discipline and some knowledge of camp life. The whole of the Northern States is one vast recruiting ground. Should the present civil war continue it is contended by some that there will be full employment for these forces at the south, but vulnerable as Canada now is she invites attack from that surplus force which now exists. But when this contest ends, and end it must—even should no conflict with us mark the interval—either by exhaustion by conquest or by the interference of foreign powers, there will remain in the Northern States two or three hundred thousand trained soldiers, with a fair proportion of ambitious military chieftains, emulous of distinction, or it may be, not indisposed to wipe out in foreign fields the remembrance of discomfitures experienced in civil strife. Besides disciplined masses of soldiers the United States will have accumulated vast stores of warlike material. Enormous quantities of small arms and of cannon have been purchased or manufactured, and the establishments founded by a lavish expenditure can readily supply as many more. The United States thus have been suddenly transformed from peaceful communities, pursuing lawful commerce, to a military republic.

The British Provinces survey these phenomena without fear but not without emotion, and they ask, as the first measure of

P

indispensable precaution and obvious defence, that the Intercolonial Railroad shall be completed without delay. Without that road the Provinces are dislocated and almost incapable of defence for a great portion of the year, except at such a sacrifice of life and property, and at such an enormous cost to the mother country, as makes the small contribution which she is asked to give towards its construction sink into insignificance. With that railroad we can concentrate our forces on the menaced points of our frontier, guard the citadels and works which have been erected by Great Britain at vast expense, cover our cities from surprise, and hold our own till reinforcements can be sent across the sea; while without the railway, if any attack were made in winter the mother country could put no army worthy of the national honor and adequate to the exigency upon the Canadian frontier without a positive waste of treasure far greater than the principal of the sum, the interest of which she is asked to contribute or rather to risk.

The British government have built expensive citadels at Halifax, Quebec and Kingston, and have stores of munitions and warlike material in them. But their feeble garrisons will be inadequate for their defence, unless the Provincial forces can be concentrated in and around them. An enterprising enemy would carry them by *coups de main* before they could be reinforced from England; and once taken the ports and roadsteads which they have been erected to defend would not be oversafe for the naval armaments sent out too late for their relief.

Since this subject was pressed upon the attention of the British government in 1851, taking the very moderate military expenditure of last year as the basis of an estimate, £4,417,590 have been expended in the British Provinces for the maintenance of a few thousand troops in time of profound peace. Of what avail is this expenditure? With what object has it been incurred or are similar disbursements to be continued, if the only work which during five months of the year will furnish the means of securing the Provinces is to be neglected? Why spend so much money if it is to be of no use hereafter, and if proper precautions are not taken to protect the property which has been made thus valuable.

Therefore we desire to strengthen our frontier by the completion of a work indispensable to its defence. It is not too much to say that the construction of the Intercolonial Railroad might save us the cost of a war, for the Americans are themselves sagacious enough to see that with that work completed surprise is impossible, and the results of a protracted war at least extremely doubtful. Without it Canada and the Maritime Provinces may be cut asunder and outflanked at any moment, without the possibility of their population leaning upon common points of support, and aiding and strengthening each other. We are reluctant to believe, then, that Her Majesty's government will forget the opinion expressed by Lord Durham in his report, or will even, if disposed to, construe strictly the terms of the offer made in 1851 by Lord Grey, overlook the momentous interests now at stake, or the altered circumstances which at the present moment invest this subject with so much of national interest and importance.

Though the undersigned argue this question upon higher grounds than those of mere finance, they repeat that they are not indifferent to the financial aspect of it. The Colonies unaided have themselves, since 1851, already made nearly one-half of the railway route, and the construction of about 350 miles more by the joint action of the Imperial and Colonial governments, will complete the Intercolonial Railway. Our governments and people, having done so much already, now propose to contribute more than one-half of the liability of what remains, and thus to be responsible for £60,000 a year, and also for the right of way. The mother country is now asked to give £60,000 a year, so long only as the revenue of the railway is inadequate to meet the interest. What is she to get or to save? is not, however, an unreasonable question. We will endeavor to supply an answer.

The British government now pay to two lines of steamers, one of which carries the mails and passengers past the British Provinces, £189,500. Make the Intercolonial Railroad and there cannot be the slightest pretence under any circumstances for continuing these subsidies beyond the port of Halifax, and the subsidy ought not to exceed £112,000, the amount of postage now actually received.

If the contract for the Galway Line is renewed the subsidy should only cover the sea service from the nearest point in Ireland to the nearest port on the continent of America. It is a mistake to suppose that subsidies are required to maintain communication between the Maritime Provinces and the United States. Steamers run all summer from Halifax and St. John to Portland and Boston, maintained by private enterprise, and will soon be adequate for the winter service, if left to a fair field of open competition. Subsidies to a reliable line of ocean steamers may, by the British government, notwithstanding the difference of opinion existing, be considered indispensable, but these, if limited to the amount of postage (£112,000), would save £77,500 a year, so soon as the Intercolonial Railroad is completed to Halifax. This saving would more than cover the entire sum which the Imperial government is now asked to risk to insure the construction of the work.

But in addition to the cost of ocean steamers the British people now pay for the transmission of their correspondence with their own Provinces twelve and a half cents per ounce on letters, and two cents on newspapers sent through the United States, amounting on the whole to a large sum per annum, which could be saved to the country.

The cost of conveying by land a single regiment from Halifax to Quebec in 1838 is stated to have been £30,000. The cost of transportation in winter was so great in 1855 that the regiments, so much wanted in the Crimea, and not required in Canada at all, had to be left over there till the war was over.

Were the Intercolonial Railway built troops could be forwarded from Halifax to Quebec in four and twenty hours. If to the amount which may be fairly deducted from the steamship subsidies be added the amount paid to the Post Office of the United States, and the actual cost of moving troops and material on an average of ten years, the figures will show an amount of saving far beyond the aid asked for, and which ought to satisfy the most rigid economist; that while what we urge secures Imperial interests now in peril, it saves the resources of the English people.

There is one view of this subject which surely should not be overlooked. Within the last ten years but 235,285 emigrants from the British Islands went to the Provinces, while more than six times the number, or 1,495,243, went to the United States, and are now citizens of that country, whose commercial policy is seen in the Morrill tariff, which shuts out the manufactures of this country. Let us hope that it is not too late to turn the tide of emigration elsewhere, that the life blood of the parent state may not be drained off to extend the power of a people who alone can threaten or endanger the British rule in America, and whose jealous sensitiveness renders a continuance of their friendship towards Great Britain at all times uncertain.

The proposal made to the British government is to join the three Provinces in a guarantee of four per cent. upon £3,000,000 Sterling, the assumed cost of the proposed works, less the cost of the right of way, which the Provinces will provide. The Provinces are ready to pass bills of supply for £60,000 a year if the Imperial government will do the same, and as no doubt this Imperial route will gradually work on with increasing returns, the sum of the risk will gradually diminish, until at last, and perhaps before many years are over, the liability may cease altogether. The Canadian Railway Companies are open to treat for the working of the line so as to avoid any liability beyond the gross amount of the joint guarantee. The selection of the route of the line is left solely to the British government.

Should the British government prefer to raise the capital for building the road their outside responsibility under such arrangements would be three and a quarter per cent. on £3,000,000, or about £97,500 a year, and the Provinces would still be responsible for one-half, leaving a net liability to the British government of only £48,750 a year ; but if they are not disposed thus to increase their nominal and decrease their real responsibility, the sum required for the estimated length of 350 miles of railway, namely £3,000,000, can be raised on the terms named, viz., by the mutual guarantee of £120,000 a year, or £60,000 a year from the Provinces and £60,000 a year from the British government, which guarantee will enable the issue at par of £3,000,000 of four per cent. stock.

And now, believing that in this and former papers submitted to the Imperial authorities, all the arguments in detail in favor of the Intercolonial policy sought for have been fully set forth, the undersigned have only to add that it appears to them that such arguments are conclusive, that the subject should be looked upon and dealt with mainly in regard to the consideration of permanent connection between Great Britain and the Provinces, and the relative positions of England and the United States in the event of hostilities between them.

Is or is not the completion of the line of railway between Halifax and Quebec essential, or at least of infinite importance, as enabling England to carry on by land as well as by sea a war with the only power in America that can assail her, as enabling her to protect a portion of her own dominions? Should war with the United States of America break out during the present or any winter, how is England to cope with her adversary by land? How can she transport a month hence to the points of strategy in Canada the necessary troops and material of war? and to what mortification and disaster may not her few soldiers, usually in garrison there, be subjected for want of that aid which the Intercolonial Railway could bring them? Again, England has pledged herself, and without a formal pledge would doubtless strive, that the whole force of the Empire should be put forth for the defence of the Provinces in the event of a foreign invasion, and how can that strength be put forth in Canada without the means of reaching it in winter? And while she may by her navy hold the American seaboard in terror, the American forces can enter Canada, and three millions of people will be left to cope with twenty millions in a war in the cause of which they would have had no concern, and in the conduct of which they could have no voice.

A dispute in the China seas may involve the United States and England in war, and Canada, without this means of protection, will have to bear the brunt and suffering of it, without having provoked the difference or being directly interested in the quarrel.

The undersigned most desire it to be understood that the financial position of the Provinces does not enable them to hold out any hope that more than is herein proposed can be offered by the Provinces themselves. The heavy responsibilities for her railway undertakings now pressing upon her have compelled Canada, in order to preserve her credit with her debenture holders, to impose import duties on a scale which has already raised discussion in England, and laid her under the imputation of having had resort to a system of commercial protection, when in fact she was simply straining her resources to preserve her credit and good faith. To her, therefore, as well as to the other Provinces, greater sacrifices are impossible.

As the selection of the route to be adopted has been confided by the Provinces to the British government, and all local disputes in regard to it thus removed, the undersigned would urge the importance of making use of the coming winter to select and locate the line of Railway ; and if it were possible to lay upon the ground some of the heavier material, most valuable time would also be gained. The line can be completed in two summers, if the coming winter be used, and in such a case the railway may be completed by the fall of 1863.

The reply of the British government to the propositions embodied in the above was contained in a despatch from the Colonial Secretary to the Lieutenant Governor of New Brunswick, and was as follows :—

DOWNING STREET, April 12, 1862.

SIR,—

I have already acknowledged the receipt of your despatches, the one accompanied by a joint address to Her Majesty from both Houses of the Legislature of New Brunswick, expressive of their wish that Imperial aid may be afforded to the completion of the Intercolonial Railway between Halifax and Quebec, the other reporting that the Hon. Samuel Tilley had been appointed to represent New Brunswick in the Provincial delegation which was intended to visit England on this subject. Not long afterwards Mr. Tilley arrived and associated himself with the Hon. Philip Vankoughnet, who had been appointed delegate on behalf of Canada, and the Hon. Joseph Howe, on behalf of Nova Scotia. I had several interviews with these gentlemen, who urged with good ability the project committed to their charge, and eventually embodied their views in a Memorandum communicated to me in a letter dated December 2nd, 1861, but owing to the urgency of business connected with the threatening aspect of affairs in the United States, I was unable to bring the subject under the consideration of Her Majesty's government before the deputies were obliged to return to their homes, and other urgent matters have hitherto prevented the adoption of a decision. The subject has now been before Her Majesty's government, and I need scarcely assure you that they have examined it with the care due to the importance of the question, of the high authorities from whom it has emanated in the Provinces, and to the character and position of the delegates by whom it has been so powerfully presented to notice in this country.

The length of railway necessary to complete the communication between Halifax and Quebec is estimated at 350 miles, and the cost, after deducting the right of way, which the Provinces will provide, is estimated at £3,000,000 Sterling, such being the data supplied by the deputation. The project is that the Imperial government should join the three Provinces in a guarantee of four per cent. upon £3,000,000, in which case the Provinces are to pass bills of supply for £60,000 a year, £20,000 in each Province, if the Imperial government will do the same. The selection of the route is left solely to the British government. Should the sum of £3,000,000 be found insufficient, nothing very definite is said on the essential point of the provision to be made for the completion of the railway.

I much regret to inform you that, after giving the subject their best consideration, Her Majesty's government have not felt themselves at liberty to concur in this mode of assistance. Anxious, however, to promote, as far as they can, the important object of completing the great line of railway communication on British ground, between the Atlantic and the westernmost parts of Canada, and to assist the Provinces in a scheme which would so materially promote their interests, Her Majesty's government are willing to offer to the Provincial government an Imperial guarantee of interest towards enabling them to raise by public loan, if they should desire it, at a moderate rate, the requisite funds for constructing the railway. This was the mode of action contemplated by Earl Grey, in the year 1851, and is the same method which was adopted by Parliament in the Act of 1842, in order to afford to Canada the benefit of British credit in raising the money with which she has completed her great system of internal water communications.

The nature and extent of the guarantee which Her Majesty's government could undertake to recommend to Parliament must be determined by the particulars of any scheme which the Provincial governments may be disposed to found on the present proposal, and on the kind of security which they would offer. I fear that this course will not be so acceptable to the Provincial governments as that which the delegates were authorized to propose for consideration. It is, however, the only one in which Her Majesty's government, after anxious deliberation, feel that they would be at liberty to participate. I trust that the proposal will, at all events, be received as a proof of their earnest wish to find some method in which they can co-operate with the Provinces in their laudable desire to complete a perfect intercolonial communication over British territory, and it will be a source of sincere pleasure to me if, adverting to all the different bearings of the subject, and to the condition of their respective finances, the Provincial governments should end by finding it in their power to make use of the present offer and to propound some practical scheme for applying it to the attainment of the desired object. I have addressed a similar despatch to the Governor General of Canada and the Lieutenant Governor of Nova Scotia, and I must now leave the subject in the hands of the several Provincial governments, who will best know, in case they prosecute the subject further, how to provide for the requisite mutual consultations.

I have the honor to be,

Sir,

Your most obedient humble servant,

NEWCASTLE.

Delegates, representing the three Provinces, met at Quebec in September, 1862, to consider the proposal of the Duke of Newcastle as to the aid the Imperial government were prepared to give in the construction of the Intercolonial Railway. New Brunswick was represented by Messrs. Tilley, Steeves and Mitchell. Having discussed with the gentlemen present the immediate questions which had brought them together, the delegates from the Maritime Provinces declared their willingness to propose to their respective governments to accept the proposition of the Duke of Newcastle, if the government of Canada would bear one-half of the expense of the rail-

way instead of one-third.   After a day's deliberation
the Canadian Council communicated their ultimatum,
which was an offer to assume five-twelfths of the liability
of the construction and working of the Intercolonial Railway, provided the two other Provinces would assume the
remaining seven-twelfths.   After serious and anxious
deliberations the delegates from Nova Scotia and New
Brunswick decided to assume the responsibility.   The
following Memoranda were then agreed upon :—

MEMORANDUM No. I.

The undersigned, representing the three governments of Canada, Nova Scotia and New Brunswick, convened to consider the
despatch of His Grace the Duke of Newcastle, of April 12th,
1862, with reference to the Intercolonial Railway, having given
the very important matters contained in that despatch their
attentive consideration, are agreed :—

1.—That while they have learned with very great regret that
Her Majesty's Imperial government has finally declined to
sanction the proposal made on behalf of these Provinces, in
December, 1861, and at previous periods, they at the same time
acknowledge the consideration exhibited in substituting the
proposal of "an Imperial guarantee of interest towards enabling
them to raise by public loan, if they should desire it, at a moderate rate, the requisite funds for constructing the railway."

2.—That with an anxious desire to bind the Provinces more
closely together, to strengthen the connection with the mother
country, to promote their common commercial interest, and to
provide facilities essential to public defences of these Provinces
as intregal parts of the Empire, the undersigned are prepared to
assume, under the Imperial guarantee, the liability for the
expenditure necessary to construct this great work.

3.—That the three governments are agreed that the proportion of liability for the necessary expenditure shall be apportioned as follows, namely : Five-twelfths for Canada and seven-twelfths to be equally divided between the Provinces of New Brunswick and Nova Scotia.

4.—But it is understood that the liability for principal and interest shall be borne by each Province to the extent only of the proportion hereby agreed upon.

5.—That in arriving at this conclusion the undersigned have been greatly influenced by the conviction that the construction of the road between Halifax and Quebec must supply an essential link in the chain of an unbroken highway, extending through British territory from the Atlantic to the Pacific, in the completion of which every Imperial interest in North America is most deeply involved ; and the undersigned are agreed that to present properly this part of the subject to the Imperial authorities, the three Provinces will unite at an early day in a joint representation on the immense political and commercial importance of the western extension of the projected work.

J. S. McDONALD,
L. V. SICOTTE,
J. MOSSIS,
W. P. HOWLAND,
WM. McDOUGALL,
M. J. TESSIER,
THOS. D'ARCY McGEE,
F. EVANTURAL,
ADAM WILSON.
} Representing Canada.

JOSEPH HOWE,
J. McCULLY,
WILLIAM ANNAND.
} Representing Nova Scotia.

S. L. TILLEY,
W. H. STEEVES,
P. MITCHELL.
} Representing New Brunswick.

MEMORANDUM No. II.

Agreed at the conference of the delegates of Nova Scotia and New Brunswick and the government of Canada:

1.—If it should be concluded that the work shall be constructed and managed by a joint commission of the three Provinces, it shall be constituted in the proportion of the two appointed by the government of Canada, and one each by the governments of Nova Scotia and New Brunswick, the four to select a fifth before entering upon the discharge of their duties.

2.—That a joint delegation proceed with as little delay as possible to England to arrange with the Imperial government the terms of the loans, the nature of the security required, the amount to be paid for the transport of troops and mails, and, if possible, to obtain a modification of the terms proposed to the extent of the interest accruing during the construction of the work.

3.—That no surveys be authorized until the laws contemplated shall have been passed and the joint commissioners appointed; that any profit or loss, after paying working expenses, shall be divided in proportion to the contribution of the several Provinces.

4.—That such portions of the railways now owned by the governments of Nova Scotia and New Brunswick, which may be required to form part of the Intercolonial road, shall be worked under such joint authority as may be appointed by the three Provinces; that the rates collected shall be uniform over each respective portion of the road. That all net gain or loss resulting from the working and keeping in repair of any portion of the road constructed by Nova Scotia and New Brunswick and to be used as a part of the Intercolonial Railway shall be received and borne by the said Provinces, respectively, and the surplus, if any, after the payment of interest, shall go in abatement of interest on the whole line between Halifax and River du Loup.

5.—That the Crown Lands required for the line and for stations shall be provided by each Province.

(Signed),

THOMAS D'ARCY McGEE, for Canada.
JOSEPH HOWE, for Nova Scotia.
S. L. TILLEY, for New Brunswick.

The delegation to England was composed of the following gentlemen :—The Hon. Mr. Howland and the Hon. Mr. Sicotte for Canada ; Hon. Joseph Howe for Nova Scotia, and the Hon. S. L. Tilley for New Brunswick.

The departure of the Canadian delegates was delayed by a prolonged session of Parliament, but after their arrival in London an early conference was arranged with Mr. Gladstone. The objections taken at this conference by the delegates to the proposed terms were mainly to the Sinking Fund provisions. Mr. Gladstone desired that £3,000,000 should be set aside for this purpose, and it appeared that this was to be a first charge upon the revenues of the several Provinces. The delegates presented fully their objections to the Sinking Fund, and asked that their reasons as stated should have the favorable consideration of the Imperial government. This Mr. Gladstone promised a week later. In the meantime the Canadian delegates left for Paris. Before the week expired Mr. Gladstone sent his reply to the delegates. He held to his demand for a Sinking Fund, but explained that he did not wish the guarantee to take precedence of the then existing liabilities of the several Provinces. A copy of Mr. Gladstone's reply having been submitted to Mr. Howe and Mr. Tilley, then in London, and it being necessary for Mr. Tilley to return to New Brunswick at the earliest date possible, they prepared and submitted to the Duke of Newcastle a Memorandum, of which the following is a copy :—

As the Intercolonial Railroad is a work in which the Imperial and Colonial governments are assumed to have a joint interest, as the undersigned regard it as indispensable to national defence, and to the transportation to this country of breadstuffs, in case war with the United States should ever arise, they hope Mr. Gladstone may be induced to reconsider the matter of the Sinking Fund and trust that the Cabinet may be enabled to convince Parliament that under all the circumstances of the peculiar case, a Sinking Fund should not be insisted upon.   But if it is, the undersigned will not assume the responsibility of periling or delaying this great enterprise by neglecting what the Chancellor of the Exchequer seems to regard as an indispensable condition. If they did they do not believe that such a course would meet the approbation of the governments they represent.

(Signed),

JOSEPH HOWE,
S. L. TILLEY.

It is understood that on receipt of Mr. Gladstone's reply by the Canadian delegates, they left England without an acceptance of the terms proposed, and without a formal rejection.   Previous to the meeting of the Canadian Parliament Mr. Tilley was requested to proceed to Quebec and urge upon the Canadian government the preparation of the necessary bills to carry out the agreement entered into for the construction of this great railway.   Mr. Tilley reported to the Lieutenant Governor of New Brunswick, and to Mr. Howe, that the government of Canada, for reasons stated by them, could not then undertake to have passed the legislation required, which they greatly regretted, but that they had not abandoned the arrangements or the construction of the railway, and would be willing to ask for a vote of money to cover their share of the cost of its survey.   It was, therefore, a matter of great surprise and regret to the friends of this international work in Canada and England that the government, during the session, declared that they had abandoned this important enterprise. The feeling in England on hearing this may be understood by a communication sent to the government of Canada by a representative organization in London, urging the speedy completion of the proposed railway and the passage of the needed legislation :—

BRITISH NORTH AMERICAN ASSOCIATION,
185 GRESHAM HOUSE,
LONDON, January 29th, 1863.

SIR:—

In pursuance of the wish expressed to the Secretary of this Association, the Association addressed the Colonial Minister under date the 8th inst., as per copy enclosed, urging that the surveys preliminary to the submission of the question of the Intercolonial Railway to the Imperial Parliament, should be proceeded with as soon as possible. I am instructed confidentially to say that in reply to this application, the Association have received under date of 21st January, a letter by direction of the Colonial Minister, in which it is stated that "Her Majesty's Government can have no objection to the commencement of the surveys necessary in order to determine the line of railway and ascertain the cost, as soon as the Colonial governments shall have authorized the advance of the requisite funds and shall have come to an arrangement respecting the appointment of the officers to be employed."

Thus it will be seen that the request which the Association was desired to make is at once consented, and it will now rest with the Provinces by a very small outlay of money to make the preliminary survey and obtain that estimate of cost, which are all that in the first instance Her Majesty's government will require. In fact it is the desire, as the Association believe, of the Imperial government to throw no technical obstacle in the way, but if the provinces will enable them to do so, to bring the whole

question before Parliament in the coming sessions. To this end
the surveys and estimates are not required to be those final
and elaborate documents upon which the works would be let by
contract, but merely reliable general facts which practical men
would require in order to guide their judgment as to the feasa-
bility and costs of the project.

But the Association regret to learn that while the delegates
from Nova Scotia and New Brunswick expressed a concurrence
in the general scheme proposed by the treasury, the delegates
from Canada sent to His Grace the Duke of Newcastle, on the
day of their leaving England, and to quote the words of the letter
from the Colonial office above alluded to, "without seeking any
further discussion or the removal of any misapprehension or uncertainty in which they might be involved," a Memorandum
conveying their dissent to the above named treasury minute and
giving counter proposals which the Association cannot think
differ essentially from the scheme proposed by Her Majesty's
government.

The Association believe that the three points of difference are :
First, as to the proposed rate of interest on the debentures ;
Second, as to the Sinking Fund, and Third, as to the suggestion
that Her Majesty's government shall be satisfied that the railway
can be constructed without the Imperial government being asked
for further assistance.

As regards the latter point, that will be determined with the
greatest ease by the estimates of cost which the preliminary
surveys proposed may exhibit, and the Association believe that
the faith of Her Majesty's government in the entire solvency of
the Provinces will satisfy them on this head so soon as such survey and estimate be presented to them, and more especially so as
the Association believe that Her Majesty's government are ready
to agree to the appointment of an Engineer, and that the plans
and estimates may be in England, if immediate dispatch is exercised, by the first week in June.

As regards the second point, it appears that the Chancellor of
the Exchequer proposed a definite scheme of Sinking Fund, while
the Canadian delegates proposed a Sinking Fund in another form,
namely, "In which profits of the road shall be applied towards
extinction of the loan."

As regards the first point, it will be obvious, on reading carefully the treasury minute alluded to, that the illustrative calculations therein made are merely hypothetical, while on the other hand it is, as the Association believe, a fact that money can be raised, if the Imperial guarantee is proposed, at the rate named by the delegates, namely 3½ per cent., and if this be so then the most material difficulty of all is clearly disposed of.

Under these circumstances the Association would hope that the Canadian government, in view of the present state of political and other circumstances, may see their way to a frank explanation with Her Majesty's government, and that the misapprehensions —for the Association will not believe they are more—which have arisen may be removed without delay.

The Association are all the more anxious on this head because experience has proved that misunderstandings of this nature are very difficult to remove when once established. The Association have learned with very great regret that the leading organ of a large political party in Canada has declared that Messrs. Sicotte and Howland have succeeded in their real mission, namely, the indefinite postponement of the Intercolonial Railway.

The Association will not believe that this statement possesses any color of truth, but they allude to it in order to show how, connected with what has taken place, so vigorous an allegation may be used to damage, in the opinion of the people of this country, a great enterprise which the Association hope all true patriots,both in Great Britain and Canada, have sincerely at heart.

I have the honor to be, Sir,

Your very obedient servant,

A. D. HAY, Chairman.

To the Honorable, the Provincial Secretary of Canada, Quebec.

The engagements entered into by the governments of Nova Scotia and New Brunswick were discharged to the letter by the passage of the necessary legislation, though with some opposition. No further steps were taken by the government and Legislature of Canada to secure the construction of this railway until the Confederation negotiations were commenced in 1864. Q

CHAPTER IX.

We now come down to an event of the greatest interest, in which Mr. Tilley took part, and one of such vast and widely reaching importance that it overshadows every other part of his distinguished career. The confederation of the Canadian Provinces was beyond all question the most notable movement that had been taken by any Colony of the British Empire since the Declaration of Independence of the thirteen Colonies. It changed at once the whole character of the Colonial relation which had subsisted with the mother country, and substituted for a few weak and scattered Colonies a powerful Dominion, able to speak with a united voice, and stand as a helpmeet to the nation from which most of its people had sprung. No man, whatever his views as to the wisdom of that political union may have been at the time, can now deny that it was timely and necessary, if the Colonies and the mother country were to preserve their connection with each other. It is safe to say that if Confederation had not taken place in 1867, British interests on this continent would have suffered, and possibly some of the Colonies would now have been a part of the United States. The policy of separating the Colonies from England, which has been so much advocated by many leading public men in the great republic, would have found free scope, and by balancing the interests of one Colony against those of another, promoting dissensions and favoring those Provinces which were disposed to a closer union with the United States, something might have been done to weaken their allegiance to the British Empire, connection with which is now the glory and the strength of the Dominion of Canada.

The question of the union of the several Colonies of British North America was by no means a new one when it came up for final settlement. It had been discussed at a very early period in the history of the Provinces, and indeed it was a question which it was quite natural to discuss, for it seemed but reasonable that Colonies of the same origin, owning the same allegiance, filled with people who differed but little with each other in any respect, and with many commercial interests in common, should form a political union. No doubt it might have been brought earlier to the front as a vital political question but for the fact that the British government, which was most interested in promoting the union of the Colonies, took no step towards the end until almost compelled by necessity to move in the matter. The Colonial policy of England, as represented in the Colonial office and in the royal instructions to Colonial governors, has seldom been wise or far-seeing, and the British Colonies which now girdle the world have been built up mainly as the result of private enterprise; for the part taken by the government has, in most cases, been merely a concurrence in what private individuals have already done, and to assist in protecting British interests when they have become important, especially in new regions of the world. When we consider the manner in which Cabinet appointments have been and arc still arranged in England, this weakness on the part of the Colonial office need not surprise us. The English Prime Minister, in filling up his Cabinet, can give but little attention to the question of merit and fitness, as compared with availability on the score of influence and family connection. Until recently the system of government in England has been mainly aristocratic, and leading families, who were supposed to be able to lend political strength to the Cabinet, were able to force inefficient members upon it, thus making it an aggregation not of talents but of money and titles. Until the year 1801, the business of the Colonies was carried on at the home office, but in that year it was transferred to the Secretary of State for War, and so continued until 1854, when the offices were divided, and Sir George Grey became first Secretary of State for the Colonies. Under such circumstances we need not feel any surprise that the business of the Colonies was done in a very imperfect fashion, and that very absurd notions prevailed in regard to the manner in which they ought to be treated.

It has been seen that in the early years of New Brunswick's history the government was largely controlled by the Lieutenant Governor, who received his commands from Downing street, and who made things pleasant for himself by entering into alliance with leading families in the Province, among whom the offices were divided, and who enjoyed the distinction of being his advisers in all matters. The home authorities seemed to think that if these families were pleased everything was well, and they claimed as a right the distribution of offices and the control of legislation in a manner which no Colonial Minister in his senses would now dream of attempting to exercise. When the Earl of Durham was sent out as Governor General of Canada after the rebellion there in 1838, he suggested in his report that the union of the Colonies of British North America was one of the remedies which ought to be resorted to for the pacification of Canada and the reconstruction of its constitution. Lord Durham, although of high descent and an earl of the United Kingdom, was a strong Liberal, and in fact a Radical in his political notions, and as a consequence incurred the hatred of all the aristocratic nobodies who formed British society, and who even at this day are ready to hiss a British Prime Minister of Liberal tendencies. Lord Durham was made the object of bitter attacks by the entire Tory body in England, and some actions of his, in which he seemed to have strained the constitution, were made a pretext for his dismissal from office and his disgrace. He died a broken-hearted man, but the principles which he enunciated in his report did not die, but survived to find their full fruition a quarter of a century later at a time when Toryism had less ability to injure, and when it had somewhat modified its views with regard to the Colonies.

While a large proportion of the people of the Colonies looked with favor upon the idea of a political union, there was in all of them a large body of objectors who were steadily opposed to it. People of that kind are to be found in all countries, and they have existed in all ages of the world's history. They are the persons who see in every new movement a thousand difficulties which cannot be surmounted. Their minds are constructed on the principle of rejecting all new ideas, and hanging on to old forms and systems long after they have lost their vitality. They are a class who look back for precedents for any step of a political character which it is proposed to take, and who judge of everything by the standard of some former age, and by the answer to the question whether such a thing has ever been heard of before or not. They seem to forget that precedents must be created some time or another, and that the nineteenth century has as good a right to create precedents as any of its predecessors. To these people every objection that could be urged against Confederation was exaggerated and magnified, and whenever any proposal was made which seemed to tend towards the union of the Colonies their voices were heard upon the other side. We need not doubt the honesty or loyalty of these objectors, or consider that they were either unfavorable to British connection or to the building up of the Empire. It was merely their misfortune that constitutionally they were adverse to change, and could not see any merit in a political movement which involved the idea of novelty.

The principal advocate of Confederation in the Maritime Provinces was Hon. Joseph Howe, a man of such ability and force of character that on a wider stage he might have risen to great eminence, and have been regarded as one of the world's mightiest statesmen. When we contrast the noble figure of Joseph Howe with some of the nobodies who have been thrust into high office in England, even into the Premiership, it is impossible to restrain a regret that so great a man, one so imperial in his instincts and views, should have been condemned to spend his whole life in a small Province, and to become so dwarfed by its party politics as for a time to lose his character as a statesman and sink to the level of a mean politician looking for office rather than for the good of his country. When the Confederation question came up for final discussion in the Maritime Provinces, Joseph Howe, who had awakened in these Provinces the desire for such a union, was found arrayed against it, and used all his eloquence and power to defeat the measure of which he had been himself the leading advocate, and which he had taught the people of Nova Scotia and New Brunswick to consider essential to their well-being. No more striking instance than this can be recorded of the disastrous effect of small Provincial politics on the mind of a great man.

The question of the politicial union of the British North American Provinces was brought up in the House of Assembly of Nova Scotia in 1854, and then the leaders of both parties, Hon. Mr. Johnston for the Conservatives,

and Hon. Mr. Howe for the Liberals, united in advo-
cating the measure and in depicting the advantage which
would accrue from it not only to Nova Scotia, but to every
British Province in North America. In 1858 the question of Confederation was brought up in the Parliament of
Canada, and such a union was made a part of the policy
of the government, for Mr. A. T. Galt, on becoming
a member of the administration, insisted upon it being
made a Cabinet question, and Sir Edward Head, the
Governor General, in his speech at the close of the session,
intimated that his government would take action in the
matter during the recess. Messrs. Cartier, Galt and Ross,
who were in England, representing the government of
Canada, waited upon the Colonial Secretary, Sir Edward
Bulwer Lytton, asking the authority of the Imperial
government for the meeting of representatives from each
of the Colonies to take the question of union into consideration, but met with a rebuff, which no doubt was the
result of a conference with the other members of the
government on the subject. The Earl of Derby, whose
son afterwards became Governor General of the Dominion
of Canada, was then Prime Minister, and his government
had no inclination at that time to enter into so vast a
question as the union of the British North American
Colonies. The Colonial Secretary informed the Canadian
delegates that the question of Confederation was necessarily one of an Imperial character and declined to authorize
the meeting, because no expression of sentiment on the
subject had been received from any of the Maritime

Provinces except Nova Scotia. The Earl of Derby's
government fell a few months after this declaration of its
policy in regard to the Colonies, and was succeeded by the
government of Lord Palmerston, which was in office at
the time when the negotiations, which resulted in the
Confederation of the Colonies, were commenced. At first
Lord Palmerston's government seemed to have been no
more favorable to the union of the Colonies than its predecessor; for in 1862 the Duke of Newcastle, then Colonial
Secretary, in a despatch to the Governor General of
Canada, after stating that Her Majesty's government was
not prepared to announce any definite policy on the
question of Confederation, added that " If a union, either
partial or complete, should hereafter be proposed, with the
concurrence of all the Provinces to be united, I am sure that
the matter would be weighed in this country both by the
public, by Parliament and by her Majesty's government,
with no other feeling than au anxiety to discern and
promote any course which might be the most conducive
to the prosperity, strength and harmony of all the British
communities of North America." It must always be a
subject of astonishment that the British government for so
many years should have had no definite policy on a matter
so momentous, and that they should have sought to dis-
courage, rather than otherwise, the project which has been
of such vast importance to the Empire as a consolidating
force, not only by the manner in which Canada itself has
been made to serve Imperial needs, but also for the
example which it showed to other Colonies of the way in

which they could preserve their connection with the mother country, and at the same time enjoy freedom of action in the administration of their affairs, while acquiring that consideration and respect which is due to strength and unity.

The first impulse in favor of Confederation in the minds of the members of Lord Palmerston's Cabinet seems to have developed about the time when it became evident that the result of the civil war in the United States would be the defeat of the southern Confederacy and the consolidation of the power of the great republic in a more effectual union than that which had existed before. No one who was not blind could fail to see that this change of attitude on the part of the United States would demand a corresponding change in relation to the British Colonies towards each other; for from being a mere federation of States, so loosely connected that secession was frequently threatened by States both north and south, the United States, as the result of the war, had become a nation with a strong central government which had taken to itself powers never contemplated by the constitution and which added immensely to its offensive and defensive strength. In 1863, Thomas D'Arcy McGee, a member of the Canadian Cabinet and a man of great eloquence and ability, visited St. John and delivered a lecture in the Mechanics' Institute hall on the subject of the union of the Colonies. His lecture was fully reported in the "Morning News," a paper then published in that city, and attracted a wide degree of attention because it opened up a new subject of interest for the contemplation of the people of the Provinces. Shortly afterwards a series of articles on the same subject, written by the author of this book, appeared in the columns of the "Morning News," and were widely read and quoted. These articles followed closely the lines laid down for the union of the Colonies by the late Peter S. Hamilton, a writer of ability, whose articles on the subject were collected in pamphlet form and extensively circulated. Thus in various ways the public mind was being educated on the question of Confederation, and the doctrine that the union of the British North American Colonies was desirable was generally accepted by the persons who gave any attention to the subject. It was only when the matter came up in a practical form, and as a distinct proposition to be carried into effect, that the violent opposition which afterwards developed itself against Confederation began to be shown.

The failure of the negotiation for the construction of the Intercolonial Railway had convinced the people of New Brunswick that there was nothing to be hoped for at that time in regard to the completion of that great work. Their minds, therefore, were naturally turned towards obtaining railway connection with the United States, and completing the original scheme of the European and North American Railway, which was designed to run from Halifax to Bangor by way of St. John, and there connect with the railway system of the United States. The government of Nova Scotia had already constructed as a part of that work the line from Halifax to Truro, while the government of New Brunswick had built the line from Shediac to St. John, but the portion between Moncton and Truro, which was necessary to connect with Halifax, and the portion between St. John and Bangor, which was necessary to connect with the United States, still remained unbuilt, and indeed no step had been taken towards its construction. In St. John a demand arose for the construction of the railway to the Maine border as a government work, it being understood that the line from Bangor to the New Brunswick boundary, "would be built if our people would meet the Maine people on the border." A numerously signed petition was sent up to the government on the subject, at the session of 1864, and such a strong pressure was brought to bear upon the administration that it was clear something had to be done to assuage the threatened storm and to give the people of the Province such railway facilities as they demanded. It was clearly impossible for the government to comply with the request of the St. John people and their representatives, unless something was done also to aid railway construction in other parts of the Province. There always has been in New Brunswick a very considerable amount of sectional jealousy on such subjects, and it was not to be supposed that the people of the North Shore and up river counties would view with complacency the proposal to expend a very large sum of money in building the railway to the Maine boundary, while nothing was being done to enable them to obtain railway facilities.   Under these circumstances the government resolved upon the introduction of a Railway Facility Act, giving a bonus of $10,000 a mile for the construction of certain railways.   The lines embraced in this Act were a line from St. John to the Maine border, with a branch to Fredericton ; a line from St. Stephen to the St. Andrews line, and from the terminus of that line to Woodstock ; a line from some point between Moncton and Shediac to the Nova Scotia boundary ; a line from some point on the European and North American Railway to Hillsboro and Hopewell ; and a line from Moncton north to the Miramichi.

This bill, when it made its appearance in the House of Assembly was considered by the opposition to be a very absurd measure, and some of the wits of that side of the House named it the Lobster Act, because its provisions seemed to extend to all parts of the Province, like the claws of a lobster.   But the result has amply justified the wisdom of Mr. Tilley and his colleagues, by whom the Act was framed and carried in the Legislature.   The person who predicted that no railway would ever be built under it found that they had greatly mistaken the temper and enterprise of our people ; because no sooner was it passed than measures were taken to render it operative. Under this act, in the course of a few years, the line was built to the Maine border with a branch to Fredericton ; the connection with Woodstock and St. Andrews was completed ; a line from Painsec Junction to Sackville was constructed, and also a line into Albert County.   In fact practically all the lines contemplated by this Act have since been built, either under its terms, or in other ways which rendered the facilities it gave unnecessary.

At the same session of the Legislature a highly important subject was taken up which aided very materially in the movement which afterwards culminated in the confederation of the British North American Colonies. Resolutions were passed authorizing the government to enter into negotiations and hold a convention for the purpose of effecting the union of the Maritime Provinces. Similiar resolutions were carried in the Legislatures of Nova Scotia and Prince Edward Island, and the convention thus authorized was appointed to meet at Charlottetown, in the latter Province, in the month of September following. This movement for Maritime Union arose as the result of negotiations which had been going on for some time between the governments of Nova Scotia and New Brunswick.

Previous to the year 1861 a number of factories of various kinds had been established in the Maritime Provinces, but the limited market they then enjoyed prevented their extension and crippled their operations. To remedy this, Mr. Tilley, with the approval of his colleagues in the government, visited Nova Scotia and Prince Edward Island and proposed to the governments of both Provinces the free exchange of the manufactures of the three Provinces, free admission of their natural products and a uniform tariff on dutiable goods. In Halifax he had a lengthy and satisfactory conference with Mr.

Howe, the then leader of the government, and with Dr. Tupper, the leader of the opposition. Both gentlemen agreed that the proposed arrangements would be in the interests of the three Provinces, and Mr. Howe agreed to submit the matter to his government with the view of legislative action at the next session. Mr. Tilley then proceeded to Charlottetown, Prince Edward Island. At the conference held with the government there his proposal was not so favorably entertained, the objection being that the then tariff of Prince Edward Island was lower than the tariff of either Nova Scotia or New Brunswick, and sufficient for the financial wants of the Island, and that the necessary advance would be imposing taxation beyond their requirements. Notwithstanding the failure to secure the co-operation of the Island government it was decided that the joint action of the Nova Scotia and New Brunswick Legislatures in the direction named was desirable. When the Nova Scotia Legislature met and the public accounts were proposed, it was found that a reduction of the tariff was not practical, and Mr. Howe informed Mr. Tilley that the scheme would have to be postponed, though in other respects desirable. One of the objects of the conference later on, to consider the union of the Maritime Provinces, was the securing of the trade arrangements proposed by the conference referred to. The step taken in 1861 led up to the larger questions presented in 1864.

Another event occurred in the summer of 1864 which had its effect on the question of Confederation. Up to that time the people of Canada and New Brunswick had been almost wholly unknown to each other because the difficulties of travelling between the two Provinces were so great. Any person who desired to reach Montreal at that time from St. John, had to take the International steamer to Portland and was then carried by the Grand Trunk Railway to his destination. Quebec could be reached in summer by the steamer from Pictou which called at Shediac, but in winter the journey had to be made by the Grand Trunk Railway from Portland, the only alternative route being the road by which the mails were carried from Edmundston north to the St. Lawrence. [Under these circumstances the people of the Canadian Provinces had but few opportunities of seeing each other, and the people of both Provinces knew much more of their neighbors in the United States than they did of their fellow Colonists.] One result of Hon. D'Arcy McGee's visit in 1863 was an invitation by the City of St. John to the Legislature of Canada to visit the Maritime Provinces. The invitation was accepted and a party of about a hundred, comprising a number of the members of the Legislature, newspaper men and others, visited St. John in the beginning of August, 1864. Their trip was extended to Fredericton, where they were the guests of the government of New Brunswick, and to Halifax where they were the guests of that city and of the government of Nova Scotia. This visit produced a good effect upon the public mind and enabled our people to see what kind of men their fellow Colonists of Upper and Lower Canada were.

In the meantime a great crisis had arisen in the government of Canada which was the immediate cause of the active part which that Province took in the Confederation movement. When Upper and Lower Canada were united in 1841 it was arranged that the representation of each Province in the united Legislature should be equal. The arrangement at that time was favorable to Upper Canada, which had a smaller population than Lower Canada, but in the course of time as the population of Upper Canada increased faster than that of the Lower Province, the people of Upper Canada felt that they had much less representation than they were fairly entitled to, and this state of affairs raised a cry of "Representation by Population" which was so often heard in that Province prior to the era of Confederation. In 1864 Upper Canada had half a million more people than Lower Canada, and yet was only entitled to the same number of members in the Legislature. Another serious difficulty, which arose out of the Act of Union, was the necessity of the government having a majority in the Legislature of each Province. This in time grew to be so flagrant an evil that the successful government of Canada became almost impossible, for the majority for the government in one Province might at any time be disturbed by some local feeling of jealousy, and as a consequence the government overthrown. To trace the history of the difficulties which arose from this cause would be to recite twenty years of the history of Canada, but it is only necessary to point out thus plainly the reasons for the willingness of the

R

people of Upper and Lower Canada to resort to Confederation as a means of getting rid of their embarrassments.
In 1863 the Hon. John Saufield McDonald was leader
of the government, but he was compelled to resign when
Parliament met in the early part of 1864, and in March
of that year a new administration under the Premiership
of Sir E. P. Tache was formed. This new government
developed very little strength and was threatened with
defeat. But on the 14th of June, the following entry is
found in the journals of the Legislature of Canada :—

"The Hon. Mr. Brown from the select committee appointed to
enquire into the important subjects embraced in a despatch to
the Colonial minister, addressed to him on the 2nd of February,
1864, by the Hon. Geo. E. Cartier, the Hon. A. T. Galt, and the
Hon. John Ross, then members of the Executive Council of the
Province, while in London acting on behalf of the government of
which they were members, in which they declared that very
grave difficulties now present themselves in conducting the government of Canada in such a manner as to show due regard to the
wishes of its numerous population; that 'differences exist to an
extent which prevents any perfect and complete assimilation of
the views of the two sections;' that the progress of population
has been more rapid in the western section, and claims are now
being made on behalf of its inhabitants for giving them representation in the Legislature according to their numbers; that the
result is shewn by an agitation, fraught with great danger, to the
peaceful and harmonious working of our constitutional system,
and consequently detrimental to the progress of the Province, and
that the necessity of providing a remedy for a state of things that
is yearly becoming worse, and of allaying feelings that are daily
being aggravated by the contention of political parties, has impressed the advisers of Her Majesty's representative in Canada
with the importance of seeking such a mode of dealing with the
difficulties as may forever remove them; and the best means of
remedying the evils therein set forth, presented to the House

the report of said committee, which was read as followeth : 'That the committee have held eight meetings, and have endeavored to find some solution for existing difficulties likely to receive the assent of both sections of the Province.' A strong feeling was found to exist among the members of the committee in favor of changes in the direction of a federation system applied either to Canada alone or to the whole of the British North American Provinces, and such progress has been made as to warrant the committee in recommending that the subject be again referred to a committee at the next session of Parliament.

The whole respectfully submitted,

GEORGE BROWN,

Chairman."

On the same day that this entry was made the Tache government was defeated by a vote of 60 to 58, on a question relative to some transaction connected with bonds of the City of Montreal. A deadlock had come and, as it was evident that no new government which could be formed was likely to command sufficient support, it became a necessity to make some new arrangements in regard to the system of administration. Immediately after the defeat of the government, Mr. George Brown, leader of the opposition, spoke to several supporters of the administration, strongly urging that the present time should be utilized for the purpose of settling forever the constitutional difficulties between Upper and Lower Canada, and assuring them that he was prepared to co-operate with the existing or any other administration that would deal with the question promptly and firmly, with a view to its final settlement. Messrs. Morris and Pope, to whom he spoke, asked and obtained leave to communicate this conversation to Mr. John A.

Macdonald, the Attorney General, and Mr. Galt. Messrs. Brown, Macdonald and Galt met on June 17th at the St. Louis Hotel and discussed the situation. Mr. Brown stated that nothing but the extreme urgency of the crisis and the hope of settling the sectional difficulties of the Province would, in his opinion, justify him in meeting with the members of the government, with a view to common political action. He was informed by Messrs. Galt and Macdonald that they were charged by their colleagues formally to invite his aid in strengthening the administration, with a view to the settlement of those difficulties. Mr. Brown stated that it was quite impossible for him to become a member of any administration then, and that he thought the public mind would be shocked by such an arrangement; but he felt very strongly that the crisis presented an opportunity of dealing with this question that might never occur again. He thought that another general election presented no prospect of a much altered result, and he believed that both political parties were better prepared than ever before to look the true cause of all the difficulties in the face, and endeavor to settle the representation question on an equitable and permanent basis. Mr. Brown added that, if the administration were prepared to do this and would pledge themselves clearly and publicly to bring in a measure next session that would be acceptable to Upper Canada, he would heartily co-operate with them and endeavor to induce his friends to sustain them until they had an opportunity of presenting their measure. Mr.

Macdonald thought that it would be necessary for Mr. Brown himself to become a member of the Cabinet, with a view to give guarantees to the opposition and to the country of the earnestness of the government. In reply to a question by Mr. Brown as to what the government proposed as a remedy for the injustice complained of by Upper Canada, Mr. Macdonald and Mr. Galt replied that their remedy was a federal union of the British North American Provinces. Mr. Brown replied that this would not be acceptable to the people of Upper Canada as a remedy for existing evils ; that he believed that the federation of all the Provinces ought to come and would come, but it had not been thoroughly considered by the people, and there were so many parties to be consulted that its adoption was uncertain and remote. He proposed as an alternative remedy parliamentary reform based on population, without regard to the dividing line between Upper and Lower Canada.

Mr. Brown's proposal was declared to be impossible by both Mr. Macdonald and Mr. Galt and after much discussion it was found that a compromise might be had in the adoption either of the Federal principle for all the British North American Provinces or for Canada alone, with provision for the admission of the Maritime Provinces and the North Western Territory, when they should express the desire. After some further negotiations, Mr. Brown requested to have the views of the administration as expressed to him reduced to writing, for the purpose of being submitted confidentially to his friends. This was done, and the result was the following Memorandum to which Mr. Brown gave his assent :—

The government are prepared to pledge themselves to bring in a measure next session for the purpose of removing existing difficulties, by introducing the federal principle into Canada, coupled with such provision as will permit the Maritime Provinces and the North West Territory to be incorporated into the same system of government.

And the government will seek, by sending representatives to the Lower Provinces and to England, to secure the assent of those interests which are beyond the control of our own legislation, to such a measure as may enable all British North America to be united under a general Legislature based upon the federal principle.

Mr. Brown was very reluctant to enter the Cabinet for the purpose of carrying out this proposal, but his presence in it was considered indispensable, and on the thirtieth of June when the House was prorogued a new government was announced of which the Hon. George Brown and Messrs. Mowatt and MacDougall, two other prominent Reformers, were members, they having taken the place of Messrs. Foley, Buchanan and Simpson in the existing administration. Thus a coalition had been formed between the leaders of the Reform and Conservative parties, for the purpose of carrying a measure for the confederation of the British Provinces of North America. It is easy to see from the tenor of the negotiations that nothing short of the emergency which had arisen in Canada could have induced the leaders of the Reform party there to join with Conservatives in this movement, nor is it likely that the latter would have troubled themselves about the matter had they not been influenced by the same motive. The necessities of Canada, in a political sense, alone brought about the existence of the present great Dominion which stretches from ocean to ocean.

The delegates appointed by the government of New Brunswick for the purpose of representing this Province at Charlottetown in the convention for a union of the Maritime Provinces, were the Hon. Messrs. Tilley, Steeves, Johnson, Chandler and Gray. The first three were members of the government, while Messrs. Gray and Chandler were leading members of the opposition, so that the arrangement had the assent of the leaders of both political parties and was in no sense a party movement. The Nova Scotia delegation consisted of Hon. Chas. Tupper, the leader of the government, the Attorney General, Mr. Henry, and Mr. Dickey, a Conservative supporter, and also the Hon. Adam G. Archibald and Jonathan McCulley, leaders of the Liberal party. The Prince Edward Island delegates were also chosen from both sides of politics. The convention was opened in due form at Charlottetown on September 8th, in the chamber of the House of Assembly. The delegations had no power to decide finally on any subject, because any arrangements they made were necessarily subject to the approval of the Legislatures of the three Maritime Provinces. But at this time the sentiment in favor of Maritime union was so strong it was confidently believed that whatever was agreed upon at Charlottetown would become the basis of a future union.

The government of Canada had full knowledge of
what was going on at Charlottetown, and they considered
the time opportune for the purpose of bringing to the
notice of the delegates from the Maritime Provinces the
subject of a confederation of all the British North American colonies.   A telegram was received while the
delegates were in session announcing that representatives
of the government of Canada had left Quebec for the
purpose of meeting the delegates of the Maritime
Provinces, and placing certain proposals before them,
and on the receipt of this message the further consideration of the question which they had met to
discuss was deferred until after the Canadian delegates had arrived.   They came in the government
steamer "Victoria" on the day following the receipt of the
telegram announcing their departure, and were found to
embrace the leading men then in Canadian public life,
the Hons. J. A. Macdonald, George Brown, George E.
Cartier, Alex. T. Galt, Thomas D'Arcy McGee, Hector
L. Langevin, William MacDougall and Alex. Campbell.
Those delegates represented the Reform as well as the
Conservative party, and were therefore able to speak
with authority with regard to the views of the people of
both Upper and Lower Canada.   They were accorded
seats in the convention, and at once submitted their
reasons why in their opinion a scheme of union, embracing the whole of the British North American colonies,
should be adopted.   The Hon. John A. Macdonald and
Messrs. Brown and Cartier were heard on this subject,

the financial position of Canada was explained, and the sources of revenue and wealth of the several Provinces were discussed. Speeches were also made by Messrs. Galt, McGee, Langevin and MacDougall, and after having commanded the attention of the convention for two days the Canadian deputation withdrew. Before doing so they had proposed that if the convention concluded to suspend its deliberations upon the question of Maritime Union, they should adjourn to Quebec at an early day to be named by the Governor General, to consider the question of Confederation. On the following day the convention adjourned upon the ground that it would be more for the general interest of British North America to adopt the larger union than a mere union of the Maritime Provinces, and it was thought that this might be effected without any very great difficulty, for there was then no strong feeling evinced in any quarter against Confederation.

From Charlottetown the members of the convention and the Canadian deputation went to Halifax, where they were received most cordially and entertained at a banquet at the Halifax hotel. They then took their departure for St. John where they were entertained at a public dinner at which many leading men of the city were present. The chair was occupied by the Hon. John H. Gray, one of the delegates, and the expressions in favor of the proposed confederation were strong and hearty. No one could have suspected at that time that the movement for Confederation would meet with so much opposition in New Brunswick. All seemed plain sailing, but, as the result showed, the battle for Confederation had yet to be fought and it was only won after a long and doubtful struggle.

According to arrangement the delegations from the other provinces met in Convention at Quebec on the 10th of October, all the colonies, including Newfoundland, were represented and the delegates were as follows:—

Canada—Hon. Sir Etienne P. Tache, Premier M. L. C.; Hon. John A. Macdonald, Attorney General West, M. P. P.; Hon. George E. Cartier, Attorney General East, M. P. P.; Hon. George Brown, President of the Executive Council, M. P. P., Hon. Alex. T. Galt, Finance Minister, M. P. P., Hon. Alex. Campbell, Commissioner of Crown Lands, M. L. C.; Hon. William MacDougall, Provincial Secretary, M. P. P., Hon. Thomas D'Arcy McGee, Minister of Agriculture, M. P. P., Hon. Hector Langevin, Solicitor General East, M. P. P., Hon. J. Cockburn, Solicitor General West, M. P. P., Hon. Oliver Mowatt, Post Master General, M. P. P., Hon. J. C. Chapais, Commissioner of Public Works, M. L. C.

Nova Scotia—Hon. Chas. Tupper, Provincial Secretary, M. P. P., Hon. W. A. Henry, Attorney General, M. P. P., Hon. R. B. Dickey, M. L. C., Hon. Adam G. Archibald, M. P. P., Hon. Jonathan McCully, M. L. C.

New Brunswick—Hon. Samuel L. Tilley, Provincial Secretary, M. P. P., Hon. John M. Johnson, Attorney General, M. P. P., Hon. Edward B. Chandler, M. L. C., Hon. John Hamilton Gray, M. P. P., Hon. Peter Mitchell, M. L. C., Hon. Chas. Fisher, M. P. P., Hon. William H. Steeves, M. L. C.

Newfoundland—Hon. F. B. T. Carter, M. P. P., Speaker of the House of Assembly, Hon. Ambrose Shea, M. P. P.

Prince Edward Island—Hon. John Hamilton Gray, Premier, M. P. P.; Hon. Edward Palmer, Attorney General, M. P. P.; Hon. W. H. Pope, Provincial Secretary, M. P. P.; Hon. George Coles, M. P. P.; Hon. A. A. Macdonald, M. L. C.; Hon. T. H. Haviland, M. P. P.; Hon. Edward Whelan, M. L. C.

Sir Etienne P. Tache, who was then Premier of Canada, was unanimously chosen President of the conference, and Major Hewitt Bernard, of the staff of the Attorney General West, Private and Confidential Secretary. It was arranged that the convention should hold its meetings with closed doors, and it was laid down as a principle of the discussion, that as the matters to come up for debate were all of a novel character, no man should be prejudiced or held liable to the charge of inconsistency because he had changed his views in regard to any particular matter in the course of the discussion. It was also agreed that the vote, in case of a division, should be by Provinces and not by numbers, Canada having two votes, representing Canada East and Canada West, and each of the other Provinces one. This arrangement made it quite certain that the interests of the Maritime Provinces were not likely to be prejudiced by the result of the vote or the work of the convention. It was soon decided that a federal union was to be preferred to a legislative union, and on the second day of the meeting the outlines of the proposed confederation were submitted in a series of reso-

lutions by the Hon. John A. Macdonald. The general
model of the proposed confederation was that of the
United States, but with this difference, that whereas in
the United States all powers, not expressly given by the
constitution to the federal government, are held to
belong to the several states, in the Canadian con-
titution all powers not expressly reserved to the several
Provinces were held to belong to the federal parliament.
Thus in the United States the residuum of power is in the
several states, and in Canada the residuum of power is in
the federal union, and in the Parliament of the Dominion.
No doubt the recent example of the civil war in the
United States, which was the result of an extreme assertion of state rights, was largely responsible for this feature
of the Canadian constitution. It is clear, however, that
it is a feature that is to be commended, because its tendency is to cause Canadians to regard themselves rather
as Canadians than as belonging to any particular
Province, while in the United States the feeling of state-
hood is still very strong, as has been shown by recent
events in that country, and in the discussion of such
matters as the silver question, which at some future time
may become as dangerous to the unity of the Republic as
the slavery question once was. There are, of course,
many other contrasts between the Canadian Confederation
and the federal union of the United States, arising from
radical differences in the system of government. Nothing
like responsible government, as understood in the British
Empire, exists in the United States, while this essential

feature had to be preserved in the Canadian constitution, not only with reference to the Dominion Parliament, but also in the Legislatures of the several Provinces. It is quite safe to assert that viewing the Confederation in all its aspects, it is a much more efficient and satisfactory form of government than that which exists in the United States, and that our Provincial governments are superior in every respect to the state governments of that country.

It does not fall within the scope of this volume to deal exhaustively with the proceedings at Quebec in which Mr. Tilley, as the Finance Minister of New Brunswick, took a very prominent part. One great difficulty which arose was with respect to the amount of money to be given by the federal government to the several Provinces for Legislative purposes, in lieu of the revenue which they had been accustomed to obtain from customs duties and otherwise. The whole customs establishment was to be transferred to the central government, and as most of the Provinces would have no other means of obtaining a revenue except by direct taxation, this feature of the matter became of very vital importance. The difficulty was increased by the fact that by the municipal system then prevailing in Upper Canada, the local needs of the municipalities, in the way of roads, bridges, schools and other matters, were provided for by local taxation, whereas in the Maritime Provinces the Provincial government had been accustomed to bear these burdens. It was therefore an essential requisite to any scheme of union, to make it acceptable to the people of the Maritime Provinces, that sufficient money should be given to the Provincial governments to enable them to continue these services as before.   It was difficult to convince the representatives of Upper Canada of this, and it appears that the conference came near breaking up without arriving at any result, simply because of the apparently irreconcilable differences of opinion between the representatives of the Maritime Provinces and those of Canada in regard to this point.   Finally these differences were overcome, and the conclusions of the conference were embodied in a series of seventy-two resolutions, which were agreed to, and which were to be authenticated by the signatures of the delegates, and to be transmitted to their respective governments, and also to the Governor General, for the Secretary of State for the colonies.   These resolutions formed the first basis of Confederation and became what is known as the Quebec scheme.

It was perhaps inevitable that during the discussion of the scheme of Confederation by the Quebec convention, the proceedings should be secret, but this restriction as to secrecy should have been removed as soon as the convention adjourned.   That this was not done was the principal reason for the very unfavorable reception which the Quebec scheme met with from the people of New Brunswick, when it was placed before them.   It was agreed at the Quebec conference that the scheme should not be made public until after the delegates had reported to their respective governments for their approval, but it was impossible that a document, the terms of which were known to so many men, should be kept wholly concealed from the public, and so the details of the scheme leaked out and soon became a topic for public discussion. These discussions would have been conducted in a much more friendly spirit if the Quebec scheme had been given freely to the world, but as it was, prejudices and jealousies in many cases darkened the question, and made men who were otherwise friendly to Confederation assume an attitude of hostility to the Quebec scheme.

One of the points which at once attracted the attention of the opponents of the scheme was the sum allowed to the several Provinces for the purpose of conducting their local affairs. As the Provinces had to surrender to the general government their right to levy customs and excise duties, it became necessary to make up in some way a sum sufficient to enable them to carry on these services which were still left to the Provincial Legislatures. It was arranged that this sum should be eighty cents a head of the population of the Provinces, as established by the census of 1861, which would give to the Province of New Brunswick something more than $200,000. This feature of the Confederation scheme was eagerly seized upon as being a convenient club with which to strike it down. [The cry was at once raised that the people of New Brunswick were asked to sell themselves to Canada for the sum of eighty cents a head, and this parrot-like cry was repeated with variations throughout the whole of the election campaign which followed in New Brunswick.] It has often been

found that a cry of this kind, which is absolutely mean-
ingless when reduced to reason, is more effective than the
most weighty arguments for the purpose of influencing
men's minds, and this proved to be the case in New
Brunswick, when the question of Confederation was placed
before the people.   It was conveniently forgotten by those
who attacked the scheme in this fashion that if the people
of New Brunswick were selling themselves to Canada
for the sum of eighty cents a head, the people of Canada
were likewise selling themselves to us for the same sum,
because the amount set apart for the Provincial Legislatures was precisely the same in each case.   It would
not however, have suited the enemies of the Confederation
scheme to view the matter in this light; what was wanted
was a cry which would be effective for the purpose of
injuring the scheme, and making it distasteful to our
people who were asked to vote upon it.   It is not necessary
to assume that those who opposed Confederation were all
influenced by sinister motives.   Many honest and good
men whose attachment to British institutions could not
be questioned were opposed to it, because their minds
were of a conservative turn, and because they looked
with distrust upon such a radical change which would
alter the relations which existed between the Province and
the mother country.   Many, for reasons which it is not
easy to understand, were distrustful of the politicians of
Canada, whom they looked upon as of less sterling honesty
than our own, and some actually professed to believe that
the Canadians expected to make up their financial deficits

by drawing on the many resources of the Maritime Provinces through the Confederation scheme. On the other hand Confederation was opposed in the Province of New Brunswick by a number of men who could only be discribed as adventurers or discredited politicians, and who saw in this contest a convenient way of restoring themselves to influence and power. There were also among the opponents of the scheme some men who recognized in its success the means of perpetrating British power on this continent, and who being annexationists naturally looked with aversion upon it for that reason. The vast majority of the people, however, had given the matter but the slightest degree of attention, and their votes were cast in accordance with prejudices hastily formed which they had an opportunity of reconsidering before amother year and a half had elapsed.

It had been arranged at the convention that the first trial of the scheme before the people should be made in the Province of New Brunswick, the Legislature of which was about expiring, and accordingly the appeal was made to the people and the elections came on in the month of March, 1865. The enemies of Confederation were very active in every part of the Province, and they left no stone unturned to defeat the measure. The great cry upon which they based their opposition to the union with Canada was that of taxation, and, as the voters of New Brunswick were not inclined to favor any policy which involved high taxation, the appeals made in this way had a powerful effect. All through the rural constituencies the opposition candidates told the electors that if they united themselves with Canada direct taxation would be the immediate result. That every cow, every horse and every sheep which they owned would be taxed, and that even their poultry would not escape the grasp of the Canadian tax gatherers.] In the City of St. John Mr. Tilley and his colleague, Mr. Charles Watters, were opposed by Mr. J. V. Troop and Mr. A. R. Wetmore. Mr. Troop was a wealthy shipowner, whose large means made him an acceptable addition to the strength of the anti-Confederate party, although previously he had taken no active part in political affairs. Mr. Wetmore was a lawyer of standing in St. John, who was considered to be one of the best *nisi prius* advocates at the bar, and who carried the methods of the bar largely into his politics. [Mr. Wetmore never pretended to have any political principles, or any views whatever of a fixed character in regard to Confederation, or any other political subject. Indeed it was his boast on a later occasion that, as he had been on both sides of the Confederation question he had the assurance that he was at least right once.] He rushed into the contest for the purpose of bettering his own fortunes, and he succeeded in doing so by becoming in the course of time Attorney General of the Province, and later on a judge of the Supreme Court. Mr. Wetmore when haranguing St. John audiences used to depict the dreadful effects of Confederation in a manner peculiarly his own. His great plea was an imaginary dialogue between himself and his little son, that precocious infant asking him in lisping tones, "Father what country do we live in?" to which he would reply "My dear son you have no country, for Mr. Tilley has sold us all to the Canadians for eighty cents a head."

In the county of St. John the Hon. John H. Gray, Chas. N. Skinner, W. H. Scovil and Mr. Quinton, who ran as supporters of Confederation, were opposed by John W. Cudlip, T. W. Anglin, the Hon. R. D. Wilmot and Joseph Coram. Mr. Cudlip was a merchant who at one time enjoyed much popularity in the city of St. John, but who was wholly unfit for political life. Mr. Cudlip was an impulsive man, easily carried away by his feelings, and after Confederation had become a fixed fact, he so far forgot himself as to become an open advocate of annexation to the United States. He enjoys the distinction of being the only member of our Legislature who has ever moved a resolution in that body in favor of annexation. Mr. Anglin was a clever Irishman, a native of the County of Cork, who had lived several years in St. John and edited a newspaper called the Freeman, which enjoyed a great popularity among his co-religionists. Mr. Anglin was admitted to be the leader of the Irish Catholics of St. John and had acquired an ascendancy over them which was not easily shaken. Yet he was not as a politician a great success, nor did his efforts to improve the condition of his countrymen always lead to satisfactory results. The Hon. R. D. Wilmot had been a prominent Conservative politician, but was defeated and had retired to his farm at Belmont, and for some years had been devoting

his abilities to the raising of calves and swine. But at the
first note of alarm on the Confederation question he
abandoned his agricultural pursuits and rushed into the
field to take part in the contest, which he thought might
inure to his political advantage. Mr. Joseph Coram
was a leading Orangeman, a highly respected citizen,
whose sole claim to distinction was that he had person-
ated King William in an Orange procession which had
resulted in a riot some years before, and that his features
were supposed to resemble those of the Prince, whose
memory the Orange body has been created to honor.

In the County of York the Hon. George L. Hatheway,
who was then Chief Commissioner of the Board of Works,
appeared in the field as an opposition candidate, in company with John C. Allen, John J. Fraser and William
H. Needham. Mr. Hatheway deserted the government
in its hour of need, apparently through mere cowardice,
because he judged from the cries that were raised against
Confederation that the current of public opinion was
strongly adverse to the Quebec scheme. He thought that
by deserting his colleagues he might retain his office in
the new government which was to be formed, and in this
view he was correct, but the final result showed that he
was as ready to desert his new allies as he had been those
with whom he had been before associated. He left Mr.
Tilley in the lurch on the eve of the Confederation contest, and he deserted the Smith government sixteen
months later when the second Confederation election
came to be run, thereby inflicting upon them a blow from

which it was impossible they could recover. Hatheway
was nothing more than a loud-mouthed demagogue, with
a large body and a small heart.] William H. Needham,
whose name has already appeared in this volume, did not
pretend to have any political principles, but having been
for some time retired to private life, the Confederation
struggle gave him a good opportunity of getting into the
Legislature.   Needham was a man of very considerable
ability, and had his principles been only equal to his
knowledge and talents he would have risen to the highest
position in this Province.   But his shifty course on many
occasions made the public distrustful of him, and
he died without having enjoyed any of those honors
which men of far less ability, but of more political
honesty, have obtained.   John James Fraser, now
Governor of this Province, was a man of a different
stamp, and seems to have been a sincere opponent of
Confederation from conviction.   The same may be said
of John C. Allen, now Chief Justice of this Province, a man whose sterling honesty has never been
questioned.

The result of the election was the most overwhelming
defeat that ever overtook any political party in the Province of New Brunswick.   Out of forty-one members the
friends of Confederation only succeeded in returning six,
Hon. John McMillan and Alexander C. DesBrisay for the
county of Restigouche ; Abner R. McLellan and John
Lewis for the county of Albert, and William Lindsay and
Charles Connell for the county of Carleton.   Every

member of the government who held a seat in the House of Assembly, with the exception of the Hon. John McMillan, the Surveyor General, was defeated. The majorities against the Confederation candidates in some of the counties were so large that it seemed hopeless to expect that any future election would reverse the verdict. Both the City and County of St. John and the County of York made a clean sweep and returned solid delegations of anti-Confederates. With the exception of the two Carleton members, the entire block of counties on the River St. John and the County of Charlotte, forming the most populous and best settled part of the Province, declared against the Quebec scheme. On the North shore, Westmorland, Kent, Northumberland and Gloucester, pronounced the same verdict, and on the day after the election the strongest friends of Confederation must have felt that nothing but a miracle could ever bring about a change in the opinion which had been pronounced with such emphasis and with such apparent unanimity. Yet fifteen months later the verdict of March, 1865, was completely reversed, and the anti-Confederates were beaten as badly as the advocates of Confederation had been in the first election ; such are the mutations of public opinion.

Mr. Tilley and his colleagues resigned immediately after the result of the elections, and the Hon. Albert J. Smith was called upon to form a new government. Mr. Smith had been Attorney General in Mr. Tilley's government up to the year 1862, when he resigned in consequence of a difference with his colleagues in regard to the negotiations which were being carried on for the construction of the Intercolonial Railway. Mr. Smith was a fine speaker and a man of good ability, and at a later period when Confederation had been established, became a Cabinet Minister in the government of the Hon. Alex. McKenzie. His powerful influence was largely responsible for the manner in which the North shore counties declared against Confederation, and he also did much to discredit the Quebec scheme by his speeches delivered in the City of St. John. Mr. Smith did not take the office of Attorney General in the new government, but contented himself with the position of President of the Council, Hon. John C. Allan, of York, becoming Attorney General, and Hon. A. H. Gilmour, of Charlotte, becoming Provincial Secretary. The Hon. Bliss Botsford, of Westmorland, was made Surveyor General, the Hon. W. H. Odell Postmaster General; and the Hon. George L. Hatheway retained his old office as the Chief Commissionor of the Board of Works. The other members of the government were the Hon. Robert Duncan Wilmot of Sunbury, the Hon. T. W. Anglin of St. John, and the Hon. Richard Hutchinson of Miramichi. The new government looked strong and imposing, and seemed to be secure against the assaults of its enemies, yet it was far from being as compact and powerful as it appeared to the outward observer. In the first place it had the demerit of being founded solely on a negative, and upon opposition to a single line of policy. The reason why these men were assembled together in council as a government was that they were opposed to Confederation, and this question having been disposed of left them free to differ upon all other points which might arise. Some of the men who thus found themselves sitting together at the same council board had all their lives been politically opposed to each other. The Hon. R. D. Wilmot, an old Conservative, could have little or no sympathy with Mr. A. H. Gilmour, a very strong Liberal. The Hon. A. J. Smith, also a Liberal, had little in common with his Attorney General, Mr. Allen, who was a Conservative. Mr. Odell, the Postmaster General, represented the old family compact more thoroughly than any other man who could have been chosen to fill a public office in New Brunswick, for his father and grandfather had held the office of Provincial Secretary for the long term of sixty years. As he was a man of no particular capacity, and had no qualification for high office, and as he was more-over a member of the Legislative Council, his appointment to such a position was extremely distasteful to many who were strongly opposed to Confederation. The Hon. Bliss Botsford of Moncton, who became Surveyor General, was another individual who added no strength to the government, being hopelessly dull by nature, and however honest in his intention, wholly unable to outline or even follow intelligently any distinct line of policy. With four men in the government who might be classed as Liberals, and five who might be properly described as Conservatives, room was left for many differences and quarrels over points of policy after the great question of Confederation had been disposed of. Local feelings also were awakened by the make up of the government, for the North Shore people could not but feel that their interests had been grossly neglected, as instead of having the Attorney Generalship and the Surveyor Generalship which had been theirs in the previous government, they had to be content with a single member in the government, without office, in the person of Mr. Richard Hutchinson, who as the representative of Gilmour, Rankine Co., was extremely unpopular even in the county which had elected him. Hon. Robert Duncan Wilmot was perhaps the most dissatisfied man of any with the new cabinet in which he found himself. He had not been a fortnight in the government before he began to realize the fact that his influence in it was quite overshadowed by that of Mr. Smith and Mr. Anglin, although neither of them held any office. Mr. Wilmot was a man of ability, and of strong and resolute will, so that this condition of affairs became very distasteful to him and his friends and led to consequences of a highly important character.

The new government had not been long in existence before rumors of dissensions in its ranks became very common. Mr. Wilmot made no secret to his friends of his dissatisfaction, and it was also understood that other members found their position equally unpleasant. An element of difficulty was early introduced by the resignation of the Chief Justice, Sir James Carter, who found it

necessary, in consequence of failing health, to retire from
the Bench. Sir James Carter resigned in September,
1865, and it immediately became requisite to fill his
place. The Hon. Albert J. Smith, the leader of the
government, had he chosen might have then taken the
vacant position, but he did not desire to retire from
political life at that time, and the Hon. John C. Allen, his
Attorney General, was appointed to the Bench as a puisne
Judge, while Hon. Robert Parker was made Chief Justice.
The latter, however, had but a few weeks to enjoy his new
position, dying in November of the same year, and leaving
another vacancy on the Bench to be filled. Again as
before, the Hon. Mr. Smith declined to go on the Bench,
and the Hon. John W. Weldon, who had been a long
time a member of former Legislatures, and was at one
time Speaker, was appointed to the puisne judgeship, and
the Hon. William J. Ritchie made Chief Justice. The
entire fitness of the latter for the position of Chief Justice
made his appointment a popular one, but he was the
junior of the Hon. Lemuel A. Wilmot as a Judge, and
the Hon. R. D. Wilmot, who was a cousin of the latter,
thought the senior judge should have received the
appointment of Chief Justice. His disappointment at
the office being given to another, caused a very bad feeling on his part towards the government, and he would
have resigned his seat forthwith, but for the persuasions
of some of those who were not friends of the government,
who intimated to him that he could do them a great deal
more damage by retaining his seat, and resigning at the

proper time than by abandoning the government at that moment. Mr. Wilmot remained in the government until January, 1866, but although of their number his heart was estranged from them, and he may properly be regarded as an enemy in their camp.

Mr. Anglin also had difference with his colleagues with regard to railway matters, and he resigned his seat early in November, 1865; still he gave a general support to the government although no longer in its councils. But the most severe blow which the government received, arose from the election in the County of York which followed the seating of the Hon. John C. Allen on the bench. The Confederation party had been so badly beaten in York at the general election that no doubt was felt by the government that any candidate they might select would be chosen by a very large majority. The candidate selected to contest York by the government was Mr. John Pickard, a highly respectable gentleman, who was engaged in lumbering, and who was extremely popular in that county, in consequence of his friendly relations with all classes of the community and the amiability of his disposition. Mr. Pickard would have been an ideal candidate had he been a better speaker, but he never pretended to be an active politician, and therefore stood at a disadvantage as compared to some men of no better ability but of greater eloquence. The Hon. Chas. Fisher was brought forward by the Confederation party as their candidate in York, although the hope of defeating Mr. Pickard seemed to be desperate, for at the previous election Mr. Fisher had only received 1226 votes against 1799 obtained by Mr. Needham, who stood lowest on the poll among the persons elected for York. Mr. Fisher's abilities have already been sufficiently referred to in this work, and it need only be said that by his conduct in the York campaign, which resulted in his election, he struck a blow at the anti-Confederate Government from which it never recovered. His election was the first dawn of light and hope to the friends of Confederation in New Brunswick, for it showed clearly enough that whenever the people of this Province were given another opportunity of expressing their opinion on the question of Confederation, their verdict would be a very different one from that which they had given at the general election. Mr. Fisher beat Mr. Pickard by 710 votes, receiving 701 votes more than at the general election, while Mr. Pickard's vote fell 572 below that which Mr. Needham had received on the same occasion.

CHAPTER X.

Among the causes that had assisted to defeat Confederation in New Brunswick, when the question was first placed before the people, was the active hostility of the Lieutenant Governor, Mr. Arthur Hamilton Gordon, a son of that Earl of Aberdeen who was Prime Minister of England at the outbreak of the Crimean war. Mr. Gordon had been a strong advocate of Maritime Union and had anticipated that he would be the first Governor of the United Province of Acadia, or by whatever name the Maritime Union was to be known. He was therefore greatly disappointed and annoyed, when the visit of the Canadians to Charlottetown, in September, 1864, put an end to the conference which had met for the purpose of arranging the terms of Maritime Union. While a Governor cannot take a very active part in political matters in this Province, he may stimulate others to hostility or to a certain course of action, who under other circumstances would be neutral or inactive, and there is reason to believe that some of the men who were most prominent in opposing Confederation at the general election of 1864 were mainly influenced by the example of the Lieutenant Governor. Confederation, however had been approved by the British Government after the terms

arranged at Quebec had been submitted to it in a despatch
from the Governor General, and those officials in New
Brunswick and elsewhere who expected to find support
in Downing street in their hostility to Confederation were
destined to be greatly disappointed. Not long after the
new government was formed in New Brunswick, Mr.
Gordon returned to England, and it is generally believed
that he was sent for by the home authorities. Instead of
meeting with a flattering reception on the ground of his
opposition to Confederation, he is believed to have been
compelled to submit to a stern reproof for his anti-consti-
tutional meddling in a matter which did not concern him,
and to have been given decidedly to understand that if he
returned to New Brunswick, to fill out the remainder of
his term of office, it must be as one pledged to assist in
carrying out Confederation and not to oppose it. When
Mr. Gordon returned to this Province he was an entirely
changed man, and whatever influence he was able to
exert from that time forward was thrown in favor of Confederation.

Another cause which made Confederation more acceptable to the people of this Province arose from the threats
of the Fenians to invade Canada, which were made during the year 1865 and which actually resulted in armed
invasions during the following year. Although there
was no good reason for believing that the opponents of
Confederation were less loyal than its supporters or less
inclined to favor British connection, it was remarked that
all the enemies of British connection seemed to have got

into the anti-Confederate camp. The Fenian movement had its origin in the troubles in Ireland, arising out of oppressive land laws and other local causes, and it soon extended to America where the politicians found it useful as a means of increasing their strength among the Irish people. At that time there were in the United States many hundreds of thousands of men who had recently been disbanded from the army at the close of the civil war, and who were only too ready to embrace any new opportunity of winning for themselves fame and rank on other fields of glory. Among these disbanded soldiers were many Irishmen, and it soon came to be known that bands of men could be collected in the United States for the invasion of this country with the avowed object o driving the British flag from this continent and substituting the stars and stripes. It was impossible that the people of Canada could view without emotion these preparations for their undoing, and in New Brunswick especially, which was the first Province to be threatened, the Fenian movement materially assisted in deciding the manner in which our people should vote on the great question of Confederation when it came a second time to be submitted to them.

The House of Assembly met on the 8th March, 1866, and the speech from the throne, delivered by the Lieutenant Governor, contained the following paragraph :—" I have received Her Majesty's commands to communicate to you a correspondence on the affairs of British North America which has taken place between Her Majesty's principal Secretary of State for the Colonies and the Governor General of Canada; and I am further directed to express to you the strong and deliberate opinion of Her Majesty's government that it is an object much to be desired that all the British North American Colonies should agree to unite in one government. These papers will immediately be laid before you." This paragraph was not inserted in the speech without considerable pressure on the part of the Lieutenant Governor, and it excited a great deal of comment at the time because it seemed to indorse the principle of Confederation, although emanating from a government which had been placed in power as the result of an election in which Confederation had been condemned. When this portion of the speech was read by the Lieutenant Governor in the Legislative Council Chamber the crowd outside the bar gave a hearty cheer, a circumstance which never occurred before in the Province of New Brunswick, and perhaps not in any other British Colony.

The members of the House favorable to Confederation immediately took up the matter and dealt with it as if the government had thereby pledged themselves in favor of that policy, and indeed there was considerable excuse for such inferences. When the secret history of the negotiations between the Lieutenant Governor and his advisers, prior to the meeting of the Legislature, comes to be told, it will be found that at least some of the members of the government had given His Excellency to understand that they were prepared to reverse their former action and to adopt Confederation. The difficulty, however, with them was that they feared their own supporters, and thought that if they made such a movement they would lose the favor of those who had placed them in power, and this inference was certainly a very natural one.

As soon as the House met it was discovered that Mr. A. R. Wetmore, one of the prominent supporters of the government who had been elected to represent the City of St. John as an anti-Confederate, was no longer in sympathy with them. Mr. Wetmore's long experience as a *nisi prius* lawyer and his curt and imperturbable manner, rendered him a most exasperating and troublesome opponent, and at a very early period of the session he commenced to make it unpleasant for his former friends. He cross-examined the members of the Government in the same fashion which he had learned from long experience in the courts. Such attacks proved extremely damaging as well as very annoying.

The address in reply to the speech from the throne was moved in the House of Assembly by Colonel Boyd, of Charlotte County, and when the paragraph relating to Confederation was read, Mr. Fisher asked him what it meant. Mr. Boyd replied that the Government had no objection to Confederation provided the terms were satisfactory. This reply still further strengthened the feeling that the Government were inclined to pass the measure which they had been elected to oppose. Mr. Fisher moved an amendment to the fourth paragraph of the address which

T

referred to the Fenian conspiracy against British North America, expressing the opinion that while His Excellency might rely with confidence on the cordial support of the people for the protection of the country, his constitutional advisers were not by their general conduct entitled to the confidence of the Legislature. This amendment was seconded by Mr. DesBrisay of Kent, who had been a supporter of the Government and it was debated at great length. The discussion upon it continued from day to day for about three weeks, when on the 9th of April the Government resigned in consequence of difficulties with His Excellency in regard to his reply to the address of the Legislative Council. The Legislative Council had gone on and passed the address in reply to the speech, but in consequence of the delay in the House of Assembly, this reply had not before been presented to the Governor. In answer to the address of the Legislative Council which was presented to him on the same day that the resignation of the Government took place, His Execllency said: "I will immediately transmit your address to the Secretary of State for the Colonies, in order that it may be laid at the foot of the Throne. Her Majesty the Queen has already been pleased to express deep interest in a close union of her North America colonies and will no doubt greatly appreciate this decided expression of your opinion and the avowal of your desire that all British North America should unite in one community, in one strong and efficient government, cannot but tend to hasten the accomplishment of this great measure."

The resignation of the Government was announced in the House of Assembly on the thirteenth of April, 1866, by Hon. A. J. Smith, and the following the documents were placed before that body, and are here reproduced because they explain fully the causes which led to the resignation of the government :

To His Excellency the Hon. Arthur Hamilton Gordon, C. M. G., Lieutenant Governor and Commander in Chief of the Province of New Brunswick, etc., etc., etc.

The Executive Council in Committee beg to acknowledge the receipt of Your Excellency's memorandum of the 7th inst., and the reply therein referred to, which are as follows:

His Excellency the Lieutenant Governor transmits to his Council a copy of the reply which he has this afternoon returned to an address of the Legislative Council requesting His Excellency to transmit to Her Majesty an address praying that Her Majesty will be pleased to cause a measure for the union of the British North American Provinces to be introduced into the Imperial Parliament.

(Signed),

Arthur H. Gordon.

Frederictou, April 7th., 1866.

Mr. President and Honorable Gentlemen of the Legislative Council :

I will immediately transmit your address to the Secretary of State for the Colonies, in order that it may be laid at the foot of the Throne. Her Majesty the Queen has already been pleased to express a deep interest in the union of her North American Dominions, and will no doubt graciously appreciate this decided expression of your opinion. I rejoice to believe that the avowal of your desire that all British North America should unite in one community, under one strong and efficient government, cannot but tend to hasten the accomplishment of this great measure.

The Council would subjoin a copy of the address referred to in the above.

"TO THE QUEEN'S MOST GRACIOUS MAJESTY :

"MOST GRACIOUS SOVEREIGN,—We, Your Majesty's faithful and
loyal subjects, the Legislative Council of New Brunswick, in
Provincial Parliament assembled, humbly approach Your Majesty with the conviction that a union of all Your Majesty's
North American Colonies, based on the resolutions adopted at
the conference of delegates from the several colonies had at
Quebec on the 10th day of October, 1864, is an object highly to be
desired, essential to their future prosperity and influence, and
calculated alike to strengthen and perpetuate the ties which bind
them to Your Gracious Majesty's Throne and Government, and
humbly pray that Your Majesty may be graciously pleased to
cause a measure to be submitted to the Imperial Parliament for
the purpose of thus uniting the colonies of Canada, Nova Scotia,
New Brunswick, Newfoundland and Prince Edward Island in
one government."

The Council in reply would respectfully remark that in their
opinion it was incumbent upon Your Excellency to consult your
constitutional advisers in regard to the answers so given, and in
assuming to yourself the right to reply to such address without
consulting them, Your Excellency has not acted in accordance
with the true spirit of the constitution.

In this connection the Council would beg to refer to the statement appended herewith, giving an account of the two interviews
between Your Excellency and the Attorney General. The reply
so given by Your Excellency to the Legislative Council is a distinct and emphatic approval of their proceedings, the responsibility of which your advisers are unwilling to assume for the
following reasons :

1st.   That in any measure involving an organic change in the
constitution and political rights and privileges of the people, they
should be consulted, and unless approved of by them, no such
measure should be adopted or forced upon them.

2nd.   That in March last a dissolution took place, professedly
with a view to ascertain the sense of the people upon the Quebec
scheme, and they pronounced unmistakably against its adoption
by large majorities.

3rd. That the representation of the people at the last session of the Legislature passed resolutions condemnatory of such scheme by a majority of 29 to 10.

4th. That the Legislative Council are not elected by the people and are not constitutionally responsible to them for their legislative conduct and have no rightful authority to pray Her Majesty to give effect by Imperial legislation to any measure which the people have rejected.

5th. That such proceeding violates every principle of responsibility and self government, and is subversive of the rights and liberties of the people, and seeks to take from them their constitution not only without their consent, but against their clearly expressed wishes.

6th. That such a course is calculated to bring the Legislative Council and House of Assembly into collision and disturb the harmony that should subsist between them, and manifests an entire disregard of the power and majesty of the people.

That the Legislative Council have a legitimate right to express their opinion upon any public question the Council do not deny, but to invoke the aid of the British Government to coerce the people into Confederation is a proceeding, in the opinion of this Council, without parallel and wholly unwarrantable. The Council would further remark that they have good cause to believe Your Excellency has, ever since the opening of the legislature, consulted and advised with gentlemen of the opposition and made known to them matters which they think should be regarded as confidential. This we feel Your Excellency has continued to do notwithstanding the repeated objections of one or more members of the Council, who told Your Excellency that it was not right and that it gave the opposition a decided advantage in the debate then pending, and Your Excellency having taken the advice, as they truly believe, of a gentleman of the opposition as to the answer given to the Legislative Council on Saturday last, instead of that of your constitutional advisers, they would respectfully express their conviction that such a course was unconstitutional and without precedent in any country where responsible government exists.

The Council would further state that the Government were supported by a majority of the members of the House of Assembly, of which fact Your Excellency was fully aware. Under these circumstances the undersigned would beg respectfully to tender to Your Excellency the resignation of their offices as Executive Councillors.

Respectfully submitted,

> A. J. SMITH,
> B. BOTSFORD,
> JOHN W. CUDLIP,
> GEORGE L. HATHEWAY,
> W. H. ODELL,
> J. V. TROOP.

MEMORANDUM OF CONVERSATION BETWEEN HIS EXCELLENCY AND MR. SMITH.

On Saturday the 7th inst., about 11 o'clock, I called at Government House and had an interview with His Excellency, and in the course of conversation the proceedings of the Legislative Council were referred to, when I spoke in terms of disapproval of the course which they adopted in reference to the subject of union. Something was said about the presentation of the address and His Excellency's reply thereto, when he asked me what answer I would advise. I replied that in my opinion the answer to be given should simply be that he would transmit it to Her Majesty. His Excellency said that he would think of it and see me again. He did not state that he intended to receive them that day and I had not the most distant idea that he intended to do so. I then parted from him. A few minutes before three o'clock of the afternoon of the same day, in my place in the House of Assembly, I received a note from him saying that he wished to see me at once. I immediately repaired to Government House, and after a short conversation with him upon other matters, he informed me that he was going to receive the Legislative Council with their address at three o'clock. I expressed my disapproval of it and complained that he had not advised with his Council before preparing it; that as they were responsible for it they should at least be consulted before it was given. He remarked that if they did not approve of it they could relieve themselves of responsibility. I replied, even if that were true was it courteous and fair that the Council should be treated in that way; that what they asked from His Excellency was fair play, not as a favor, but as a matter of right. He then proposed that I should drive down to the House of Assembly and see my colleagues and return in half an hour and he would keep the Legislative Council, who in the meantime had arrived at Government House, waiting until I returned. I said I could not do this; that the debate of the vote of want of confidence was going on, and that they could not leave the House. He replied, "I suppose not." I further stated that it was unfair and ungenerous, and not such treatment as the Council had a right to expect, to be called upon in this sudden and extraordinary way, in a matter so important. I expressed my condemnation of the course adopted by the Legislative Council and urged the impropriety of their praying Her Majesty, the Queen, to cause a law of the Imperial Parliament to be passed, giving effect to a scheme of union, which both the people and House of Assembly had rejected by overwhelmning majorities, and that I never would consent to any address which authorized the Imperial Parliament to pass an act of union without reference to the people. I thought His Excellency seemed disposed to yield the point and strike out the last paragraph of the answer, which I considered very objectionable. He then asked me to excuse him and left the room to consult—as I thought at the time, and from information received since, I am confirmed in that opinion—a gentleman of the opposition, and a member of the Legislative Council, who was in the house at the time. He returned in a few minutes, and after some conversation similiar to that already detailed, told me that he would deliver the answer as it was, and send me a copy in the evening. I remonstrated against such conduct, but concluded by saying that if he had resolved upon such a course, it was in vain to protract the interview. I then left him.

(Signed),

A. J. Smith.

THE GOVERNOR'S REPLY.

FREDERICTON, April 13th.

The Lieutenant Governor has received from the members of the Executive Council a minute, tendering their resignation of their seats at the Council Board. The reason assigned by them for this step is a disinclination to accept the responsibility of a reply made by His Excellency to the Legislative Council, when requested by that body to transmit to Her Majesty an address, praying that a scheme for the union of the British North American Provinces may be introduced into the Imperial Parliament.

Several causes for this disinclination are enumerated by the Council. They may, however, all be resumed in the objection that the Legislative Council in adopting the address in question over-stepped the limits of action prescribed to it by constitutional principles and usage.

In this view His Excellency cannot at all concur, and he perceives with regret the name of a member of the Upper House, for whose character and abilities he has a sincere respect, appended to reasoning, which would in His Excellency's opinion go far to destroy the position of that chamber as an independent and co-ordinate branch of the legislature.

The papers on which the address in question was founded were laid before both houses of the legislature by Her Majesty's express commands, at the commencement of the present session. It had at that time long been known to Her Majesty's government that the general election in New Brunswick of 1865 had terminated unfavorably to the cause of union, and the communication was made to the Provincial Parliament in the avowed hope that the question might be again considered and more favorably received.

The address in answer to His Excellency's speech at the opening of the session, even as originally proposed, conveyed an assurance that those papers should receive a careful and respectful attention from the Legislative Council; but the chief documents which the members of the body thus pledged themselves to consider, were the resolutions adopted at Quebec, the approval of that scheme by Her Majesty, and the expression of a hope on the part of Her Majesty's government, that its provisions might be favorably considered in New Brunswick.

On the questions thus submitted to them, by Her Majesty's command, the Legislative Council were bound to inform and to express an opinion. In so doing they have intimated their approval of a union of the British North American colonies and indicated the basis on which it might, in their opinion, be accomplished.

It is neither constitutional to maintain that the Legislative Council is incompetent to act with reference to a scheme thus submitted to them until after its previous approval by the House of Assembly, nor can it be imagined that the Legislative Council alone is debarred from that right of appeal which is accorded to all Her Majesty's subjects without distinction.

The Council also take exception to His Excellency's having delivered this reply without previously communicating to them the terms in which it was couched. Without inquiring how far their ministerial responsibility (from which it is always in their power to escape) requires that the Council should possess a previous knowledge of all the Lieutenant Governor's words and actions, His Excellency must observe that the non-communication to the Council of the reply in question was the result, not of design, but of accident, and that it was his intention and desire to have afforded his Council a sufficient opportunity for its consideration. The language employed by His Excellency to the Legislative Council was not, however, inconsistent with the policy the Council had informed him they were inclined to follow, or in his judgment with the reply which with the knowledge and consent of his Council he had returned a few days previously to an address from the same body. His words were that he "Rejoiced to believe that the avowal of your desire that all British North America should unite in one community under one strong and efficient government cannot but tend to hasten the accomplishment of this great measure." This by no means conveys an approval of the particular scheme, to the provisions of which his Council made objection, although it does express a hope that a union of the British North American Provinces might shortly be accomplished. But from previous communications with the leader of the government His Excellency was fully entitled to assume that this hope was shared by his Council.

On the eighth of January His Excellency received from the Hon. R. D. Wilmot a letter tendering the resignation of his seat in the Executive Council, and assigning as his chief reason for doing so the indisposition of his colleagues to entertain propositions for a closer union of the British North American Provinces. To that resignation His Excellency declined to reply until after the return of the President of the Council from Washington, which took place on the 1st of February. On the following day His Excellency had several communications with that gentleman. His Excellency observed that the resignation of Mr. Wilmot and the fact that the legislature had now been summoned for dispatch of business rendered it necessary that a distinct understanding on the subject of union should be arrived at between His Excellency and his advisers. It would be His Excellency's duty in accordance with the instructions to submit the question again to the Legislature on its assembling, and to express the conviction of Her Majesty's government with respect to the benefits likely to attend the measure. If Mr. Wilmot was mistaken in supposing that the government had rejected all measures of union, and Mr. Smith and his colleagues were prepared to consent to the introduction into the speech at the opening of the session of the recommendation of Her Majesty's government conveyed in Mr. Cardswell's despatch of the 24th July, 1865, it would have been His Excellency's duty to accept the proffered resignation so tendered, and whether His Excellency would not be bound to enquire whether Mr. Wilmot was prepared to undertake the responsibility of recommending to the people the adoption of a measure which was in the opinion of Her Majesty's government calculated to confer benefits on Her Majesty's subjects in this Province, and the accomplishment of which I was directed by every means in my power to promote. The Lieutenant Governor also endeavored to the best of his ability to point out to Mr. Smith the advantages of a union of the British American Provinces and the urgent necessity under existing circumstances for effecting such a measure. His Excellency stated his confident belief that if, after being accepted as a basis, it were found that the details of the scheme agreed to at Quebec were open to just and serious objections on the part of the Maritime Provinces, the representation of their legislatures to that effect would be certain to receive a respectful attention from Her Majesty's government and from that of Canada. His Excellency concluded by handing to Mr. Smith the following Memorandum :

CONFIDENTIAL MEMORANDUM.

The Lieutenant Governor has been instructed by a despatch from the Secretary of State for the colonies, bearing date July 24th, 1865, to express to the legislature of New Brunswick on its next re-assembling, "The strong and deliberate opinion of Her Majesty's government that it is an object much to be desired that all the British North American colonies should agree to unite in one government."

The Lieutenant Governor has now fixed the 8th proximo as the day upon which the general assembly is to meet for business, and before that period it is highly desirable that he should be informed whether his advisers are prepared to recommend the legislature to give effect to the opinion thus expressed by Her Majesty's government.

(Signed),

A. GORDON.

Fredericton, February, 1866.

This memorandum in compliance with Her Majesty's urgent request was not formally transmitted to the Council, but it was carefully read by him, and its substance communicated to his colleagues.

Mr. Smith must have preceived, although His Excellency abstains from any expression calculated to wound the susceptibility of the Council, that had that memorandum received a negative response, His Excellency was prepared to decline to accede to the recommendation that Mr. Wilmot's resignation should be accepted, and to entrust to that gentleman the responsibility of attempting to carry into effect the policy, on account of his adherence to which he desired to quit the government.

After several communications with the members of the Council, Mr. Smith ultimately informed His Excellency that whilst unable to accept in its integrity the scheme adopted at Quebec, he and his colleagues were not indisposed to meet the wishes of Her Majesty's government, and that it appeared to him that the requisite sanction for the adoption of such a course might be obtained if the message transmitting the papers on that subject to the legislature, were referred to a joint committee of both houses, with an understanding that that committee should report in favor of a measure of union.

His Excellency replied that he had no objection to such a course, provided it was already understood beforehand, but that reference was to be made only with a view of rendering it easier for the government to adopt a course which they had themselves in any case resolved to pursue, and with no intention to cast upon the committee the duty of finding a policy for the government, for that a reference of such a description, besides involving an abdication of their proper functions as a government, would cause much delay, and might after all terminate in a report unfavorable to union, in which case it was needless to point out to him, that so far from any progress having been made in the desired direction, the position of the cause would have been materially injured.   Mr. Smith answered that he could not beforehand formally pledge a committee of the legislature, but that in making himself responsible for the recommendation of such a course, it would be with the view of honestly carrying out the policy so indicated. The committee having reported, the next step to be taken appeared to His Excellency to be the introduction by the government of an address to the Queen, praying Her Majesty to take steps for the accomplishment of the union, and His Excellency drew out the rough outline for such an address, similar in substance to that adopted by the Canadian Parliament, but adding a representation that portions of the scheme agreed to at Quebec were received with apprehension and alarm by a great part of the people of this and the adjoining Provinces, and a prayer that Her Majesty would be pleased in the preparation of any Imperial act to effect the desired union, to give just weight to the objections urged against such provision on their behalf, to which proposal His Excellency understood Mr. Smith to assent, and his impression to that effect is confirmed by finding it so stated in a note made at the time and read by His Excellency a few days subsequently to Mr. Smith, and in the despatches based on these notes, addressed by His Excellency to the Secretary of State for the Colonies. Mr. Smith has lately, however, assured His Excellency that he only meant that such an address might grow out of the committee, but he did not intend to pledge himself in the first instance to propose it.

A controversy in respect to the words used in conversation and the meaning intended to be conveyed by them is seldom capable of satisfactory settlement, and it is not His Excellency's intention to discuss the greater accuracy of Mr. Smith's memory or his own. Whatever the precise nature of the course agreed to on the 17th February was, it was one to which it was felt that it would be more difficult to reconcile the friends and supporters of the government than its actual members, and Mr. Smith left Fredericton in order to prepare all his principal adherents for the altered policy he professed to pursue, asking His Excellency to observe the strictest secrecy on the subject until his return to report either the acquiesence of his friends or the failure of his efforts. Mr. Smith on his return informed His Excellency on the 2nd of March that his party generally were willing to assent to the course which he had consented to pursue. It was accordingly agreed to insert in the speech on the opening of the session the recommendation of Confederation made by Her Majesty's government, as early as possible, to move the appointment of such a joint committee of both houses of the legislature as should ensure the adoption of the scheme of union, whilst the objections to the Quebec scheme should be carefully weighed and examined at the same time by the committee.

What the precise alterations in that scheme were which would have satisfied Mr. Smith, His Excellency was never able exactly to learn, but he found that representation according to population, to which he entertained a strong objection, would not be regarded by him as an insuperable obstacle to union, should a larger share of representation be secured to New Brunswick in the upper branch of the proposed Federal legislature. His Excellency considering that the speedy accomplishment of a measure of union was now a matter of absolute certainty, addressed to Mr. Smith on the 7th of March, a letter of which the following is an extract:

"I have been much gratified, though not surprised to find that you are disposed to approach the question of union as it now presents itself in a large and statesman like spirit, and to realize as facts the necessities which are imposed by the actual condition of affairs. There is nothing which more distinguishes a statesman from a man incompetent to deal with great affairs than this power of appreciating the changes, the mode and the obligation, often a most irksome one, of acquiesing in a course which he considers open to objection, in order to prevent evils of yet greater magnitude.

"You have it in your power to render the Province the inestimable service of depriving its accession to the principle of union of that character of a party triumph, which it must otherwise wear, and of those feelings of bitterness which such a triumph would engender."

Mr. Smith did not deny the assumption which this letter contains and verbally acknowledged the terms in which he was therein spoken of.

Having thus, therefore, as he presumed, ascertained that his Council were not indisposed in their own way, and at their own time, to recommend to the legislature the adoption of a union policy, His Excellency felt that much forbearance was requisite in order that this change of course might be accomplished in the manner which the Council might think least injurious to themselves and most calculated to ensure the ultimate success of the measure, and with this view, he sought to secure the co-operation of some of the leading friends of Confederation ordinarily hostile to the government. In doing so it was His Excellency's desire to strengthen the hands of his administration in the conducting of a difficult enterprise, believing it to be of the highest importance that this measure should not be carried as a mere party triumph, but as the expression of a national wish ; nor did he suppose that the course he then took could so be misunderstood by those in whose interests it was taken. It is true that Mr. Smith, and on one occasion one other member of the government, remonstrated against this course, and Mr. Smith observed that it was unnecessary, as he felt that he could carry out his plan without any assistance from political opponents, an assertion the correctness of which His Excellency at that time felt disposed to question, and which, even if accurate, appeared to him of doubtful policy, as it was desirable the union should be accomplished in virtue of as general an agreement as possible among the leading men of every political section in the community, and His Excellency more than once suggested that the principal advocates of Confederation should be called upon to meet Mr. Smith and his collegues in order that a line of action might be adopted by common consent on a question of such general importance and with regard to which, now that the government had adopted the principle of union, it seemed difficult to believe that a common understanding might not be reached.

Upon the distinct understanding, therefore, that the government was endeavoring to procure the passage through the legislature of resolutions affirmative of the principle of union, and with the impression that an address praying Her Majesty to move the resolutions was to be subsequently adopted, His Excellency felt justified in omitting, at the request of the Council, from his speech at the opening of the session the strong recommendation of union which he intended to introduce, but the responsibility for which his ministers felt they could not so suddenly assume. To what extent the other members of the Executive Council agreed with their president His Excellency cannot say, as, except on a few occasions in February, he had little communication with any of them on the subject, but His Excellency is convinced that when Mr. Smith returned to Fredericton on the 5th of March he imagined that he would be able to carry out the pledges he had given and that he fully intended to do so. Since the commencement of the session, however, the course of the government has shown little indication of a movement in this direction.

His Excellency has never ceased to urge on Mr. Smith the expediency and even the necessity of a bold avowal of his intended policy, nor has he failed to express his apprehension as to the consequence of delay in doing so, believing that until that avowal was made Mr. Smith would become daily more and more entangled in contradictory pledges, from which he would find it impossible to extricate himself, and which might act most prejudicially on the prospects of the cause, whilst at any time circumstances might call for such action on the part of His Excellency as would place him in a position of apparent antagonism to the Council and prove productive of very serious embarrassment. This course, however, the government did not pursue, and it became more and more clearly apparent to His Excellency that they lacked the power—he will not say they lacked the will —to carry out their original intention. Their hostility to the particular form of union agreed to at Quebec was distinct and emphatic, whilst their approval of even an abstract union of an indefinite character became daily more vague and uncertain. Declarations were publicly made that no proposition for a union would be made during the present session, and arguments were used by members of the government and their supporters which were not only unfavorable to the Quebec scheme but equally directed against any plan of whatever description for a closer union with Canada. On more than one occasion His Excellency noticed these facts to Mr. Smith, who replied that the reports received by His Excellency as to the language used were inaccurate, that it was desirable not to indicate too soon the line he meant to take, as it would give an advantage to his opponents and might estrange some of his friends. In the desire to avoid giving cause of embarrassment to the government, and at their request, His Excellency delayed for nineteen days the reception of the address of the Legislative Council in reply to the speech from the throne, nor was it until it became evident to His Excellency that further delay in this respect would seriously imperil the harmony of the relation between himself and the Legislative Council and House of Assembly that he fixed a day for its reception. Mr. Smith frequently expressed a hope that the Lieutenant Governor did not entertain any doubt as to the honesty of his intention of carrying out to the letter the understanding between them as to the passage of resolutions on the subject of union. At length the presentation of the address to the Queen by the Legislative Council brought the question to a decided issue. Up to that time the government had given no public sign of an intention to grapple with the question or to substitute any amended scheme of union for that adopted at Quebec, and the Lieutenant Governor, in accordance with his instructions as the representative of the Queen and as an officer of the Imperial Government, could not but feel it his duty to express satisfaction at the approval by one branch of the Provincial Legislature of the policy, the adoption of which had been recommended by him in his Sovereign's name and by her command at the commencement of the session.

If the Lieutenant Governor's advisers cannot concur in these sentiments, and decline to become responsible for their utterance by His Excellency, it is no doubt their duty to tender, as they have done, the resignation of the offices held by them. His Excellency accepts those resignations with regret. His relations with his advisers during the past year have been harmonious and cordial ; for many among their number he entertains strong feelings of personal esteem ; nor can he forget to acknowledge the attention which his views have generally received at their hands, or the readiness with which his wishes have on most occasions been met by them, but he has no doubt as to the course which it is his duty to pursue in obedience to his Sovereign's commands and in the interests of the people of British North America. His Excellency may be in error, but he believes that a vast change has already taken place in the opinions held on the subject in New Brunswick. He fully anticipates that the House of Assembly will yet return a response to the communication made to them, not less favorable to the principle of union than that given by the upper house, and in any event he relies with confidence on the desire of a great majority of the people of the Province to aid in building up a powerful and prosperous nation under the Sovereignity of the British Crown. To this verdict His Excellency is perfectly ready to appeal.

His Excellency thinks it right, also, to state that his reply was prepared by himself alone, and that the Council are in error in supposing that its terms were the subject of advice from any member of the opposition. His Excellency does not admit the entire accuracy of Mr. Smith's reports of his conversation with him appended to the minute of Council, but at the same time readily acknowledges that the difference between his own impression of these conversations and that of Mr. Smith, is only such as might naturally arise under the circumstances. Mr. Smith has, however, omitted to state that at his first interview His Excellency pointed out, as he had frequently done before, the embarrassing results of the non-avowal of his union policy, and observed that the Legislative Council had now passed an address, at the adoption of which he would probably feel obliged to express satisfaction.

U

This is a matter of infinitely less importance to the public, and will be very shortly dealt with by His Excellency. Although His Excellency has met at all times with the utmost courtesy and consideration from the members of his government, it would be a source of sincere regret to him to believe that he was justly liable to any imputation of such a nature. That a leading member of the opposition was more than once communicated with by His Excellency is perfectly true. This communication was made with Mr. Smith's full knowledge, and in the belief on His Excellency's part that it would facilitate Mr. Smith's accomplishment of the end in view. Nor was it until a very late period that his Excellency relinquished the hope of seeing a combination effected to smooth the passage of the contemplated resolutions.

The Lieutenant Governor of course feels that previous communications between himself and his advisers, as to any step he is about to take, when practicable, both desirable and convenient, and it was His Excellency's full intention to have afforded the Council ample opportunity for the consideration of his reply, and he much regrets that accident should have frustrated his intention. The committee of the Legislative Council did not wait on His Excellency till about 12 o'clock, and until that address was before him he could not officially communicate with the Council on the subject of his reply. Immediately on its reception he sent for Mr. Smith, intending to put the draft reply into his hands and request him to communicate it to his colleagues. Mr. Smith, however, appears not to have received His Excellency's note until half past two o'clock. So strong was His Excellency's wish that the contents of his reply should be known to the Council before its delivery, that when His Excellency left the room, as stated by Mr. Smith, it was not as that gentleman supposes to consult with a member of the opposition respecting the omission or retention of a paragraph in his reply, a point on which His Excellency received no advice from any other person than Mr. Smith, but for the purpose of ascertaining whether it might not even then be possible to postpone the reception of the address for a few hours. He found, however, that it would have been impossible to do so without gross discourtsey to the Legislative Council.

[Signed]   ARTHUR GORDON.

Fredericton, April 12, 1866.

The Lieutenant Governor called upon the Hon. Peter Mitchell, who was a member of the Legislative Council, to form a government. Mr. Mitchell had been very active in the cause of Confederation, and was the moving spirit in the Legislative Council in all the proceedings in favor of Confederation in that body; but when asked to form a new government, he advised the Lieutenant Governor that the proper person to undertake that responsibility was the Hon. Mr. Tilley. The latter, however, declined the task on the ground that he was not a member of the Legislature, and then Mr. Mitchell associated with himself the Hon. Mr. Wilmot for the purpose of forming a new government. The government was announced on the 18th of April, and it was formed as follows :—Hon. Peter Mitchell, President of Council; Hon. S. L. Tilley, Provincial Secretary; Hon. Charles Fisher, Attorney General; Hon. Edward Williston, Solicitor General; Hon. John McMillan, Post Master General; Hon. A. R. Mc-Clelan, Chief Commissioner of Public Works; Hon. R. D. Wilmot and Hon. Charles Connell, members without office. The latter afterwards became Surveyor General.

While this government was being formed in New Brunswick a Fenian army was gathering upon the border for the purpose of invading this Province. This force consisted of four or five hundred young men, most of whom had been in the army of the United States. It was recruited at New York, and its chief was a Fenian named Doram Killian. A part of his force arrived at Eastport on the 10th of April, and a schooner laden with arms for the Fenians soon after reached that place. From this schooner, which was afterwards seized by the United States, one hundred and seventeen cases of arms and ammunition were taken, a clear proof that the intentions of the Fenians were warlike and that their presence on the border was not a mere demonstration. The Fenians appeared to have been under the impression, as many residents of the United States are to this day, that the people of Canada and of New Brunswick were dissatisfied with their own form of government, and were anxious to come under the protection of the stars and stripes. This absurd idea was responsible largely for the war of 1812, and it has been responsible since then for many other demonstrations with respect to the British Provinces of North America, in which residents of the United States have taken part. There never was a greater delusion than this, and in the instance referred to the Fenians were doomed to be speedily undeceived. The presence of a Fenian force on the border sounded like a bugle blast to every able-bodied man in New Brunswick, and the call for troops to defend the country was instantly responded to. About one thousand men were called out and marched to the frontier. The troops called out consisted of the three Battalions of the New Brunswick Regiment of Artillery, seven companies of the St. John Volunteer Battalion, one company of the First Battalion of the York County Militia, one company each of the First and Third Battalions of the Charlotte County Militia, and two companies each of the Second and Fourth

Battalions of the Charlotte County Militia. These troops remained in arms on the frontier for nearly three months, and were disembodied by general order dated the 20th of June. The Fenian raid on New Brunswick proved to be a complete fiasco. The frontier was so well guarded by the New Brunswick Militia and by British soldiers, and the St. Croix so thoroughly patroled by British warships that the Fenians had no opportunity to make any impression upon the Province. It ought to be added that the United States government was prompt to take steps to prevent any armed invasion, and General Meade was sent down to Eastport with a force of infantry and a ship of war to prevent the Fenians from making that place a base of operations against these Provinces.

The general elections to decide whether or not New Brunswick was willing to become confederated with Canada were held in May and June. The first election was that for the County of Northumberland, on the 25th of May, and the result was that the four candidates who favored Confederation, Messrs. Johnson, Sutton, Kerr and Williston, were elected by large majorities. The same result followed in the County of Carleton, where the election was held on the 26th of May, Messrs. Connell and Lindsay being elected by a vote of more than two to one over their anti-Confederate opponents. The third election was in Albert County on the 29th, and there Messrs. McClelan and Lewis, the two candidates in favor of Confederation, were triumphantly returned. On the 13th day of May, elections were held in Restigouche and Sunbury,

and in these counties the candidates in favor of Confederation were returned by large majorities. The York
election came next. In that county the anti-Confederates
had placed a full ticket in the field, the candidates being
Messrs. Hatheway, Fraser, Needham and Brown. Mr.
Fisher had with him on the ticket Dr. Dow and Messrs.
Thompson and John A. Beckwith. Every person expected a vigorous contest in York, notwithstanding the
victory of Mr. Fisher over Mr. Pickard a few months before. But to the amazement of the anti-Confederates in
other parts of the Provinces, the Hon. George L.
Hatheway and Dr. Brown, another anti-Confederate candidate, retired after nomination day and
left Messrs. Fraser and Needham to do battle alone.
Mr. Hatheway's retirement at this time was a death
blow to the hopes of the anti-Confederates all over
New Brunswick, affecting not only the result in the
County of York, but in every other County in which an
election was to be held. A few nights before his resignation, Mr. Hatheway had been in St. John, addressing a
packed meeting of anti-Confederates in the hall of the
Mechanics' Institute, and he had spoken on that occasion
with all the insolence and apparent confidence which
were a part of his political stock in trade. When his
friends in St. John, who had been so much moved by his
vigorous eloquence, learned that he had deserted them,
their indignation was extreme, and they felt that matters
must indeed be in a bad way when this blatant and un-
principled demagogue did not dare to face the York

electors. The result was that in York, Messrs. Fraser and Needham were simply snowed under, and the Confederate candidates elected by a vote of more than two to one. The election in the County of St. John was held on the 6th of June and that in the City on the 7th. For the County the Confederate candidates were Messrs. C. N. Skinner, John H. Gray, James Quinton and R. D. Wilmot, and the anti-Confederate candidates were Messrs. Coram, Cudlip, Robertson and Anglin. The former were elected by very large majorities, Mr. Wilmot who stood lowest on the poll among the Confederates, having a majority of 600 over Mr. Coram, who stood highest among the defeated candidates. The election for the City was an equally emphatic declaration in favor of Confederation. The candidates were the Hon. S. L. Tilley and A. R. Wetmore on the Confederate side, and J. V. Troop and S. R. Thompson opposed to Confederation. Mr. Tilley's majority over Mr. Troop, who stood highest on the poll of the two defeated candidates, was 726. The only Counties which the anti-Confederate party succeeded in carrying were Westmorland, Gloucester and Kent, three counties in which the French vote was very large, so that of the forty-one members returned only eight were opponents of Confederation. The victory was as complete as that which had been recorded against Confederation in the beginning of 1865.

The battle of Confederation had been won, and the triumph was largely due to the efforts of Hon. Mr. Tilley. That gentlemen, as soon as the defeat of Confederation took place in March, 1865, had commenced a campaign for the purpose of educating the people on the subject of Confederation. Being free from his official duties and having plenty of time on his hands, he was able to devote himself to the work of explaining the advantages of the proposed union to the people of this Province ; and during the years 1865 and 1866 he spoke in almost every county on the subject which was so near to his heart. He had embraced Confederation with a sincere desire for the benefit of his native Province, and with the belief that it would be of the greatest advantage to New Brunswick. If the fruits of Confederation have not yet all been realized that has been rather due to circumstances over which neither Mr. Tilley nor anyone else had any control, than to any inherent vice of Confederation itself. If union is strength then it must be admitted that the union of the British North American Provinces which consolidated them into a powerful whole was a good thing, and there cannot be a doubt that if the Provinces had remained separate from each other their present position would have been much less favorable than it is now.

One of the great objects of Confederation was the construction of the Intercolonial Railway from St. John and Halifax to Quebec. It was thought by our people that there could be no real union between the several Colonies of British North America unless a good means of communication existed, and such a means was to be found only in the construction of this line of railway. The In-

tercolonial railway, as we have seen, had been a part of the
policy of successive governments in the Province for many
years, and it became an essential part of the scheme of
Confederation. When Confederation was accepted by the
people of New Brunswick in 1866, the Intercolonial Railroad had yet to be built. Western Extension, as the line
to the Maine border was called, had only been commenced;
Eastern extension, from Shediac line towards Halifax,
was in the same condition; in fact the total mileage of
the railways in New Brunswick did not exceed 200, and
these lines were isolated from each other and formed no
part of any complete system. New Brunswick now has
three separate lines of railway leading to Quebec and Montreal; it is connected with the great railway system of this
continent; there is no county in the Province which has
not a line of railway traversing it; and the mileage has
risen from less than two hundred to more than fourteen
hundred. If Confederation had produced no other fruits
than the increase of our railway facilities surely it must
be admitted to have been useful to this Province. Mr.
Tilley realized with the eyes of a statesman that the time
had come when the communities which form the British
Provinces of North America must either become politically connected with each other or else fall one by one beneath the influence of the United States. After Confederation had been brought about between Quebec, Ontario,
New Brunswick and Nova Scotia, enough was seen in
the conduct of American statesmen towards Prince Edward Island to show that their design was to divide and

conquer, and to try to create a separate interest in these
colonies apart from the general interest of Canada.   The
acceptance of the scheme of Confederation by Prince Edward Island at a comparatively early period, put an end to
the plots in that quarter, but in the case of Newfoundland
the same thing has been repeated, and an attempt was
made by American statesmen to cause the people of that
Island to believe that their interests and those of Canada
are not identical, and that they would be favored by the
United States if they showed themselves hostile to the
great Dominion.   The attitude of the people and Congress
of the United States towards Canada has generally been
one of hostility.   They saw in Confederation an arrangement that was likely to prevent this country from
ever becoming annexed to their own, and they believed
that by showing hostility to us with respect to the tariff
and other matters, and limiting the area of our commercial
relations, they could put such pressure upon Canada as
would compel our people to unite with them.   This
scheme has failed because it was based on a mis-
conception of the spirit of our people, but who will say
that it would not have succeeded if the several
Provinces, which now form Confederation had been
disunited and unharmonious in their relations and pursued different lines of policy ?

It is unfortunate that the reporting arrangements of
the newspapers during the campaign of Confederation
have made it impossible to reproduce any of Mr. Tilley's
speeches during that eventful time.   No Speaker that

New Brunswick has ever produced has been more generally acceptable than was Mr. Tilley, his speeches being pointed and addressing themselves to his hearers in such a clear fashion that they really could not be misunderstood. Mr. Tilley possessed to a very large extent that magnetism which enabled him to retain the attention and awaken the sympathy of his audiences. At all the meetings which he addressed there were many who regarded themselves always as his friends and supporters and who formed a phalanx around him, giving him a confidence and political strength which few statesmen have ever enjoyed to a like extent. Although his addresses frequently provoked the bitter animosity of his enemies he had always enough friends to counteract their influence, and during the many contests which he had to fight for his seat in the city of St. John he was always able to rely on the loyalty of those who were his early associates and who remained his supporters until the end of his career.

It is quite safe to assert that Confederation could not have been carried out had it not been for the personal efforts of Mr. Tilley. As the leader of the government, which had consented to the Quebec scheme, he was properly looked upon as the chief promoter of Confederation in New Brunswick, and his name will go down to future generations identified with that large and necessary measure of Colonial statesmanship.

After the elections were over and Confederation had been carried, the "Morning Telegraph" of St. John, which had been an ardent supporter of the scheme, made up a statement which showed that 55,665 votes had been cast throughout the Province for candidates in favor of Confederation, while only 33,767 votes had been cast against it. That was a sufficiently emphatic endorsement of the scheme of union, and it was accepted as a proof that the people of New Brunswick ardently desired the constitutional change which a union with Canada would involve. But although the vote had been taken on the question, much remained to be done before Confederation could become an accomplished fact. The last elections, which were those of Kings and Charlotte, were held on the 12th of June, but more than a year was to elapse before the union was effected and the result which the election was intended to bring about realized. The first thing to be done was to call the Legislature together and complete the business of the Province, which had been interrupted by the dissolution. The Legislature met on the 21st of June and the Hon. John H. Gray, who had been an active advocate of Confederation, and who was one of the members for the County of St. John, was made speaker. In the speech from the throne the following reference was made to the question of Confederation:

"The address of the Legislative Council to Her Majesty the Queen, on the subject of the union of the British North American Provinces, agreed to during the late session, was duly transmitted by me to England to be laid at the foot of the throne, and I am commanded to inform you, Her Majesty has been pleased to accept the same very graciously. The adoption and the reception by me for transmission to Her Majesty of this address led to events which rendered it, in my opinion, expedient to dissolve the then existing General Assembly. I have now much satisfaction in resorting to your assistance and cooperation at the earliest possible moment, although I regret that it should be necessary to call you together at a period of the year which must, I fear, render your assembling a matter of much personal inconvenience to some of you.

"Her Majesty's government have already expressed their strong and deliberate opinions that the union of the British North American Provinces under one government is an object much to be desired. The Legislatures of Canada and Nova Scotia have formed the same judgment, and you will now shortly be invited to express your concurrence with or dissent from the view taken of this great question by those Provinces.

"The question which you are now called together especially to consider is one of the most momentous ever submitted to a Colonial Legislature."

In the address in answer to the speech from the throne the following reference was made to the question:

"It is satisfactory to learn that the adoption and reception by Your Excellency of the address led to events which rendered it expedient to dissolve the then existing General Assembly and most gratifying to believe that the country has sustained that conclusion, and, although we unite with Your Excellency in regretting that it should have been necessary to call the Assembly together at a season that may cause personal inconvenience to some of us, we rejoice to have the opportunity of aiding by our counsel and co-operation in the consummation of those national objects which have led to our meeting.

"We learn with satisfaction that Her Majesty's government, having already expressed their strong and deliberate conviction that the union of the British Provinces under one government is an object much to be desired, and that the Legislatures of Canada and Nova Scotia having passed the same judgment, we will shortly be called upon to express our concurrence with or dissent from the view taken of this question by those Provinces, and we confidently look forward to a similar decision here."

This address was moved by Mr. Kerr, of Northumberland, and seconded by Mr. Beveridge of Victoria, and its consideration was made the order of the day for the following Saturday. When it came up for discussion the Hon. Albert J. Smith was not in his place, and Mr. Botsford, one of his colleagues from Westmorland, endeavored to have the consideration of the matter postponed, but the House was in no humor to await the convenience of any single member, and the address was passed the same day by a vote of thirty to seven. Mr. Tilley's name was not recorded in this division, because he had to leave for St. John on public business; the other absentees were Messrs. Smith and Skinner. Attorney General Fisher, immediately on the passage of the address, gave notice of the Confederation resolution, which was to be made the order of the day for Monday, June 26th. This resolution was in the following terms :

"*Resolved*, That an humble address be presented to His Excellency, the Lieutenant Governor, praying that His Excellency be pleased to appoint delegates to unite with delegates from the other Provinces, in arranging with the Imperial Government for the union of British North America, upon such terms as will secure the just rights and interests of New Brunswick, accompanied with provision for the immediate construction of the Inter-colonial Railway ; each Province to have an equal voice in such delegation, Upper and Lower Canada to be considered as separate Provinces."

On that day Mr. Fisher moved the resolution in question in a very brief speech, and was replied to by Hon. Mr. Smith, who spoke at great length and continued his speech on the following day. Mr. Smith took exception to giving delegates power to fix the destinies of the Provinces forever, without again submitting the scheme of union to the people. He proceeded to discuss the Quebec scheme, but took exception to the construction of the upper House of the proposed legislature of the Confederation, declaring that each Province should have an equal number of representatives in it, as was the case in the United States. After going over the ground pretty thoroughly and criticising most of the terms of the scheme of Confederation, he moved an amendment to the effect that no act or measure for a union with Canada take

effect until approved by the Legislature or the people of
this Province.

The Hon. Mr. Tilley replied to the leader of
the opposition in one of the most effective speeches
that he ever delivered in the Legislature. He
first took up Mr. Smith's allusion to the constitutional
question, and, with immense .power and solemnity, he
charged that any want of constitutional action which
existed was due to Mr. Smith and his colleagues. He
stated that the Governor's sympathies were with the late
government, and that he had endeavored to aid
and not to injure them. Mr. Smith had alluded to
the Hon. Joseph Howe, who was then an opponent of
Confederation, in terms of praise, and Mr. Tilley in reply
read from Mr. Howe's speech, made in 1861, a magnifi-
cent paragraph on the union of British America. Mr.
Tilley stated that the government would take the Quebec
scheme for a basis, and would seek concessions to meet
the views of those who found difficulty as to parts of it.
He went over the Counties of the Province to show that
they were either for the Quebec scheme or substantially
for it. He was convinced that even his friend, the ex-
Attorney-General and member for Westmorland, was
hardly against union. He asked, Was there one anti-
unionist on the floors of the House ? Where was Mr.
Anglin ? Mr. Needham ? Mr. Hill and all the rest of
the anti-unionists ? They were all swept away and
unionists had taken their places, and when the arrangements for union were carried out, the feeling in its favor

would be deeper and deeper. Mr. Tilley showed the great advantages which would accrue to New Brunswick eventually in consequence of Confederation. He combatted the statement made by Mr. Smith that after Confederation the Provincial Legislature would become a mere farce, showing that of all the Acts passed during the previous two years there were only seven which would have come under the control of the general Legislature. Mr. Tilley closed by dwelling on the impression of power which union would have on the minds of those abroad who were plotting our ruin. The speech was listened to with the utmost attention by the members of the Legislature and by a very large audience, which completely filled the galleries, and it was generally considered to have been one of his greatest efforts.

Quite a sensation was created by the speech delivered by Mr. Charles N. Skinner, one of the members elected for the County of St. John as a supporter of Confederation. Mr. Skinner took the position that the government did wrong in introducing a bald resolution, and showing an unwillingness to take the suggestions of the House as to what kind of a scheme the country wanted. He believed it was the duty of the representatives to deliberate upon this question, and give the delegates instruction as to what they desired. The position taken by the government was that the House had better not say anything about what they or the country wanted, but clothe the delegates with power to do as they pleased irrevocably, and give them no instructions. This he

v

deplored in strong language. The country, he said, had
not elected the men in favor of Confederation to be mere
automatons, to move as they were moved, and to say only
such words as should be put into their mouths. He
thought on a question of such vast importance as this
the fullest deliberation should be had. He would not tie
the delegates down to the letter of their instructions. He
would leave them a margin to go and come upon. He
also complained that the House did not know the number of delegates that were to be sent, neither did they
know who the delegates were to be. He said unless the
men who were going on this mission were men of great
ability and integrity he would lack confidence in them.
There were men in the Legislature and government that
he would trust with this great responsibility, but there
were others whom he would not. He then proceeded to
show that while he was dissatisfied at the manner the
government were pushing the question before the House,
he still would vote for the resolution, because the policy
of the government, although to his mind a wrong policy,
was the only policy before the country on the question
of Confederation, and to vote against the resolution and
with Mr. Smith's amendment was to vote against Confederation altogether. He would vote for the resolution and hold the government responsible for their
conduct in bringing the matter down as they did. He
then proceeded to enlarge upon the Quebec scheme ; he
made several objections to it and reasoned them out. He
said he made the objections that the delegates might know

what his opinions were, and, if they were worth anything, they might profit by them. His speech was said to be the best he ever delivered in the House, and was listened to with marked attention, scarcely a member leaving his seat while he was speaking. The resolution was finally carried by a vote of 30 to 8, Mr. Glazier, of Sunbury, and Mr. W. P. Flewelling, of Kings, both of whom would have voted for the resolution, being absent. As soon as the Confederation resolution was passed the Hon. A. J. Smith moved a resolution which, after reciting the steps which had already been taken in favor of union with Canada, continued as follows:

" *Therefore resolved*, As the deliberate opinion of this House is that no measure for such union should be adopted which did not contain the following provisions, viz. : 1st—An equal number of Legislative councillors for each Province ; 2nd—Such Legislative councillors to be required to reside in the Province which they represent and for which they are appointed ; 3rd—The number of representatives in the Federal Parliament to be limited ; 4th—The establishment of a court for the determination of questions and disputes that may arise between the Federal and Local governments as to the meaning of the act of union ; 5th—Exemption of this Province from taxation for the construction and enlargement of canals in Upper Canada, and for the payment of money for the mines and minerals and lands of Newfoundland ; 6th—Eighty cents per head to be on the population as it increases and not to be confined to the census of 1861 ; 7th—Securing to the Maritime Provinces the right to have at least one executive councillor in the Federal Parliament ; 8th—The commencing of the Intercolonial Railroad before the right shall exist to increase taxation upon the people of the Province."

Mr. Smith supported his resolution in a lengthy speech in which he predicted increased taxation as the result of Confederation. He said that the House, instead of being a deliberative assembly, had to surrender its judgment to the government. Confederation was a great experiment at best and called for the exercise of other men's judgment. The government was going on in the most high-handed manner and were not justified in withholding information asked for. He elaborated the idea that Canada was pledged to issue treasury notes to pay present liabilities, and asserted that the government was altogether under the control of Canadian politicians. He insisted particularly on a provision in the Act of Union that each of the Maritime Provinces have an executive councillor in the Federal government. Finally the vote was taken and the following amendment, which had been moved by Hon. Mr. Fisher, was carried, only eight members voting against it :

" *Resolved*, That the people of this Province having, after due deliberation, determined that the union of British North America was desirable, and the House. having agreed to request His Excellency the Lieutenant Governor to appoint delegates for the purpose of considering the plan of union upon such terms as will secure the just rights of New Brunswick, and having confidence that the action of His Excellency under the advice of his constitutional advisers will be directed to the attainment of that end, sound policy and a due regard to the interests of this Province require that the responsibility of such action should be left unfettered by an expression of opinion other than what has already been given by the people and their representatives."

This ended the battle for Confederation in New Brunswick, for what remained to be done was merely the arrangement of the details of the union by the delegates who had received full power for that purpose. The session of the Legislature, which must be considered one of the most important ever held in New Brunswick, came to a close on Monday, the 7th of July. At a meeting of the government held immediately after the prorogation of the Legislature, the Hon. Messrs. Tilley, Wilmot, Fisher, Mitchell, Johnson and Chandler were appointed to go to England as delegates, for the purpose of meeting delegates from Canada and Nova Scotia, and arranging the bill which was to be passed by the Imperial Parliament for the consummation of Confederation. It was understood at that time that there would be no delay on the part of the delegates from Canada, but owing to causes which perhaps are a little obscure, Sir John A. Macdonald and the other Canadian delegates were unable to leave at the time appointed, and did not meet our delegation in England until many months after the latter had arrived there. This unfortunate circumstance produced much comment at the time, because it looked as if the government of Canada was treating the delegates of New Brunswick and Nova Scotia with gross discourtesy. The business, instead of being completed promptly, as was expected, and the bill passed by the Parliament during the autumn session, was thrown over until the following year, and our delegates, most of whom were prominent members of the government, had to remain in England for about ten months at great expense and inconvenience. It has been stated that the ill health of Sir John A. Macdonald was responsible for that condition of affairs, he being subject at that time to attacks of indisposition which prevented him from attending to his duties as a Minister of the Crown. Whatever the cause of the trouble it was a very unfortunate beginning, and but for the good sense and moderation displayed by the representatives of the Maritime Provinces, might have greatly prejudiced the movement in favor of Confederation.

CHAPTER XI.

The delegates from the three Provinces, Canada, Nova Scotia and New Brunswick, met at the Westminster Palace hotel, London, in November, 1866, Hon. John A. Macdonald in the chair ; C. W. Bernard acting as Secretary. The resolutions passed at the Quebec Conference held in 1864, were read, and amendments were moved in accordance with the suggestions made in the several Legislatures during the discussions at the previous sessions. It was conceded on all hands that the Intercolonial Railway, by which facilities for interprovincial commercial intercourse could be secured, must be built by the united Provinces and without a delay. It was also conceded that in the Provinces where separate schools were established by law, that principle should not be disturbed. Mr. Galt was the special advocate of this concession from the Province of Quebec, and the Roman Catholic members of the convention on behalf of the minority in Canada West. In the discussion it was claimed that the sole right of imposing an export duty should be vested in the Federal authority. This was objected to by the New Brunswick delegates, as the people of that Province had expended a large sum of money in the improving of the navigation of the upper St. John, and had, to recoup themselves,

imposed an export duty on lumber shipped from the Provinces. A considerable portion of the income thus received was paid by the lumbermen of the State of Maine,
the advantage derived by them from such improvements
being very great. The claim thus presented by the New
Brunswick delegates was conceded and the Province permitted to retain the right. This right was abandoned
since Confederation, the Dominion paying therefor $150,-
000 per annum to the New Brunswick government. Up
to the present time no export duty on lumber going from
New Brunswick has been demanded since the passage
of this last legislation.

During the sitting of the delegates, which extended to
over a period of two months, many conferences were held
with Lord Carnarvon, then Secretary of State for the
Colonies, and the law officers of the Crown in regard to
objections which were taken to some of the resolutions
adopted by the delegates. Valuable assistance was
rendered during this Conference by Lord Monk, who
was then in London, but who was Governor General of
Canada when the Conference was held at Quebec. The
arrangements there made in regard to the strengthening of
the central authority as compared with the constitution
of the United States, the result of the experience of that
country during the rebellion, were adhered to in the London resolutions and accepted by the Imperial authorities.
When the bill reached Parliament some amendments were
suggested, but when it was pointed out that the bill as
presented was the result of the most careful consider-

ation of both the Imperial authorities and the Colonial representatives, the suggested amendments were not pressed and the measure passed through Parliament with very little discussion. But one spirit seemed to animate both the Imperial authorities and the members of Parliament and that was to give the Provinces interested the fullest liberty consistent with the new relations they were about assuming. The Parliamentary opposition to the measure was much less than might have been expected when it is remembered that the opponents of Confederation had representatives in London, well able to present objections from their standpoint, who had the ear of Mr. Bright and other members of Parliament. Her Majesty took a deep interest in the measure when before Parliament, and expressed that interest to members of the delegation, adding that she felt a great affection for her Canadian subjects, they being so loyal. While the bill was before the House of Lords Messrs. Macdonald, Cartier, Galt, Tupper and Tilley, were honored by a private presentation to her Majesty, at Buckingham Palace. Later on all the members of the Conference were presented at a drawing room at the same place.

The New Brunswick delegates returned to England in the spring of 1867, having completed their labors, and the Legislature was called together on the 8th of May. The business before it was of great importance, for the Province was entering upon a new era as a member of the Canadian Confederation, and the Legislature was about to lose a portion of its powers which were delegated to the Federal Parliament. It is not, however, necessary to enter into any details of the work of the session which was done without any particular difficulty, the opposition being too weak to oppose seriously the measures of the government. It was felt on all sides that as twelve members of the Legislative Council were about to become members of the Senate of Canada, and as fifteen representatives were to be elected to the House of Commons, most of whom would come from the House of Assembly, a striking change would take place in the composition of the Legislature, which would be deprived of the services at once of a large number of its ablest men. One of the important bills of the session was the passage of the Act establishing County Courts in the Province, and in respect to this measure a difference of opinion took place between Mr. John M. Johnson, one of the delegates, and member for Northumberland, and his fellow delegates to England. He thought that the Legislature had no authority under the terms of Confederation, or from any understanding between the delegates while in England, to create County Courts, while the other delegates held a different view. The Act was passed, however, and has proved to be one of the most useful ever placed upon the statute book, relieving the Supreme Court of many cases, both civil and criminal, which would otherwise block its business, and enabling them to be disposed of more rapidly than before. The County Court judges appointed under this Act were, with one exception, members of the Legislature, and this made another serious drain upon its experienced members.

During the last session of the old New Brunswick Legislature, measures were also taken to secure the completion of the line of railway from St. John to the border of Maine, generally known as the Western Extension. The government of New Brunswick, which had already given a subsidy of ten thousand dollars a mile to the enterprise under the Act passed in 1863, agreed to take three hundred thousand dollars worth of the stock of the road. Under the stimulus of this additional subsidy the work rapidly advanced and railroad connection between St. John and Bangor, where it joined the American system of railroads, was established. The Legislature prorogued on the 17th day of June, thus bringing to an end the old independent Legislature of the Province which had done its work for so many years, to be replaced by a Legislature, shorn of a considerable part of its powers, but still efficient for good or evil because of its ability to pass laws profoundly affecting the material and moral welfare of the Province. Many men looked upon this dissolution of old ties with something like sadness, but to others it appeared like the dawning of a better day for the Province of New Brunswick as well as for the other Provinces of British North America.

The British North America Act, by which the Provinces of Upper and Lower Canada, New Brunswick and Nova Scotia were bound into a Confederation, came into force by royal proclamation on the first day of July, 1867. When it is considered how vast and vital a change this measure brought about it is surprising that it produced

so little excitement anywhere. With the exception of
one or two demonstrations which were made with flags
by persons hostile to Confederation, in the Province of
New Brunswick, which had been so much excited
during two elections, it was received with perfect calm-
ness, and although for some years afterwards there were
always a number of persons opposed to union who predicted direful things from Confederation and thought it
must finally be dissolved, the voices of such persons were
finally silenced either by death or by acquiescence in the
situation. Now it may be safely declared that the
Canadian Confederation stands upon as secure a foundation as any other government in the civilized world, and
is much less likely to break in pieces than the great republic to the south of us, where differences of climate and
of products and resources seem to have created separate
interests, which to an outside observer appear able to
threaten the stability of the nation.

In June, 1867, the Hon. John A. Macdonald, then
leader of the government of Canada, was entrusted by
Lord Monk, then Governor General, with the formation
of a ministry for the Dominion. Mr. Macdonald naturally experienced a good deal of difficulty in making his
arrangements. In the formation of the first ministry
much care was necessary ; provincial and national interests were to be thought of and denominational claims had
to receive some attention. But the greatest difficulty arose
with respect to old party lines. Mr. Macdonald considered that to a considerable extent old party lines could

not be recognized, and selected his men from the leading advocates of Confederation belonging to both the Conservative and Liberal parties, and acting upon this suggestion, named seven Conservatives and six Liberals. The Liberals included the names of Mr. Howland and Mr. McDougal for Ontario. A large number of the Liberals of Ontario, including George Brown and Alex. Mackenzie, opposed this arrangement, called a public meeting in Toronto and passed resolutions in favor of a strictly party government on old lines. It declared hostility to the proposal for a coalition and resolved to oppose Messrs. Howland and Mr. McDougal should they accept office under Mr. Macdonald when they returned to their constituents. This decision was carried out, but both Mr. Howland and Mr. McDougal were returned with good majorities. In this first ministry there were five members from Ontario: John A. Macdonald, William McDougal, W. P. Howland, A. J. F. Blair and Alex. Campbell; four from Quebec: Messrs. George E. Cartier, Alex. T. Galt, J. C. Chapais and Hector L. Langevin; two from Nova Scotia: Adams G. Archibald and Edward Kenny; and two from New Brunswick: S. L. Tilley and Peter Mitchell. Nine of the members were Protestants and four were Roman Catholics.

The wisdom of the course adopted will be apparent when it is remembered that the question of Confederation was not settled or carried on old party lines, some of the Conservatives opposing and some Liberals supporting it. This was clearly the case in New Brunswick, as shown

by the last two elections held here.　About one-third of
the Liberal party and a like proportion of the Conservative party opposed Confederation at the second election.
To have formed the first government on old party lines
would have necessitated the selection of some men who
were opposed to the union, and whose efforts might not
have been devoted to making it a success.　The name of
Liberal-Conservative was given to the new party, composed, as it was, of men of both parties.

The first Confederation ministry was a very strong
one.　The Hon. John A. Macdonald became Premier and
Minister of Justice ; the Hon. George E. Cartier was
Minister of Militia and Defence ; Alexander T. Galt was
Minister of Finance ; the Hon. William McDougal was
Minister of Public Works ; Hon. W. P. Howland was
Minister of Inland Revenue ; Hon. A. J. F. Blair, Presi-
dent of the Privy Council ; Hon. Alex. Campbell, Post
Master General; Hon. J. C. Chapais, Minister of Agri-
culture ; Hon. Hector L. Langevin, Secretary of State.
Mr. Tilley became Minister of Customs and Mr. Mitchell
became Minister of Marine and Fisheries, while the two
Nova Scotia representatives, Messrs. Archibald and
Kenny, became respectively Secretary of State for the
Provinces and Receiver General.

It will thus be seen that the Maritime Provinces had
four representatives of the Crown out of thirteen members of the Cabinet, and this proportion has generally
been maintained since that time, so that the fears of those
who anticipated that the Provinces by the sea would not

receive fair treatment in the distribution of high offices have proved to be groundless. So far has this been from being the case that the Maritime Province members of the government appear always to have occupied a very influential position in it, and the late lamented Premier was a representative of the Maritime Provinces, while the highly important office of Minister of Finance is also held by a Maritime representative.

The office of Minister of Customs, which Mr. Tilley received, was thought by some of his friends to be less important than he deserved, they being of the opinion that he should have been made Minister of Finance. This office, however, went to Mr. Galt, who, owing to a difference with the rest of the government, resigned four months later, his place in the Cabinet being taken by Sir John Rose, who held the office of Finance Minister until October, 1869, Sir Francis Hincks then receiving the appointment. It was not until the resignation of the latter in February, 1873, that Mr. Tilley became Minister of Finance. The office to which he was appointed, however, was one of great importance, involving as it did the reorganization of the entire establishment of the Customs of Canada, and it gave ample scope for his great ability as a business man.

The elections for the House of Commons in the new Parliament of Canada took place in August, the Hon. Mr. Tilley being chosen to represent the City of St. John, and the Hon. John H. Gray the County. It had been expected that in view of the fact that these men

had been so largely instrumental in bringing about
Confederation they would have been allowed to walk the
course unopposed. This was the case with Mr. Gray,
whose candidature met with no opposition; but Mr. Tilley was opposed by Mr. John Wilson, who received a
very small vote. This needless and futile opposition to
the candidature of a man who deserved so well from the
Province, was merely one of the proofs of the existence
of political rancor in the breasts of those who had been
defeated on the Confederation question. WHATTHEHELLWHYNOT?

The first Parliament of United Canada met on the 6th
of November 1867, and the address was moved by the
Hon. Charles Fisher, who had been elected to represent
the County of York. The session was a very long one,
lasting until the 22nd of May of the following year; but
there was an adjournment, extending from December 21st,
to the 20th March. This meeting of Parliament was the
most memorable ever held in Canada, because it brought
together for the first time, the representatives of all the
Provinces, and the ablest men of all political parties.
The people of Ontario and Quebec were little known to the
people of the Maritime Provinces, and those who resided
in the larger Provinces naturally enough knew compari-
tively little of their fellow-subjects who dwelt by the
sea, and had become members of the new Confederation.
It was expected by some that our Maritime Province
representatives would be completely overshadowed by
men of greater political reputation who dwelt in the
larger Provinces, but this did not prove to be the case.

The Maritime representatives at once took a leading position in Parliament, and this position they have steadily maintained down to the present time. No man stood better in the House of Commons than the representative from St. John, the Hon. S. L. Tilley. At that time Her Majesty the Queen, in acknowledgment of his services in the cause of Confederation, had created him a Companion of the Bath, a distinction which was also given to the Hon. Charles Tupper, of Nova Scotia.

A vast amount of business had to be disposed of at the first session of the Parliament of Canada. Although the Union Act embodied the plan upon which Confederation was founded, it was necessary to supplement it by a great deal of other legislation, for the purpose of interpreting it and making preparations for the practical working of the constitution. In all the discussions relative to the necessary legislation which had to be passed at that time, Mr. Tilley took a prominent part, and, when the session was over, he had established in the House of Commons, as fully as he had in the Legislature of New Brunswick, a reputation for ability as a speaker and as a man of affairs. He was looked upon as one whose wide knowledge of the needs of the Province and whose experience in departmental work were likely to be of the greatest use to the Confederation. His high character at all times gave a weight to his words and caused him to be listened to with the most respectful attention. During the whole period that Mr. Tilley sat in the House of Commons he had the pleasure of knowing that even his

w

political enemies respected his character and attainments, and with the exception of the Premier, perhaps no man wielded a more potent influence in the councils of the Dominion than he. It is not intended in this publication to trace to any full extent the career of Sir S. L. Tilley in the Parliament of Canada; that belongs rather to the history of the Dominion than to a work of the limited scope of the present volume, and only so much of his public life in the House of Commons will be dealt with as seems necessary to complete the story of his personal history. Mr. Tilley continued to hold the position of Minister of Customs during the whole of the term of the first Parliament of Canada. This Parliament held five sessions and dissolved in the summer of 1872, the general election being in the month of July, upon which occasion Mr. Tilley was re-elected for the City of St. John without opposition.

The second Parliament met on the 5th of March, 1873. But eleven days before that time Mr. Tilley had become Minister of Finance, succeeding Sir Francis Hincks, who resigned after holding the office of Finance Minister for more than three years. The advancement of Mr. Tilley to this responsible and influential position was very pleasing to his friends, and was received with great satisfaction by the country generally.

CHAPTER XII.

The first Confederation ministry of Canada resigned office on the 5th November, 1873. The circumstances which led to that action are a part of the political history of the Dominion and need not be gone into in this volume. With regard to Mr. Tilley it is sufficient to say that whatever basis there may have been for charges of corruption in connection with the Pacific scandal against other persons in the government, none were ever preferred against him, and no one suspected or believed that he had anything whatever to do with the transactions with Sir Hugh Allan and his associates which led to the government being compelled to resign. Prior to the resignation of the government Mr. Tilley had been appointed Lieutenant Governor of the Province of New Brunswick in succession of the Hon. Lemuel A. Wilmot, whose term had expired. Every one felt that the honor thus bestowed upon Mr. Tilley was a most fitting one, for he was New Brunswick's foremost son in political life, and had reached his high position purely through his own ability and his own good character. However much people may have differed in regard to Mr. Tilley's political views, there has never been any difference of opinion in regard to his acceptability as the Governor of

the Province.   He filled that high position a greater
number of years than any of his successors are likely to
do, and it is admitted on all sides that no man could
have performed the duties of that high office better than
he has done.

Mr. Tilley took up his residence in the old government
house, Fredericton, and he must have been struck with
the changed aspect of affairs from that which existed
under the old regime, when our Lieutenant Governors
were appointed by the British Government and sent out
from England to preside over the councils of a people of
whom they knew little or nothing.   Many of these former
Governors had been military men and were more
accustomed to habits of command than to deal with per-
plexing questions of state government.   They looked
with a very natural degree of impatience on the attempts
which the people of the Province were making to get the
full control of their own affairs.   Under the old regime
the Governor was surrounded with military guards;
sentries paced the walks and stood at the entrances of the
government house, and a vast amount of ceremony had
to be gone through with before any one could see the
distinguished occupant of that building.   Government
house, under the old system, had been the scene of many
festivities, not always distinguished by their sobriety, and
strange stories are told of many, high in New Brunswick
political life, who had drunk overmuch at the dinner-table
of the Governor.   All this was now to be changed.   The
Hon. Lemuel A. Wilmot, although a life-long temperance

man and total abstainer, had kept up the old customs with respect to the use of liquor in government house, and thereby incurred no small amount of adverse criticism from those who thought he should have discouraged the use of wine and other intoxicating beverages. The temperance views of Mr. Tilley were of a more consistent order, and he carried out, in practice at government house, those principles of total abstinence which had distinguished him throughout his entire career. So long as he was Lieutenant Governor of New Brunswick no intoxicating beverages of any kind were ever used at his table. Some of the old-time frequenters of government house were at first inclined to object to this change in its customs, but the general voice of the people of the Province was in favor of the change, and it was felt that in acting as he did the Lieutenant Governor had merely given another proof of his consistency as a man and of his attachment to those principles which he had embraced so early in life. The withdrawal of the British troops from Canada before the Lieutenant Governorship of Mr. Tilley commenced relieved him of any embarrassment in regard to dispensing with military guards and sentries, but all pretentious accompaniments of authority were very foreign to his nature, and he always showed, by the severe simplicity of his life, that he felt he was one of the people, and that it was his duty as well as his pleasure to permit all who had any reason to see him to have free access to him, without the necessity of going through any formal process.

When Mr. Tilley became Lieutenant Governor of the Province, he was fifty-five years of age, and he seems to have thought that his political career was ended because, by the time his term of office expired in its natural course, he would have reached the age of sixty, a period of life when a man is not likely to make a new entrance into public life.   But circumstances, quite outside of any desire on his part, made it almost necessary for him to change his determination, and during the summer of 1878, when the general election was imminent, he found himself pressed by his old political friends to once more become the candidate of his party, for his old constituency in the City of St. John.   There was great enthusiasm amongst them when it was announced that he would comply with their wishes and that he had resigned the Lieutenant Governorship.   The result of that general election is well known.   The Liberal party, which had succeeded to the government less than five years before, with a large majority in the House of Commons, experienced a severe defeat, and the Hon. Alexander Mackenzie, seeing this, very properly did not await the assembling of Parliament, but, like the honest man that he was, sent in the resignation of the ministry, and Sir John A. Macdonald was called upon to form a new government.   In the cabinet thus constructed Mr. Tilley resumed his old office of Minister of Finance, and one of his first duties was to assist in the framing of a new tariff which was to be formed in accordance with the principles upon which the election had been run, of protection to home industries. This idea of protection had not been heard of in the Canadian Confederation as the policy of any political party until Sir John A. Macdonald took it up about a year before the general election, but it proved a winning card and was the means of giving the new government a long lease of power. Mr. Tilley's views regarding the tariff and the needs of Canada, were given very fully in his budget speech, which was delivered in February, 1879, and the following extracts from it will convey to the reader a clearer idea of them than any mere recital:

"Mr. Chairman, it is only recently, Sir, that I have fully realized the great changes that have taken place throughout the Dominion of Canada since I last had the honor of a seat in Parliament, and, to-day, I fully realize the great change that has taken place, and the increased difficulties devolving upon me, as Finance Minister, compared with the position of affairs when I submitted my financial statement in 1873. Then, Sir, my work was a very easy one indeed. Honorable members on the opposite benches were pleased, on that occasion, to compliment me on that statement, but I felt that I had earned no compliment; that if that speech was acceptable to the House at that time, it was because of the satisfactory statements I was able to make with reference to the condition of the Dominion and of the finances of the Dominion. Then, Sir, I was able to point to steady and increasing surplus and revenue, and that in the face of a steady reduction of taxation. Then, Sir, I was able to point, with some degree of confidence, to the prospective expenditures of the Dominion, extending over ten years. To-day I cannot speak of it with the same confidence.

Then the construction of the Pacific Railway was under regulations that confined and limited the liabilities of the Dominion to $30,000,000. To-day I am not in a position to say what expenditure or responsibilities we may have to incur with reference to that great undertaking. There has been a change in the policy, but it will become the duty of the Government and of Parliament to consider, while we have not reached the limit of our liabilities, whether we cannot construct that great work, with 200,000,000 acres of land lying within the wheat area of that magnificent country. Then, Sir, I could point with pride and with satisfaction to the increased capital of our banks and the large dividends they paid. To-day, I regret to say, that we must point to depreciated values and to small dividends. Then I could point to the general prosperity of the country. To-day we must all admit that it is greatly depressed. Then I could point with satisfaction to the various manufacturing industries that were in operation throughout the length and breadth of the Dominion, remunerative to the men who had invested their capital in them, and giving employment to tens of thousands. To-day many of the furnaces are cold, the machinery in many cases is idle, and those establishments that are in operation are only employed half time, and are scarcely paying the interest on the money invested. Then, Sir, we could point to the agricultural interest as most prosperous, with a satisfactory home market and satisfactory prices abroad. To-day they have a limited market, with low prices and anything but a satisfactory market abroad. Then, Sir, we could point to a very valuable and extensive West India trade; to-day it does not exist. Then, Sir, we could point to a profitable and direct tea trade, that has been demoralized and destroyed. Then everything appeared to be prosperous; to-day, though it looks gloomy, I hope there is a silver lining to the cloud, that we may yet see illuminating the whole of the Dominion and changing our present position to one of happiness and prosperity. Mr. Chairman, there has been, and very naturally so, a good deal of interest and anxiety manifested on the part of the friends of the National Policy, as it is called, in regard to its early introduction. I can quite understand that, because, believing as they do, and as a majority of this House do, that that policy is calculated to bring prosperity to the country, it was but natural that they should be anxious for its introduction, and that not a day should be lost. And it is satisfactory to know that, great and difficult as is the responsibility which rests upon me here, I trust that the propositions I am about to make will be sustained, not only by a majority of this House, but by an overwhelming majority in the country.

"I can appeal to other finance ministers, and especially to my predecessor, who, in 1874, made several changes in the tariff of that day, to speak of the difficulties there are in making even as few changes as were then made. But if we undertake, as the present Government have undertaken, to readjust and reorganize and, I may say, make an entirely new tariff, having for its object not only the realization of $2,000,000 more revenue than will be collected this year, but, in addition to providing for that deficiency, to adjust that policy, or that tariff with a view of making what has been, and is to-day, declared the policy of the majority of this House — I mean the protection of the industries of the country — the magnitude of the undertaking will be the better appreciated. Sir, we have invited gentlemen from all parts of the Dominion, and representing all the interests in the Dominion, to assist us in the readjustment of the tariff, because we did not feel, though perhaps we possess an average intelligence in ordinary Government matters, we did not feel that we knew everything. We did not feel that we were prepared, without advice and assistance from men of experience with reference to these matters, to readjust and make a judicious tariff. We, therefore, invited those who were interested in the general interests of the country, or interested in any special interests. Gentlemen who took an opposite view, met us and discussed these questions, and I may say that, down to as late a period as yesterday, though the propositions are submitted to-day, we were favored with the co-operation and opinions of gentlemen who represent their particular or general views with reference to the great questions we have under consideration. We have labored zealously and arduously, and I trust it will be found successfully, and we are now about to submit our views for the consideration of this House.

" In my opening remarks, I referred to the difficulty with which we have to grapple. We must, if we meet the expenditure of next year, our interest, the charges upon our revenue, and the necessary expenditure which the country has a right to expect, ask from this House the authority to receive a revenue from the customs of $2,000,000 more than received this year. We have also, in arranging for the levying of that duty, to consider how it can best be imposed to encourage the industries of the country. It would be well, before I enter upon the consideration of this point of the question, to ask ourselves what are the circumstances that have led to the reduction of revenue and to the present depressed condition of the country. With reference to the reduction of the revenue, I have heard it remarked that it is strange that the reduction of the revenues of late years has been so great. Perhaps there is as much prosperity here as in many other parts of the world; then why was there such a falling off in our revenue compared with the revenues of the United States and Great Britain? When we examine the case, we ascertain the fact that nearly all the revenue of the United States is from specific duties, and, therefore, the decrease in the value of imports does not, in that country materially affect the revenue, whereas in the Dominion the duties are principally *ad valorem*, and, therefore, largely affected by the decrease in the value of goods imported. It is established by comparative statements that the goods imported into the Dominion have decreased in value to the extent of 33 to 40 per cent., and the duties on those imports, being levied largely on the *ad valorem* principle, there has been a falling off in

the revenues of the Dominion in a corresponding proportion.   In the propositions I am about to make it will be
shown — and I state this fact in order that the House
may perfectly understand the nature and extent of those
propositions — that on many articles on which we propose
an increase of duty, 25 per cent. levied on the value
will not bring more per yard than we received on a 15
per cent. tariff in 1873.   We will, by way of illustration,
take 100 yards of cloth, valued in 1873 at $1 a yard,
the duty collected on it would have been $15.   The same
cloth is worth now but 60c. per yard, and it would
require a tariff of 25 per cent. to produce the amount of
revenue received from the same quantity in 1873.   It is
important to bear this fact in mind, because, while it may
be thought on the other side of the Atlantic, and by our
neighbors, that we are increasing largely our taxation,
and imposing increased duties on the products of other
countries, it is well to make it understood that, if our
duties had been specific, we would have been receiving
the same amount of revenue as in 1873.   There are
other difficulties; the volume of imports has not much
diminished.   Regarding the matter as I do, I think it is
to be regretted that the volume of imports has not been
materially reduced.   I look upon the large imports, ever
since the Dominion was organized, showing a large balance of trade against it, as one of the causes of the
troubles with which we have to contend — one of the
difficulties that it is our duty, if possible, to remedy.
They have been decreasing to a certain extent, but are

still very large, showing distinctly and clearly, in my judgment, that they ought still to be further diminished. I know there are honorable gentlemen here and elsewhere who entertain the opinion that the balance between the imports and exports is not a correct mode of judging of the condition of a country. I know that opinion is entertained by honorable gentlemen opposite. But let us, just for a few moments, turn our attention to the condition which England occupies to-day, as compared with the United States. From 1867 to 1873, the balance of trade against England amounted, in the average, to £50,000,000 sterling. It is quite true that difference was met by interest, the returns from her vessels, and in various ways, to an extent largely counterbalancing it, or leaving a balance in favor of England. By the last return I have, which covers the year 1877, the balance of trade against her is shown to be £140,000,000 sterling, or $700,000,000 per year. The balance of trade against the United States in 1872 was $116,000,000; in 1873 it was reduced to $66,000,000; but last calendar year showed that the balance in favor of the United States had reached $300,000,000 a year. I think, then, without entering into a discussion here of Free Trade and Protection, so far as it affects England and the United States, we may fairly conclude that the prosperity of the one country, at this moment, is caused in a great measure by the large surplus in its favor, and the depression in the other by the large deficiency. Under these circumstances, it appears to me, we should turn our attention to the best means of reducing the volume of our imports from all parts of the world. Let me refer to some circumstances that led to the present depression in the revenue. During and after the war in the United States, it is well understood that the country lost a large portion of its export trade, and its manufacturing industries had been to a certain extent paralyzed, and it was only about 1872 or 1873 that they really commenced to restore their manufacturing industries and endeavoured to find an extended market elsewhere for the manufactures of their country. Lying, as we do, alongside that great country, we are looked upon as a desirable market for their surplus products, and our American neighbors, always competent to judge of their own interests, and act wisely in regard to them, put forth every effort to obtain access to our market. It is well known by the term slaughter market what they have been doing for the last four or five years in Canada; that in order to find an outlet for their surplus manufactures they have been willing to send them into this country at any price that would be a little below that of the Canadian manufacturer. It is well known also that they have had their agents in every part of the Dominion seeking purchasers for their surplus, and that those agents have been enabled, under our existing laws, to enter those goods at a price, much lower than they ought to have paid, which was their value in the place of purchase. It is well known, moreover, that the United States Government, in order to encourage special interests in the country, granted a bounty upon certain manufactures, and gave to them the exclusive market of the Dominion, and, under those circumstances, we have lost a very important trade, possessed previous to 1873, in addition to the loss of the West India trade, and by the repeal of the 10 per cent. duty on tea, we lost the direct tea trade, and all the advantages resulting from it, by its transfer from the Dominion to New York and Boston. Under all those circumstances, and with the high duty imposed by the United States on the agricultural products of the Dominion, by which we are, to a great extent, excluded from them, while the manufactures of that country are forced into our market, we could not expect prosperity or success in the Dominion, so long as that state of things continued. These are some of the difficulties which have led to our present state of affairs. Now, after having made these few remarks on that head, I desire to call the attention of the House to the remedy. I know this is a difficult question — that it is the opinion of some honorable members, that no matter what proposition you may make, or what legislation you introduce, it cannot improve or increase the prosperity of the country. The Government entertain a different opinion. I may say, at the outset, it would have been much more agreeable if we could have met the House without the necessity of increased taxation. But in the imposition of the duties we are now about to ask the House to impose, it may be said we will receive from the imports from foreign countries a larger portion of the $2,000,000 we require than we will receive from the Mother Country. I believe such will be the effect, but I think that in making such a statement to this House, belonging, as we do, to and forming a part of that great country — a country that receives our natural products without any taxation; everything we have to send to her — apart from our national feelings, I think this House will not object if, in the propositions before me, they touch more heavily the imports from foreign countries than from our Fatherland. I have this to say to our American friends: In 1865 they abrogated the Reciprocity Treaty, and from that day to the present a large portion of the imports from that country into the Dominion have been admitted free. We have hoped, but hoped in vain, that by the adoption of that policy we would lead our American friends to treat us in a more liberal spirit with regard to the same articles. Well, after having waited twelve years for the consideration of this subject, the Government requiring more revenue, have determined to ask this House to impose upon the products of the United States that have been free, such a duty as may seem consistent with our position. But the Government couple with the proposal, in order to shew that we approach this question with no unfriendly spirit, a resolution that will be laid on the table containing a proposition to this effect: That, as to the articles named, which are the natural products of the country, including lumber, if the United States take off the duties in part or whole, we are prepared to meet them with equal concessions. The Government believe in a reciprocity tariff, yet may discuss Free Trade or Protection, but the question of to-day is : Shall we have a reciprocity tariff, or a one-sided tariff ?

" We found, Sir, as I stated before, that it was important to encourage the exportation of our manufactures to foreign countries, and we are prepared now to say that the policy of the Government is to give every manufacturer in the Dominion of Canada a drawback on the duties they may pay upon goods used in the manufactures of the Dominion exported. We found also, Sir, that under the bounty system of some foreign countries, our sugar-refining trade, and other interests, were materially affected. Well, Sir, the Government have decided to ask this House to impose countervailing duties under such circumstances. I trust that this proposition will receive the support of both sides of the House, because some six months since, when the deputation of sugar refiners in London waited upon Mr. Gladstone and Sir Stafford Northcote, both of them being gentlemen representing free-trade views, they declared, in the most emphatic terms, that when a Government came in and interfered with the legitimate trade of the country they were prepared to impose countervailing duties. To make this matter plain, and place it beyond dispute, the Government propose to ask the House for authority to collect on all such articles an *ad valorem* duty on their value, irrespective of drawbacks. My colleagues say, explain it. For instance, a cent and a quarter drawback per pound is granted on cut nails exported to the Dominion of Canada ; the duty will be calculated on the value of the nails,

X

irrespective of the drawback. Now a bounty is given
on sugar in excess of that which is paid by the sugar
refiners; the Government will exact an *ad valorem* duty
on the value of that sugar, irrespective of the drawback.
I may also state, Mr. Chairman, that another reason
why, I think, our American neighbors should not object to
the imposition of the duties we propose is this: It is a
fact, though not generally known, that the average per-
centage of revenue that is imposed on all imports into
the Dominion of Canada, at the present time, taking the
returns for last year as our criterion, is 13¼ per cent, the
amount of duty collected on the imports from Great
Britain, is a fraction under 17½ per cent.; while the
amount of duty collected on the imports from the United
States is a fraction under 10 per cent. If our friends
across the border will not give us the Reciprocity Treaty
again, they cannot find anything to object to in the
imposition of those duties, if it bears a little more heavily
on the articles imported from that country than they
desire."

Sir Leonard Tilley's speech in introducing the new
tariff was well received, and made a strong impression
upon those who heard it. It was admitted, even by
those who were opposed to the views he held, that he '
showed a great mastery of the details, and that he
illustrated in a very clear manner the views of those who
maintained that the country was suffering because the
duties imposed upon foreign goods were not sufficiently
high to protect Canadian manufactures. For nearly

eighteen years this tariff has been in force, and every man in Canada has had liberty to judge for himself as to how far it has answered the expectations of those who framed it. Certainly a trial of such length of one particular system ought to have supplied some criterion by which to test its value, and to enable the public to judge how far it has been advantageous to the country. The result of the recent Dominion elections would seem to indicate that public opinion in Canada is not by any means decided as to the value of the National Policy. It is not the intention of this volume to deal to any full extent with the career of Sir Leonard Tilley during his second term of office as Minister of Finance of Canada. To enter into that phase of his career would be to relate the history of Canada, for he was but one member of the government, and not its leader. It admitted, however, that in respect to all financial questions Sir Leonard showed the same ability that had characterized his career during his previous term of office, and he was looked upon by his colleagues as a man in whose judgment the utmost confidence could be placed. At this time, however, his health began to fail, and the disease, which finally carried him off, developed itself to such an extent that he was told he must cease all active work or his days would be shortened. Under these circumstances, it became necessary for him to retire from the severe duties of his very responsible and laborious office, and on the 31st day of October, 1885, he was again appointed Lieutenant Governor of New Brunswick, an office which he had filled with so much acceptance between 1873 and 1878. Sir Leonard Tilley continued Lieutenant Governor during a second term, for almost eight years, or until the appointment of Hon. John Boyd to that position.

Sir Leonard Tilley was Lieutenant Governor of New Brunswick for considerably more than twelve years, a record which is not likely to be equalled by any future Lieutenant Governor for many years to come, if ever.

There was no event of particular importance to distinguish Sir Leonard Tilley's second term as Lieutenant Governor. Hon. Mr. Blair remained Premier of New Brunswick during the whole period, and there was no political crisis of any importance to alter the complexion of affairs. The only event in connection with the Governorship, which is worthy of being mentioned, is the change that was made by the abandonment of the old Government house at Fredericton as the residence of the Lieutenant Governor. This building had become antiquated, and in other ways unsuitable for the occupation of a Lieutenant Governor, and its maintenance involved a very large expenditure annually, which the province was unable to afford. It was therefore determined that in future the Lieutenant Governor should provide his own residence, and that the amount expended on Government House annually should be saved. Sir Leonard Tilley built a residence in St. John, in which he lived for the remainder of his life, and the seat of government, so far as his presence was concerned, was transferred to that city. Sir Leonard Tilley was always on the most

cordial terms with the various premiers who administered
the government of New Brunswick during his terms of
office.   His relations with the Hon. Mr. Blair were
particularly friendly, and during the whole period of
almost eight years in which they were associated
not the slightest difficulty ever arose between them.   Sir
Leonard Tilley knew well the strict constitutional limits
of his office, and was always careful to confine his activities within their proper scope.   The lessons of responsible
government which he had learned in his early youth, and
which had been the study of his manhood, enabled him
to avoid those pitfalls which beset the steps of imported
Lieutenant Governors, who imagine that their official
position gives them an authority to which they were not
entitled.   One of the most beneficial changes which
Confederation brought to the Provinces of Canada was
the making of Canadians Lieutenant Governors of these
Provinces, and thereby avoiding those difficulties which
had been so frequent and constant in an earlier period
of their history, when military officers, without any
experience of civil government, were sent out to administer
the affairs of these colonies.   .

During Sir Leonard Tilley's last term of office, and
after its close, he abstained wholly from any interference
with public affairs in the Dominion, and although he still
remained steadfastly attached to the Liberal-Conservative
party, he gave no outward sign of his desire for their
success.   This neutral position which he assumed in
political matters had the effect of drawing towards him

thousands of his fellow-countrymen who, in former years, had been accustomed to regard him with unfriendly feelings. They forgot the active political leader, and saw only before them the aged governor, whose venerable figure and kindly face were so familiar at social or other gatherings, or whenever a good work was to be done for any good cause. In this way Sir Leonard Tilley grew to assume a new character in the public estimation, and at the time of his death the regret was as great on the part of those who had been his political opponents as among those who had been his associates in political warfare. This was one of the most pleasing features of his declining years, and one that gave him the greatest satisfaction, because it enabled him to feel that he enjoyed the affectionate regard of the whole body of the people.

CHAPTER XIII.

Sir Leonard Tilley for many years had suffered from an incurable disease, which had been mitigated by rest and medical treatment, but not removed. It was the knowledge of the fact that his life would be shortened if he continued in active political life that compelled him to leave the government in 1885. For many years before his death the malady had been so far subdued that it gave him comparatively little trouble, but any unusual exertion on his part was almost certain to arouse it again to activity, so that he was prevented on many occasions from taking part in public functions, which, under other circumstances, he would have been glad to attend. Still he always contrived to take his daily walk, and few who saw him ever suspected that he was constantly menanced by death. For three or four years before his decease his strength had been failing, he stooped more as he walked, and it was evident that he was not destined to enjoy many years more of life. Yet during the spring of 1896 there was nothing whatever to indicate that the end was so near, for he went about as usual, and was able to preside at the annual meeting of the Loyalist Society, which was held during the last week in May. On that evening he appeared very bright and cheerful, and he entered with much interest into the discussion of the details of an outing which it was proposed the society should hold during the summer. Man proposes, God Disposes. Sir Leonard had gone to Rothesay early in June to spend a few weeks in that pleasant spot, and he appeared to be in his usual health until the night of the 10th of June, when he began to suffer great pain from a slight cut which he received in the foot. The symptoms became alarming and gave indications of blood poisoning, a condition due to the disease from which he had suffered so many years. On the 11th of June he was taken to Carleton House, his town residence, and from that time the doctors gave no hope of his recovery. It was one of the sad features of his illness that his life-long friend, and physician for many years, Dr. William Bayard, was unable to attend him, being himself confined to his bed by illness.

After Sir Leonard Tilley reached his home in St. John he never rallied, and he was well aware that his end was near. He was attended by Dr. Inches and Dr. Murray McLaren, but he was beyond medical aid, and therefore the people of St. John, for several days before the event took place, were aware that their foremost citizen was dying. The time was one of great excitement, for the general election was near, yet the eyes of thousands were turned, from the moving panorama of active life which passed before them, to the silent chamber where the dying statesman was breathing his last. The regret and sympathy that was expressed were universal, and those who had been his life-long political opponents were not behind those who had been his friends in their kindly words.

Sir Leonard Tilley died at 3 o'clock on the morning of the 25th of June, and the second day after the general election, which brought about the defeat of the party with which he had been so long identified. One who watched by his bedside during his last hours, and who was present when he passed away, has furnished the following account of the event which brought so much sorrow to such a wide circle of friends:

"The last days of this great and good man were peaceful and full of faith. One of the last wishes he expressed was that a plain tomb-stone should be erected to his memory with the words inscribed: 'His trust was in Jesus,' so that passers by might be helped in their earthly pilgrimage. He desired them to know that this had been the true source of his success, the power that had influenced his life.

"There was something pathetic in the thought that, as his life was calmly passing away, the party that he dearly loved was going out as well. Through all the day of the election he watched the hours, waiting anxiously to know the result of the contest. When he was told only of the result in New Brunswick the dying statesman said, 'I can go to sleep now, New Brunswick has done well.' He went to sleep without hearing of the defeat of his party throughout the country. But he was a man who always recognized ability outside of party. He was always looking for the good and noble in human nature, and if there was any chance of bringing the possessors of those qualities to the front, he desired that it should be done. The secret of his life was that he loved his God and his country. He always said he owed so much of his success to his good mother's teachings. In his earliest days he was much with her, and he always had great admiration for her strong character. She was a woman greatly respected and esteemed in the neighborhood in which she resided; ever ready to help others in sickness or distress, and her services were much called into requisition upon all occasions. Her patient example was ever an incentive to him in his career, and when the end came it might be compared to a ship under full sail, the voyage over, with its storms all passed, quietly gliding into harbor, its pilot on board and the glory of the celestial city beaming before eyes that had looked long for it. We cannot see beyond the veil, but we know that he has entered into his reward."

The death of Sir Leonard Tilley evoked expressions of sympathy and regret from all parts of the empire and from many states of the union. The letters and telegrams of condolence which Lady Tilley received during the first days of her widowhood would of themselves fill a volume, showing how widely he was known and respected.

The funeral, which took place on the Saturday following his death, was one of the largest ever seen in St. John, and was attended by the Board of Trade, the Loyalist Society, the various temperance organizations, the members of the Provincial Government, and a vast concourse of prominent citizens. The services took place at St. John's Episcopal Church, and were conducted by the rector, the Rev. John deSoyres, assisted by the Rev. R. P. McKim, rector of St. Luke's church, with which Sir Leonard had been identified in his earlier years. The interment took place in the Rural Cemetery.

Many references from the pulpits of St. John and the province were made on the Sunday following his death, and all the newspapers had long notices of the event and editorials on his life and character. The St. John *Telegraph*, which had been politically opposed to Sir Leonard Tilley for more than twenty years, said:

" By the death of Sir Leonard Tilley, the Province of New Brunswick loses its most famous son, a man whose political career extended over a longer period and who was more successful in political life than any other statesman that this province has produced, and one whose death will be learned with regret, not only by thousands of attached friends, but by tens of thousands who never saw his face, but who looked upon him as their political leader and guide. Although Sir Leonard Tilley had been retired from active politics for more than ten years prior to his death, we are perhaps too 'near the time when he was a great political leader, to justly estimate his merits. Few people are able so far to separate themselves from their prejudices as to honestly criticise a friend or do full justice to an opponent, so that there must always be in contemporary opinions an element of weakness; yet, we

believe that the general view of the public will agree
with us in expressing the belief that Sir Leonard Tilley
was a man of high character, and of scrupulous honesty,
an honor to the land which gave him birth, and one who
had done much good for Canada.

"Sir Leonard Tilley, by birth, came from the bluest
blood of New England, for he was a descendant of one of
the Mayflower pilgrims, but he owed nothing of his success in life to this fact, and fortune showered no favors
upon his birth. A boy who, at the age of 13, has to leave
home, as he did, with an unfinished education, to seek his
living in a strange city, may fairly claim to have been
the architect of whatever fortune he succeeds in rearing
for himself. Sir Leonard was emphatically a self-made
man, and he would have been a leading citizen and an
honored and influential member of this community, if he
had never been elected to the legislature or to parliament,
and never made a political speech. Under such circumstances his great qualities would have developed themselves along different lines, but they would have led him
to fortune and to high consideration if not to as great a
degree of fame as that to which he attained. As it was,
he found himself forced into political life, almost without
his own consent, and the new path into which his steps
were thus so strangely directed led him to the highest
honors his country could give, making him the leader of
the government of New Brunswick, a cabinet minister of
Canada, twice Lieutenant Governor of his native province,

a Companion of the Bath, and a Knight Commander of St. Michael and St. George.

" It is just 46 years since Sir Leonard Tilley gained his first step in political life by being elected one of the members for the City of St. John, and it was as a representative of this city in the legislature of New Brunswick and in the parliament of Canada that he gained his fame. He represented this city in five different legislatures and in four parliaments, his legislative career covered a period of 25 years, during practically the whole of which he was in office as a member of the Provincial or Dominion Government. For thirteen years he was Lieutenant Governor, so that his official career extended over forty years, during the whole of which he was in positions of the highest responsibility and honor. Such a term of prosperous political life has had no parallel in Canada, and it is not likely that any public man now in Canada will be able to equal it.

" Yet it would be a mistake to suppose that Sir Leonard Tilley's public life was all sunshine, or that he did not experience serious reverses. He was connected with three great political conflicts — the battle for prohibition, the struggle for Confederation and the fight for the National Policy. In the first of these he was defeated, in the second, although at first worsted, he eventually succeeded, while as regards the third he was a victor at the beginning, but lived to learn of the defeat of the policy which he had labored to promote. There is surely something pathetic in the thought that on the 23rd of

June, while the voters of Canada were depositing their
ballots against the government, and recording their condemnation of the National Policy, the statesman who did
the most to create that policy was on his death bed, his
life slowly ebbing away and nearing the margin of the
dark dread river which all must cross.

"Mr. Tilley's connection with the temperance movement naturally made him the champion of prohibition,
and led to his passing a prohibitory liquor law during the
legislative session of 1855. The law worked badly and
a political crisis followed, for the Lieutenant Governor
dissolved the House of Assembly, against the wishes of
Mr. Tilley and the other members of the government,
who at once resigned. In the elections which followed
in the summer of 1856, Mr. Tilley suffered his first
defeat, but a year later he was re-elected by his old
constituency, and became the leader of a new government. The prohibition question dropped out of sight and
he suffered no further reverses until 1865, when he and
his government were defeated on the question of Confederation. A little more than a year later this adverse
verdict was reversed, and Mr. Tilley became the leader of
a government authorized to carry out the scheme of
union between New Brunswick, Nova Scotia and Canada.

"It is on this phase of the deceased statesman's career
that his friends can look back with the most satisfaction.
With respect to the prohibition question he was in
advance of his time, in respect to the protective system,
known as the National Policy, he was behind the spirit

of the age, for the attempt to make a country prosperous by a high tariff wall is an exploded fallacy. But with regard to Confederation the stand that he took was the correct one, for although Confederation has not done for us all that was claimed for it, it was a necessity, and it was the part of an enlightened statesman to do all in his power to promote it.

" There have been many criticisms of Sir Leonard Tilley on the score of his long tenure of office and the high salaries attached to the positions which he filled. It ought, however, to be understood that he was a well-to-do man, and the owner of a large amount of property before he entered political life, and it may be safely said that he would have died a much richer man if he had continued to attend to his own private affairs, rather than those of the province and dominion. Indeed, Sir Leonard Tilley was a first-class man of business, and this was one of the main elements of his success. He was essentially a man of affairs, and during the whole of his political life he was looked upon as a safe adviser by his party and as one pre-eminently qualified to conduct the financial business of the country.

" It is difficult to gauge accurately the exact position which Sir Leonard Tilley might have held as a statesman had the opportunity come to him. Sir John A. Macdonald overshadowed all his colleagues during his life-time, and prevented them from showing to the full extent their capacity for leadership. Still we have no doubt that the deceased had in him the making of an excellent premier, one who would have inspired the public with confidence, and ventured on no scheme which he regarded as dangerous. He was an excellent speaker, clear, forcible and convincing, and there was much in his voice and manner to attract an audience. His lucid exposition of financial questions was a strong point in his career as a public man, and gave his speeches a character of their own.

" It is greatly to the honor of Sir Leonard Tilley that no scandal public or private was ever attached to his name. A consistent temperance man to the end of his life, he was faithful to the cause which he had espoused when he was young, and he enjoyed the confidence and received the steady support of a vast majority of the temperance men of the province, who looked upon him as their natural leader. His capacity for friendship was great and his friends might be numbered by thousands, for he had a peculiar faculty of strongly attracting men to himself. This may be ascribed in part to the magnetism of a buoyant and strong nature, but it was more largely due to the extreme simplicity of his character, which remained wholly unspoiled by the favors which fortune had showered upon him. No man, however humble, had any difficulty in obtaining an interview with Sir Leonard Tilley, he was every inch a gentleman, and was, therefore, as polite to the poorest laborer as to the richest in the land. Such a man could not fail to be loved even by those who had been his most bitter opponents in former years, when he was in active political life.

When Sir Leonard Tilley began his public career political conflicts were conducted with a degree of personal acrimony which is wholly unknown at the present day. There was a bitterness injected into election campaigns which does not now exist. In his time he received and gave many hard blows, and many hard things were said of him. But for several years past Sir Leonard Tilley enjoyed the affectionate regard of thousands of those who have been his political opponents. He had a pleasant word and a kindly smile for all, and he passed before the eyes of man as one deserving of the highest honor for his unsullied character, and for the services which he had rendered to his country.

"It is one of the drawbacks of this human life that the wise, the learned, the good, and those whom we most love and honor grow old and feeble, fall by the wayside and pass away. So while we lament the death of Sir Leonard Tilley, we must recognize it as an event that was inevitable, and which could not long have been postponed. His life work was done; his labors were ended; his active and brilliant career was closed; he was but waiting for that dread summons which sooner or later must come to all. The summons has come and he has gone from among us for ever. His venerable, noble face will no longer be seen on our streets, his kindly greeting will no longer be heard. But his memory will live, not ony in the hearts of all his countrymen, but enshrined in the history of this his native province, and of the great dominion which he did so much to create, and which he so fondly loved."

The St. John *Sun*, in commenting on his death, said:

"While Sir Leonard Tilley had a large part in all the

Y

public events of his time, his name will be associated with three or four striking chapters of British American history.

"Sir Leonard was hardly one of the chief actors in the establishment of responsible government in this province. But the conflict was not settled when he became a prominent member of the assembly, and he afterwards did his part in securing full control for the representatives of the people.

"Sir Leonard will be remembered as the chief promoter of the only general prohibitory liquor law which has yet been adopted by any organized British colony in America. This law was almost the first achievement of the young legislator. It was hastily enacted at a time when similar legislation was passed in New England. The system was swept away a few months later, carrying the Tilley government, and Mr. Tilley's seat with it. Had the government taken more care to provide the machinery for enforcement, or the people and the governor given the experiment a more thorough test, the public of to-day might have been able to build a safer argument on this piece of history. Sir Leonard never wavered in his temperance principles, but thirty years after he introduced prohibition in this province, he told the house of commons that he would never again support prohibitory legislation unless he saw a way to its satisfactory enforcement.

"While the events mentioned were incidents in the history of a province, Sir Leonard's share in the great work of Confederation presents him as a statesman of a more imperial quality. The province, like Nova Scotia, had not been educated up to the idea of a British American union. There was a natural reluctance to surrender local autonomy, and the mass of the people could not realize the higher possibilities that union involved. Sir Leonard returned from the Quebec conference to find public sentiment against the project. He and his government were defeated. But with the help of Mr. Mitchell and other confederates he set to work arguing the case all over the province. One year of such work gave him a mandate of the people to go forward. Sir Leonard was one of those who drafted the financial part of the union scheme. After the union, when Nova Scotia was in the throes of a wild agitation for repeal, Sir Leonard Tilley, as the old friend and comrade of Mr. Howe, was the intermediary who prepared for the meeting of Mr. Howe and Premier Macdonald of the dominion. The result of the negotiations was a re-adjustment of the financial terms and the acceptance by Mr. Howe of a place in Sir John Macdonald's cabinet. Sir Leonard is almost the last of the fathers who met in London to complete the work of the conference. He leaves only four survivors of the Westminster gathering.

" In the organization of the dominion Sir Leonard Tilley was one of the chiefs. In the preparation and perfecting of the National Policy he was the chief. As finance minister it was his duty to prepare, submit, defend and operate the National Policy tariff. While the policy was

introduced as a Canadian system in 1879, it is interesting
to note that just 30 years before this time, Mr. Tilley,
then making his first appearance as a factor in New
Brunswick politics, came forward as an advocate of tariff
protection to local industries.   Two years later, when he
became a member of the assembly, he voted for protective
duties, and when after his brief retirement he came to
the front in 1854 as a minister, he brought in a schedule
of duties with a distinctly protective tendency.   New
Brunswick was a small community with a limited industrial range, and the scope of the system was much nar-
rower than that adopted in 1879 for the whole dominion.
Sir Leonard's business experience, habits of personal
investigation, great industry, almost limitless patience,
and above all, his saving common sense and freedom
from purely speculative theories, qualified him for the
great task of revolutionizing the whole system of Canadian
customs duties.

"Mention should be made of Sir Leonard's share in
railway development.   This also takes us back to the
beginning of his career, for he was one of the promoters
of our first railway, before he was elected to the
assembly.   As provincial secretary he was in England
with Mr. Howe on railway business long before confederation.   If St. John was tardy in forgiving him for
allowing the Intercolonial to be constructed by the North
Shore route, that was because St. John does not always
see the difficulties that stand in the way of her representatives.   It would hardly have been wise for Sir

Leonard to retire from public life because he was unable to control three-fourths of his colleagues, backed up by the whole imperial government. A quarter of a century has brought many changes, including a railway by a shorter route to the west than any that were then dreamed of, and another by the route that St. John first favored. The St. John representative who dared to think that a railway might be constructed from this city to Shediac, lived to promote the railway connection of the two great oceans by a line across the continent."

The St. John *Gazette*, on the eve of his death, said :

"There is dying in St. John to-day a man, who more than any other in the province, has filled the public eye for the past half a century. That man is Sir Leonard Tilley, twice governor of the province, for many years a member of the privy council of Canada, filling the most important offices in the Dominion, and prior to that a member of the council of New Brunswick. Sir Leonard Tilley was a farmer's son. Born in Gagetown, he came to this city, served an apprenticeship as a druggist, and when a comparatively young man was started in public life, more by the wish of his friends than from any desire of his own. When Sir Leonard Tilley entered upon his political career, the province was without railroads, and struggling for responsible government. The part taken by Sir Leonard Tilley in the struggle for responsible government is one that every son of New Brunswick and every true friend of government by the people should remember him, and no man played a more important part

in the railroad building epoch of the country than did
Sir Leonard Tilley. It was a gigantic enterprise which
the government of New Brunswick undertook in those
days, when the European & North American railroad was
started. The line was not very long, but railroads cost
very much more to build per mile than they do now. Sir
Leonard has lived to witness the completion of the line
through Canadian territory from ocean to ocean. Where
the journey to Montreal by land was a most difficult one,
a tourist can now board the train at North Sydney, the
most easterly point of Nova Scotia, and ride on practically
without leaving the train until he reaches Vancouver, on
the shores of the Pacific. In the Confederation struggle
which united the four separate provinces of Canada, Nova
Scotia and New Brunswick, and also the Canadas into
one Dominion, Sir Leonard Tilley played a most important part. He was one of the original commissioners who
formulated the scheme, and he was also a member of the
government of the Dominion. The area covered by
Canada in 1867 was comparatively small compared with
the area of to-day. The Great Lakes formed its western
boundary, and the great northern country, which is to
supply food for the millions of Europe, was then all
unknown. In the purchase of the Hudson Bay territory
and the construction of the Canadian Pacific railroad,
through which that territory was made known to the
world, Sir Leonard Tilley was one of the chief actors.
It was he that at that time held the purse strings of
Canada, and it was his financial ability, more than that of

any other man, which pulled through this great enterprise, which now connects each section of the Dominion.
Failing health compelled the retirement of Sir Leonard
from active politics about ten years ago. Up to two years
ago he was governor of the province. Since then his
life has been a very tranquil one. In fine weather his
figure was a familiar one on the streets of St. John, and
to young and old whom he knew, he always had a pleasant greeting. He is a man who will be greatly missed
in the community, and his place is not likely to be filled
for years to come. He has survived most of his old colleagues of the early days of Confederation, of whom
from the Maritime Provinces there are only now surviving
Sir Charles Tupper and the Hon. Peter Mitchell. Sir
Charles in the midst of the election, yesterday, sent a
very touching letter to his old friend and colleague."

The St. John *Globe* said:

"As the contest which has agitated the people for so
many weeks is closing, the sunlight falls probably on the
last days of the life of a public man of much influence
in this province. Sir Leonard Tilley's public career,
which began in 1850, ended in 1893 with his retirement
from the Governorship, a position which he had twice
filled. Since then he has lived a quiet, but by no means
inactive life in St. John. He has been interested in
business affairs and has not been wholly indifferent to
public matters, for, had his health permitted, he would
have entered upon some of the active work of the campaign in the interest of the party with which he has

acted since Confederation.   But the feelings of favor or disfavor with which his political views were regarded have given way to the feeling of respect which is ever accorded to an excellent citizen.   Sir Leonard Tilley has retained the warm regard of all his old political friends and associates, while the citizens generally, the older generation of those who fought many a battle for or with him, the younger generation who know him not as a politician, have been glad to see him about the streets, enjoying the honors which he won and the respect which all well-ordered people yield to a man who has borne his fair share of the struggles and conflicts of life, and who has been a victor in many things."

The St. John *Record* said :

" When it was announced this morning that Sir Samuel Leonard Tilley had laid down his life and had passed away by death the citizens felt that a great calamity had happened this city, province and dominion.   His public career, great and brilliant as it certainly was, did not appeal to the people so much to-day, as the great motives that actuated and shone forth in his private everyday life.

*   *   *   It is as a private citizen that St. John loved him best, because then he was virtually her own — as a public man we had to divide our claim on him with all the other provinces of Canada.   When at Ottawa he was our representative and theirs; in his home here he was our own — a lover of the city that he had done so much to extend and benefit.   So it is to this fact we allude when we say that all looked upon his death as a calamity.

It is true that a wise man in the councils of the nation has gone; but this sinks to insignificance when we consider that death has borne out from our midst one who was the particular friend of all our citizens. It was thought that having laid aside the trials and turmoils of public duty he would have been spared for some years yet to enjoy the harvest time of a life well lived, but it was not to be; but it is a consolation to know that the man who has gone out from us was a direct contradiction of that saying that an honest man is not to be found in politics. His success was due to his persistent and uncompromising perseverence. When he believed that he was right, he allowed no danger to daunt nor difficulty to deter his reaching the necessary and expected consummation; and this trait of his character was well exemplified in business as in political affairs. He went direct to the mark, in an honest and courteous way, thus changing opponents to supporters and enemies to friends."

CHAPTER XIV.

In the preceding chapters I have been considering the career of Sir Leonard Tilley as a public man, a statesman, and a man of affairs. But it would be a grave error to suppose that the whole strength of his nature was at all times devoted to matters of state, or that he in any way allowed public affairs to interfere with that home life which is always the truest source of happiness. So far was this from being the case that Sir Leonard Tilley was essentially a domestic man. He was at his best in his own study or by his own fireside. He loved his family and his friends, and it was one of his chief delights in his later years to gather the friends of his youth about him and discuss with them the happy events of bygone days. His memory was so good and his faculties so keen that the whole picture of his life spread before him like a panorama, and he lived it over again many times in a mental sense. He had a wealth of anecdote in regard to the public men whom he met in the earlier days of his active life, and a keen sense of humor which gave point and character to his reminiscences of those times. Once more the actors on the stage of life of thirty or forty years ago lived as he recalled the scenes in which he and they had taken part. His eye would brighten and his whole form become instinct with life as he related the story of other years.

When Sir Leonard Tilley came to reside in St. John in 1888, after Carleton House, his new residence, was completed, his desire to have his old friends about him caused him to hunt up all the members of the old Portland Debating Society, to which he had belonged when a young man, and to invite them to dinner once a year. The first dinner was attended by about fourteen persons, among whom were the late Sheriff Harding, the late Joseph W. Lawrence, and the late John Sears. For two or three years their meetings were cheerful enough, but death soon began to make inroads upon the survivors. Every year the number of guests was smaller than it had been the year before, and much of the conversation was of those who had passed from earth since the last meeting. Finally the survivors became so few that two or three years before Sir Leonard Tilley's own death the dinner was given up, as something better calculated to awaken sad feelings than to give pleasure.

Sir Leonard Tilley, throughout his whole life gave great attention to his religious duties. He was a devoted member of the Church of England, and his attendance at church was constant and regular. For several years before his death he was connected with St. Mark's congregation, and no cause, except severe bodily illness, was ever allowed to prevent him from going to church on Sunday morning. On many occasions, when his steps had grown feeble and his strength was failing, it was suggested to him that he should drive to church, but he always replied that he would walk to church as long as he had strength left to do so, and that he would not have people harnessing up horses on the Sabbath day on his account. This resolution he maintained to the end of his life. Sometimes, when he met an old acquaintance, as he toiled up the street which led to his favorite church, he would cheerfully greet him by saying, "John, this hill has grown steeper than it used to be," but he climbed the hill to the end, and the last Sunday he was able to be out of his bed he walked to church as usual.

Sir Leonard Tilley took a deep interest in all those humane and philanthropic objects which were for the benefit of mankind and in the great work connected with the spread of the gospel. He was a constant attendant at the annual meetings of the British and Foreign Bible Society, and was a life member of that admirable association. On a very cold night in the winter of 1895–6 the writer met him making his way along Germain street, and on inquiring where he was going on such an inclement evening, found that he was on his way to attend the meeting of the society. He had mistaken the date, for the meeting did not take place for a fortnight, but that he should go abroad in such weather to be present at this annual gathering, shows how much he was interested in its work.

The honors that Sir Leonard Tilley received from Her Majesty, in recognition of his great public services, were very gratifying to his friends as well as to himself, and when he was made a Knight Commander of St. Michael and St. George, in 1879, his temperance friends embraced the first opportunity on his return to St. John to have a banquet in his honor, at which he wore, for the first time in public, the insignia of the knightly order of which he had become a member. There was probably no public event in the whole course of his life which gave him greater pleasure than this proof of the attachment of his old friends.

Sir Leonard's last visit to England was marked by an extremely gracious invitation to visit the Queen at

Osborne, in the Isle of Wight.   While he and Lady Tilley were sojourning at Cowes a message was sent summoning them to Osborne House, where they were received by Her Majesty in the beautiful grounds that surround that palace.   The Princess Louise and Princess Beatrice, with an equerry in waiting, were the only persons present.   After an interesting conversation they were permitted to visit the private apartments of Her Majesty and the Prince Consort's farm.   A remark was made by the equerry that the honor was a very great one, as few persons in England had the opportunity that had been given to them that day.   Of course both Sir Leonard and Lady Tilley replied that the honor was highly appreciated and would never be forgotten.   During their stay in London they were entertained by the Prince of Wales at Marlborough House.   These occurrences made that visit to England a memorable one, but the foreshadowing was already that it would be the last.

Sir Leonard Tilley was first married in 1843 to Julia Ann, daughter of the late James T. Hanford, who died in 1862.   By her he had seven children, two sons and five daughters.   His oldest son, the Rev. Harrison Tilley, who died in 1877, was, at the time of his death, assistant minister to the cathedral at Toronto.   He had been previously rector of Grace Church, London, Ont., and had also been rector of St. Luke's church, Portland, the church which Sir Leonard attended when he first came to St. John.   He was a man of singularly amiable character and much ability, and his early death was deeply regretted

by the entire community, which recognized in him one
who gave great promise of future usefulness. The
other son of this marriage, Mr. L. A. Tilley, is a resident
of Sherbrooke, P. Q., where he is engaged in business.
His eldest daughter, who was the wife of Mr. A. F.
Street, of Fredericton, died in 1894. The other daughters
are: Mrs. W. H. DeWolfe, of Chilliwack, B. C.; Mrs.
Thomas Burpee, of Winnipeg; Mrs. J. D. Chipman, of
St. Stephen, and Miss Julia Tilley, of Toronto.

In 1867, after being a widower for several years, Sir
Leonard Tilley married Alice Starr, daughter of the late
Z. Chipman, of St. Stephen. By this marriage he had
two sons, Mr. Herbert C. Tilley, of the Imperial Trust
Company, who resides in St. John, and Mr. L. P. DeWolfe
Tilley, barrister, who is also a resident of St. John.
These two sons, Herbert and Leonard, were the prop and
comfort of his declining years, and were devoted wholly
to him to the end.

Sir Leonard Tilley's second marriage was contracted at
the time when he was exchanging the limited field of
provincial politics for the wider sphere which Confederation opened up to him in the Parliament of Canada. It
was a fortunate union, for it gave him a helpmeet and
companion who was in full sympathy with him in all his
hopes and feelings, and who was singularly well qualified
to preside over his household, which, in his capacity of a
minister of the crown, had become to a considerable
extent a factor in the public life of Canada. Lady Tilley
had a high ideal of her duty as the wife of a cabinet

minister, and of the governor of New Brunswick, and was not content to lead a merely ornamental life or confine her energies within a narrow range. She saw many deficiencies in our appliances for relieving human misery, and she set to work, with a zeal which could not be dampened, to seek to remedy them. The Victoria Hospital at Fredericton is her work; hers also is the Nurses' Home in connection with the Public Hospital in St. John, and the Reformatory for the care of bad or neglected boys, who are in danger of becoming criminals if they are not educated and desciplined when they are young. In every work of philanthropy Lady Tilley has always taken not only an active, but a leading part, and her position has enabled her to enlist in the cause of humanity the euergies of many who, under other circumstances, might not have taken an active part in philanthropic work. Lady Tilley has, therefore, been not only a source of good in herself, but a moving cause of good to others who, but for her, might not have enjoyed the blessed consciousness of having done something to benefit mankind. Carleton House, to which he removed in 1888, and in which he died, was named after Carleton, where he always had a strong support, and where he remained on election days until all the returns came in with their message of victory or defeat. Sir Leonard intended it to be his home for the remainder of his life, but as he continued to be governor the house was found to be too small for the proper accommodation of those whom he wished to entertain in his official capacity. An addition to it, consisting of a large dining room, was consequently built. The first persons to dine in it were the Earl and Countess of Derby, then governor general of Canada. Afterwards Sir John A. Macdonald and Lady Macdonald, Sir John Thompson, and the Earl and Countess of Aberdeen and Sir Charles and Lady Tupper were the guests of Sir Leonard and Lady Tilley at Carleton House. Thus this building, although still new, is already fragrant with pleasant memories, and half a century hence it will be one of the city's most notable landmarks, and will be called "Old Carleton House," where Sir Leonard Tilley lived and died.

THE END.